A Primer on Aristotle's *Dramatics*

A Primer on Aristotle's *Dramatics*

also known as the *Poetics*

Gregory L. Scott

ExistencePS Press

ExistencePS Press

New York, NY
USA

Softcover

Copyright © 2019

Gregory L. Scott

All rights reserved.

ISBN-13: 978-0-9997049-8-1

Library of Congress Control Number:
2018911031

This book is dedicated to D.S. Hutchinson, philosopher, mentor, and friend.

A Primer on Aristotle's Dramatics

For Updates

including any errata, reviews,
related publications & links

www.EPSpress.com/PRIMERupdates.html

Contents

Acknowledgments	xi
Introduction: Why this *Primer*?	1
Fundamental Misconceptions of the *Dramatics* .	6
In Tandem with a Translation of the Greek	20
How to Use This Book	25
The Fundamental Revisions to the Tradition	31
The Manuscript Tradition	39
The Reception of Aristotle's *Dramatics*	43
Drama at Aristotle's time (4th century BCE) .	49
Misunderstood Core Greek Terms	65
Blueprint of Aristotle's *Dramatics*	71
Chapter Overviews & Comments	85
Chapter 1	87
Overview	87
Comments	90
Chapters 2-5	141
Overview: Chapter 2	141
Comments	141

Overview: Chapter 3	146
Comments	146
Overview: Chapters 4-5	148
Comments	148

Chapter 6 157

Overview	157
Comments	158
Catharsis	166

Chapters 7-12 175

Overview: Chapters 7-11	175
Comments	175
Overview: Chapter 12	178
Comments	179

Chapters 13-14 181

Overview: Chapters 13-14	181
Comments	185

Chapters 15-19 199

Overview: Chapter 15	199
Comments	199
Overview: Chapters 16-18	200
Comments	201
Overview: Chapter 19	204

Contents

    Comments 205

Chapters 20-22 .... **207**

    Overview: Chapters 20-22 207

    Comments 208

Chapters 23-26 .... **213**

    Overview: Chapters 23-25 213

    Comments 214

    Overview: Chapter 26 224

    Comments 225

Appendix 1: Summary of Other Issues from *Aristotle on Dramatic Musical Composition* **237**

    Questions for Specialists to Answer 237

    Postscript on Catharsis, Pity and Fear 238

    Questions Aestheticians May Help Answer 244

Appendix 2: The Transmission of the *Dramatics* to the Later Peripatetics and Beyond **249**

(Corrective) Glossary **303**

Bibliography **309**

Index **321**

A Primer on Aristotle's Dramatics

Acknowledgments

Credit: The book cover is adapted from a portion of the vase *Lécythe à figures noires* (Athens, about 540 BCE), "Comastes," Collection Campana, 1861, F157, at the Louvre, Paris, France. The musical instruments being played are the *kithara*, a small lyre, and an *aulos*, a woodwind like our oboe but with two "stems" or "pipes," often badly translated as "flute" (which itself is *plagiaulos*). They are spoken of repeatedly in Aristotle's so-called *Poetics* in Chapters 1 and 2.

I acknowledge with appreciation and gratitude those scholars who have encouraged me in various ways since I not only focused on the various topics in the *Poetics* for my doctoral dissertation but expanded the research afterwards. They include: Daniel de Montmollin, Francis Sparshott, D.S. Hutchinson, Robert Crease, John Brown, Paul Woodruff, Nickolas Pappas, Claudio William Veloso, Francisco Gonzalez, Alexander Mourelatos, Brad Inwood, and Eric Csapo. Peter Simpson, Monte Ransom Johnson and Gene Fendt gave very helpful feedback for this book, as did some of the others, and warm thanks are owed to them all.

Appreciation also goes to Ivie Crawford and Jaime Cary, who, given the book's unusual approach, edited, played "testers" and offered useful suggestions.

I am most grateful to my wife, Eva, for her moral support, beautiful presence, and sunny disposition, especially during countless working nights and overtime weekends.

A Primer on Aristotle's *Dramatics*

also known as the *Poetics*

A Primer on Aristotle's Dramatics

Introduction: Why this *Primer*?

This book helps introduce newcomers to the treatise that is one of the most influential works, if not the most influential, in Western literary theory, drama, and the philosophy of art. The treatise has been known historically as *On the Art of Poetry* or *The Poetics*, despite it containing not one poem. The treatise only examines tragedy, comedy and epic, the last being a quasi-dramatic form for Aristotle that involved traditionally a singing rhapsode who gesticulated and impersonated with different facial and vocal expressions. Aristotle presents the first rigorous treatment of the formal aspects of these arts along with principles of criticism (although the final part on comedy is lost). For instance, he explains how drama and other arts are fundamentally mimetic, how mimesis can be systematically analyzed, and how all tragedies (in *his* sense of the word) have six necessary elements: plot, character, reasoning, speech, music-dance, and spectacle. His sense exactly conveys what occurred in his day and reflects his well-known empiricism. He also traces the origins of (musical) drama, gives reasons why some plays are better than others, and in the final chapter justifies a ranking of tragedy over epic.

In what follows, we see not only why Aristotle's treatise has been given an illogical title but why Aristotle does not even mention most of the Greek poetic forms, like paeans or hymns or Sapphic love poetry. In developing these points, which themselves lead to a much more extensive re-interpretation of Aristotle's work, the *Primer* essentially puts into simplified form the intricate arguments of *Aristotle on Dramatic Musical Composition: The Real Role of Literature, Catharsis, Music and Dance in the POETICS* (hereafter *ADMC*).[1] *ADMC*, which has more than three times as many words as this book, targets classi-

---

[1] Gregory Scott, *Aristotle on Dramatic Musical Composition: The Real Role of Literature, Catharsis, Music and Dance in the POETICS*, 2nd edition, 2 volumes (New York: ExistencePS Press, 2018); first published 2016.

cists and specialists of ancient Greek philosophy, especially those who focus on Plato (428-348 BCE) and his most famous student Aristotle (384-322 BCE). *ADMC* is therefore unsuitable for readers wishing to become familiar for the first time with Aristotle's little book, which comprises about 42 pages in a typical translation. Hence the need for this *Primer*. It provides a version that is accessible to students and non-specialists alike.

In brief, *ADMC* revolutionizes the 1000-year tradition of interpreting Aristotle's treatise in at least two fundamental ways. First, *ADMC* demonstrates that tragedy, the paradigmatic form of drama for Aristotle, is a species of necessarily performed "musical" theater rather than of literature, the heretofore always assumed view. Hence, the principles throughout the so-called "*Poetics*" were never intended by Aristotle to be primarily or generally applicable to either poetry or literature in the way held until now. For instance, Aristotle claims that plot is more important than character, a ranking that has upset literary theorists and novelists for generations, who think that literature often emphasizes character. For Aristotle, though, plot for tragedy is enacted on stage and could be presented without words, like in a story ballet. Indeed, Aristotle says in Chapter 4 that the early tragedies were dance-like and had little language (that was so undeveloped he calls it "silly"). Hence, Aristotle's priority of plot was not intended for literature and is very sensible on the correct interpretation of the treatise.

Then *ADMC* resolves the perennial debate about the word *katharsis* in the definition of tragedy, with *katharsis* ostensibly being tragedy's goal. According to typical translations, tragedy accomplishes through pity and fear the *katharsis* of such emotions. The problem is that none of the standard ancient Greek meanings of *katharsis*—purgation, purification, or clarification—is consistent with the rest of Aristotle's thought. Often, then, scholars simply transliterate *katharsis* as "catharsis," leaving the issue open (and, in this book, I use the English

Introduction

and Greek spellings interchangeably to mean the same concept, whatever it conveyed to Aristotle). I follow a respected modern Macedonian classicist, M.D. Petruševski, who in 1954 published a work arguing that Aristotle could not reasonably have written *katharsis* in the definition. *ADMC* goes beyond Petruševski, however, to demonstrate that Aristotle could not have written the *whole phrase* with the words *katharsis*, pity and fear. The phrase must have been interpolated by a later editor, probably one of those attested to having restored Aristotle's damaged rolls too hastily and with errors to sell them in the Roman marketplace. All of this resolves a host of related dilemmas that have never been solved since the Italians began working directly from the copies of the Greek manuscripts in the 15th century.

The fundamental misconceptions are described and corrected throughout this book with an appropriate degree of specificity but I should note immediately that I say a "1000-year tradition" even though Aristotle died about 322 BCE. The reason is that no commentary exists on the treatise from antiquity or Byzantine times. It is as if the ancients completely ignored his book, which is extremely ironic, indeed baffling, given how important it became first for Italian literature and drama in the Renaissance, then for the other European countries, and then for the world. The first commentary was produced by the Arabic scholar Avicenna, who lived in Persia (c. 970/980-1037 CE) and who worked from an Arabic translation of a Syriac translation of a copy (probably from about the 7th century CE) of the original Greek manuscript. However, Arabic culture had no type of drama similar to the ancient Greeks and the Arabic translators and commentators treated Aristotle's work as if it were poetic theory, with the second commentator, Averroes (1126-1198), the great Muslim Andalucian, compensating for the lack of poems by adding verses of the Koran! Even though the Italians dropped the verses when they began working directly from the rediscovered Greek manuscripts three centuries later, they nevertheless continued to assume Aristotle was dealing with literary theory or criticism. Everyone until my Ph.D. dissertation in 1992 followed suit.[2]

Nevertheless, this *Primer* is not merely a summary of *ADMC*. In keeping with the focus on students and non-specialists, it is designed to be used in tandem with virtually any reasonable translation of the *Poetics*, of which there are dozens or hundreds in many different languages, some for just a few dollars and some for no cost on the Internet. By reading a translation (or the ancient Greek itself) in conjunction with the chapter-by-chapter *Overviews* and *Comments* here, someone being introduced to Aristotle's philosophy of musical drama can get the more sensible understanding of his theory. *ADMC* explains thoroughly how seven of the core Greek terms and ten of the twenty-six so-called "chapters" of the *Poetics* have been gravely misconstrued over centuries; hence some of the reasons for the length of *ADMC*. By taking into consideration, though, the explanations of the misconstruals as summarized in this *Primer*, newcomers can understand much more correctly Aristotle's basic aims.

Another reason for this *Primer* relates to the simplification of *ADMC* rather than to the *Primer* being a summary of *ADMC* or being used in tandem with any translation (or with the Greek). The *Primer* allows even specialists who read ancient Greek—and who may be curious about the provocative findings in *ADMC*—to get a quick handle on the arguments without having to invest the time and effort to read a massive book. In spite of the positive reception by some internationally recognized scholars of the articles that form the foundation of *ADMC*, as published by Cambridge and Oxford University presses, specialists

---

[2] Gregory Scott, *Unearthing Aristotle's Dramatics: Why There is No Theory of Literature in the Poetics* (University of Toronto, 1992). One section of the dissertation on the theme at hand was revised and printed in Gregory Scott, "The *Poetics* of Performance: The Necessity of Spectacle, Music, and Dance in Aristotelian Tragedy," in *Performance and Authenticity in the Arts*, ed. by S. Kemal and I. Gaskell (Cambridge: Cambridge University Press, 1999) 15-48. That article is further revised and included as part of *ADMC*, Chapter 2.

Introduction

new to the debates may well have grave misgivings that any single author could have settled in one fell swoop many of the long-standing debates pertaining to the *Poetics*. Indeed, unsurprisingly, a few scholars have already printed reservations about the arguments presented in the earlier two articles (reservations that are rigorously rebutted in *ADMC*). However, once potentially interested specialists understand the basic points in this *Primer*, they can proceed (or not) to the deep arguments and evidence in *ADMC* with confidence that they would not be wasting their time on a merely clever work that cannot withstand severe scrutiny.

More details now follow for each of the first two reasons for this *Primer*; the third, pertaining to skeptical specialists, suffices as is.

Fundamental Misconceptions of the *Dramatics*

Until now, all translators, other scholars, and as a result the typical layperson have taken Aristotle's work to be about poetic theory or literary criticism. Scholars have always assumed, shockingly in retrospect, that Aristotle was using the core term *poiēsis* and its cognates as (the making of) "language and verse," which is our notion of "poetry," even though not one poem exists in Aristotle's whole treatise. Partly the translators assumed that *poiēsis* meant "poetry" in this context because drama, Aristotle's primary topic, employed verse for the script and because drama had not been performed in the Western world from the time of the repressive Christian Emperor Justinian until the 16th century. Justinian not only banned the practice of theatrical drama in approximately 528 CE but closed the schools of philosophy, effectively ruling out any grounded discussion of dramatic theory pertaining to Aristotle (or anyone else for that matter) for over 900 years.

Hence, for these and other reasons, such as only some scripts but no music and dance surviving, Avicenna and those following him like Averroes assumed that the treatise had to be about literature. This can be easily seen from their commentaries, which often either completely misconstrue the terms dealing with performance, like *opsis* (spectacle), or which drop the terms entirely.

These are merely a few of the reasons that I demonstrate Aristotle's treatise is better entitled *The Art of "Musical" Dramatic Composition* or *Dramatics* for short, and I use that title instead from now on unless it causes confusion.

Averroes, like Avicenna, did not read ancient Greek and also worked from the Arabic rendition of the Syriac translation. Even though the many verses from the Koran that he incorporated were dropped by the Italians working directly from the Greek, his commentary had significant influence as "ethical rhetoric" for the Christian West even past

Introduction

the time that the Greek manuscripts of the *Dramatics* were discovered and introduced into the universities in the late 1400's in Italy. In part, Averroes' continued influence was due to the cryptic nature of Aristotle's treatise, which notoriously confused even a number of the Italians who had learned ancient Greek.[3] For Averroes the goal of tragedy was to make one a better person, and this was something with which all religions and academics could sympathize.

However, to return to the meaning of *poiēsis*: A classicist, Noburu Notomi, published only as recently as 2011 the research essentially proving that the sophist Gorgias first used *poiēsis* in the sense of "poetry" in 415 BCE, when Aristotle's mentor Plato was already a teen.[4] Yet the sophists were typically antagonists of the philosophers like Plato, and before Gorgias coined the new meaning of *poiēsis*, it was used primarily in two senses. The first, broad sense, which all classicists know, is a "doing" or a "making," and the making could apply to pottery as much as to spear-making or to creating a song or a poem, as reported by Plato himself via the female character Diotima in the *Symposium* (she is usually discussed because she taught Socrates the meaning of love). She also stresses, however, that *poiēsis* by itself was most properly used, indeed, *only* used by the Greeks in general, as *mousikē kai metra*, adding that the maker is the cognate *poiētēs* (too often anachronistically and poorly translated as "poet").

Mousikē could mean, from broadest to narrowest: "the arts of the Muses," "music and dance," or "music." *Kai* means "and" in this context (but can mean "that is" in other contexts). *Metra* normally means "meters" or "verses," and must mean "verses" in Diotima's ex-

---

[3] All of this is covered in great detail in the Appendix of *ADMC*. Since the history there is in chronological order, with detailed sections for the commentators, I do not provide page numbers here.

[4] Noburu Notomi, "Image-Making in *Republic* X and the *Sophist*," in *Plato and the Poets*, ed. by P. Destrée and F. Herrmann (Leiden & Boston: Brill, 2011) 299-326.

planation, because, otherwise, only music would be seemingly meant. If that were the case, it would be doubly odd that she felt the need to utter *metra* redundantly, unless some music were not done with meters. Nevertheless, in that case, it would be even more illogical to translate *poiēsis/poiētēs* as "poetry"/"poet." Were *mousikē* to mean "the arts of the Muses," what would adding *metra* do? Surely not extend the arts of the Muses, because verses are part of those arts, which were not only arts in our sense but which included astronomy and history. At the best, then, *metra* would have to restrict the general arts of the Muses. However, were astronomy and history done in verse? I know of no examples of this, although natural science was expressed, as we will see, by Empedocles in verse, perhaps to help the memorization of the lines and thus of the doctrine. I show later that *mousikē* indeed best means the final choice, "music and dance," in the context of Plato and Aristotle, based on their texts, but for the moment I simply note that I call *poiēsis* (as *mousikē kai metra*) the "Diotiman (narrow) sense of *poiēsis*," in contrast to the broad sense of any doing or production.

Diotima's explanation of how the whole, simple word *poiēsis* (or *poiētēs* as maker or "musical" composer) was employed by the Greeks was opposed, we might reasonably infer, to the common Greek practice of using a cognate ending of *poiēsis* in order to categorize types of makers. That is, "*-poios*" was appended to another word in order to create the relevant label for someone, so that, for example, an epic maker, what translations improperly call for Plato "epic poet," was an *epopoios* (literally, maker of epic). Similarly, a scenery-maker was a *skeuopoios*, a sculptor *agalmatopoios* (literally, maker of sculpture), and a (portrait)-painter *eikonopoios* (literally, maker of images). Just as no classicists in their right mind would translate the last as "(portrait)-painter *poet*," so *epopoios* should not be the anachronistic "epic poet" for Plato but "epic *maker*." The difference is subtle but crucial because the "epic maker" made *songs,* and "poet" for us means some-

Introduction

one who only composes pure verse.

I discuss this topic more when examining how the core Greek terms have too often been misconstrued but, for the moment, suffice it to say that I call "language with meter" (poetry or verse) the Gorgian-English sense of *poiēsis* or, for short, the Gorgian sense.

Every classicist knows, or should know, that a "doing" or a "making" in general is too broad a meaning for *poiēsis* in the *Dramatics* and that *poiēsis* and its cognates must have another, legitimate meaning. The reason is that Aristotle explicitly theorizes about only three art forms in his treatise: tragedy, comedy, and epic. He does not care about saddle-making, candle-making, house-building, boat-production, or any of the forms of Greek poetry *per se* (what would be equivalent to, say, a Shakepearean sonnet). This is all self-evident from the whole book, as readers will easily confirm for themselves, and from what Aristotle promises at the beginning of *Dramatics* 6. However, not one commentator in print for over 1000 years, until my dissertation, even considered that Aristotle might be employing *poiēsis* as his mentor Plato does, in the Diotiman sense,—*if only* to argue that the Gorgian sense was better![5] This is despite the admiration that Aristotle had for his mentor, as shown by his written tributes. More tellingly, since actions speak louder than words (especially on Shakespeare's stage that is the world), the likelihood that Aristotle would follow his mentor rather than a sophist is shown by Aristotle's not only leaving home in Stagira in Northern Greece at 17 to enroll in Plato's Academy in Athens but by his residency there for 20 years, until Plato passed away.

Indeed, the Northern Greek's historical preference for the Gorgian meaning is in another way utterly perverse, despite any dislike Aristotle himself may have had for the sophists. As emphasized, not one

---

5   This is demonstrated in the Appendix of *ADMC* by examining the famous commentaries going back to the first one, by Avicenna.

poem exists in the treatise. Moreover, Aristotle's definition of tragedy, perhaps his most paradigmatic form of *poiēsis*, includes "music [in the Greek sense]" as an essential condition, and the tragedies from the late 6th to 4th centuries BCE, as Aristotle analyzes them, were always done with music and dance, with the verse only becoming predominant starting with Aeschylus. One would expect that if tragedy *necessarily* has "music," which is entailed by Aristotle's theory of definition, then Plato's prize student and empiricist *non plus ultra* would be using Diotima's sense of *poiēsis* (as the making of music, dance, and verse) rather than the newer sense that a sophist coins (as mere verse). This expectation will be satisfied once we go through the treatise for the first time ever with the hypothesis that Aristotle uses the Diotiman sense of the word.

Having anticipated Notomi, but only because of the behavior of the Greek terms in the text and without having done the research of earlier times that he did, in 1999 in "The *Poetics* of Performance: The Necessity of Spectacle, Music, and Dance in Aristotelian Tragedy,"[6] I presented the basic reasons why tragedy for Aristotle is not a species of literature. Rather, I argued, tragedy for him in the *Dramatics* is a species of performed musical drama, like serious Broadway plays such as *West Side Story*, with the music, dance and spectacle required along with the language. Language is not even the most important element, given Aristotle's explicit statements. If you think that the script of the Broadway play is the only crucial, or the most crucial, element, then consider instead opera, which also uses language but which is categorized under the rubric of music. I show that Aristotle is not using *poiēsis* as traditionally thought by commentators but that he employs the term in the Diotiman sense, again, given the behavior of the word in the texts. Notomi's findings, therefore, confirmed and extended my views.[7]

---

6   *Op. cit.*

7   After reading those findings, I had an inkling of the feeling that Dar-

Introduction

The ancient Greeks did not give titles to their manuscripts (which is to say, their scrolls), although they would often refer to the manuscripts by the subject or by the first couple of words in a roll. Hence, Aristotle refers to the treatise on musical drama as *peri poiētikēs*, the first two words. *Poiētikēs* is in effect a cognate of *poiēsis*, the phrase elliptical for "on the art of *poiēsis*." The titles *On the Art of Poetry* or the *Poetics* were assigned to Aristotle's work by the commentators starting with Avicenna in whatever language they were translating the work into. They never even questioned whether *poiētikēs* had the Diotiman meaning. These are just a few more of the reasons that I employ *The Art of Dramatic "Musical" Composition* or *Dramatics*. The other reasons, including why I add "dramatic" to "musical composition," are explained throughout this *Primer*, and especially with the *Comments* in *Dramatics* Chapter 1. Suffice it to say here that Aristotle conveys through the behavior of the word *poiēsis* in his treatise that he adds "(dramatic) plot" to the Diotiman sense of the term and that *poiēsis* therefore becomes a technical term for him. In other words, *poiēsis* for the Northern Greek means the making of music, dance, verse *and plot*, which reveals that he slightly restricts the Diotiman sense.

To call Aristotle's treatise the *Poetics* would be like titling a book *Cooking* when no cooking is discussed and when only hunting and farming are examined in detail, or when at most only a few remarks are made in one chapter on how the hunter dresses the kill in preparation for

---

win probably would have felt, were he alive to receive confirmation of his hypothesis that birds and bees pollinated plants with respect to one strange case, all of which I mention because of Aristotle's founding of biology and because Aristotle often uses biological metaphors and models in the *Dramatics*. Also, I believe everyone should know this. As Darwin wrote, there was probably a bird with a very long tongue (at least 9 inches long) that could pollinate the orchid *Angraecum sesquipedale* in Madagascar, because the orchid has an exceptionally long nectary, sometimes 9-11 inches. It took approximately 120 years for confirmation but a giant moth was discovered that was observed pollinating the orchid. It had a tongue about 9 inches long, which curled up when the moth was not using it.

later freezing and cooking.[8]

A few more words of background on Diotima's narrow notion of *poiēsis* as *mousikē kai metra,* and on Aristotle's addition of plot, will be helpful.

To emphasize, *ADMC* demonstrates that the Diotiman sense of *poiēsis* as *mousikē kai metra* is "music-dance and verse," and neither "the arts of the Muses and verse" nor "music and verse." *ADMC* also reveals how Aristotle himself often uses the Platonic meanings of the various terms even if he sometimes argues against his mentor on issues

---

8   When finishing both the final draft of *ADMC* (2018) and an early draft of this book, I came across yet another of the dozens of translations of Aristotle's work, Sir Anthony Kenny's new one, with a foreword, passages of Plato, and—to make it unique, I gather, for marketing purposes—some brief accounts of a few modern literary theorists (*Aristotle POETICS*, Oxford: Oxford University Press, 2013). Kenny is one of the first, or the very first, after me to write (pp. xi–xii) that the *Poetics* is a poor title, even without acknowledging that not one poem exists in the treatise and without acknowledging my earlier work from 1999 on this theme. As Kenny states: "It is many centuries too late to change the title of this treatise of Aristotle's, but '*Poetics*' gives a misleading impression of the contents of the treatise" (p. xi).

However, with all due respect to a Knight of the Commonwealth, I myself see no reason to subject new generations of readers to the same confusion that has been foisted on previous readers by bad translations and by a bad title, merely because it has been done that way for centuries. Analogously, one does not maintain discredited medical procedures just because they were done for generations; one implements the new, better procedures. Worse, Kenny does not recognize whatsoever either the Diotiman sense of *poiēsis* or any of the problems articulated in my article from 1999 and developed in *ADMC* when one construes Aristotle to be writing a theory of literature rather than a theory of an independent art of musical drama. One does a disservice to Aristotle by distorting his terms, even with the type of warning that Kenny provides. I give now merely one case for more evidence of this, if general theories of translation and the previous reasons are not sufficient. I know a professional poet and university instructor in New York City who confessed that she once started enthusiastically reading the "*Poetics*" to learn the foundations of her art. Instead, she found nothing that she was expecting, not even one poem, and never trusted another book by Aristotle.

Introduction

such as censorship. This is admirable because if the meanings of the terms change then the arguments would be at cross-purposes. The three art forms implied in Diotima's sense of *poiēsis*—music, dance, and speech—become Aristotle's famous three "means of mimesis" in Chapter 1 of the *Dramatics*, denoting the three ways in which one can "impersonate," "represent," "express," or "imitate," the common meanings of *mimēsis* in ancient Greece. *Mimēsis* for Plato was at the core of all art (cf. *Laws* II, Stephanus 669-670[9]).

However, to return to *poiēsis* and to Aristotle making it a technical term in the *Dramatics*, adding a fourth condition, plot: The cognate *poiētēs* is not a "poet" in our sense of the word, which implies the Gorgian sense, but a composer of "musical" drama (I put "musical" in quotations for brevity, implying the requisite dance). Thus, "dramatic 'musical' composer" or "'musical' dramatist" or a similar phrase is a better translation of *poiētēs* and this follows Plato's other applications of the word when he, for example, speaks in the *Laws* VII of the individual composing music by itself. Plato calls him a *poiētēs*, and translators for once realize they have no choice and render the term as "composer" or the like rather than "poet."[10] I should emphasize that

---

9 The so-called Stephanus number functions like a page number. It allows one to look at any translation of Plato's works designed for scholarly use and to find quickly the passage. Likewise, the Bekker number for the Aristotelian corpus allows the same efficient pinpointing of text. For example, 1050a2-5 in the *Dramatics* represents lines 2-5 from the first column, called "a," of the available Greek manuscript at section 1050; 1050b5 would similarly represent the fifth line in the second and final "b" column. Cf. *ADMC*, pp. 117-8 for a discussion of this section of Plato's *Laws*.

10 Stephanus 812c-e; hereafter I merely give the number and assume the reader supposes "Stephanus." The most popular of the Greek-English lexicons, by Liddell, Scott and Jones, indicates of *poiētēs* that for Plato it is "generally a writer" (Henry George Liddell and Robert Scott, *Greek-English Lexicon*, 1968 impression; first ed. 1889; revised and augmented throughout by Sir Henry Stuart Jones with the assistance of Roderick McKenzie. Oxford: Clarendon Press, 1940). They are simply wrong and have inadvertently misled researchers for generations. Usually the term for Plato conveys the Dioti-

Aristotle's sense of *poiēsis* is a technical one, for use in the Lyceum, which is reflected by a passage in his treatise that we see later proves the treatise was for use in his school. It was "esoteric" rather than "exoteric," the latter being for public consumption. Therefore, modern specialists in ancient Greek philosophy, or anyone else for that matter, should not be surprised that *poiēsis* in the *Dramatics* has a different meaning from either the commonplace Greek or from Diotima's narrow sense.

The issues pertaining to performance versus literature were absolutely new in 1992, when I finished my dissertation, because no one previously had even recognized (in print) the fundamental oddities with Aristotle being interpreted as if tragedy is mere literature rather than performed theatrical art. Much less, then, was anyone compelled to resolve any of the ensuing problems, even though Aristotle continued to be subjected to unjust criticism and his theory to inappropriate *literary* standards. One might as well judge a tennis player by the standards of ice hockey or of ping-pong.

The topic of catharsis in the famous definition of tragedy in Chapter 6, however, is different. The word *katharsis* was in the Arabic manuscript recognized by Avicenna but he could not determine its meaning and he simply drops it. It has continued to trigger many dilemmas and attempted resolutions since the very first commentaries by the Italian scholars working directly from the Greek manuscripts. In all of them, the goal of tragedy in the definition is to accomplish a *katharsis* through *and of* pity and fear. Yet how does *katharsis* get translated correctly when any and all of its three meanings in Aristotle's time—purgation, purification, and clarification—lead to grave paradoxes, given the rest of his well-known aesthetics, ethics, psychology and pol-

---

man sense and the just-noted example in the *Laws* is some evidence of this although it drops the dance-making aspect and only means "composer" in one of our common senses. Cf. *ADMC*, p. 64.

Introduction

itics? Some of these paradoxes we can address even in an introduction like this *Primer*.

I mention a few elementary points now. Pity and fear, it turns out, are legitimate and correct emotions at times for Aristotle. For example, if your ethical siblings get assaulted and crippled without just cause by a criminal gang you should feel pity for them. What about a drama along this line? If purgation is the meaning of *katharsis*, why would Aristotle want the pity purged? If purification is the meaning, what would it mean to purify an emotion like pity or fear? Does Aristotle really want the audience to have pure pity rather than, say, a mixed or moderated pity at the end of a play, and, if they have pure pity, how could they have fear too? When you have pure gold, it is not mixed with anything else. Why would pure pity be mixed with fear, whether the latter itself is pure or impure? Similarly, with *pure* fear. Finally, if *katharsis* means clarification, what would "clarify pity and fear" entail? Explain what the two emotions are? Do dramatists really teach or explain such things? The option seems absurd and indeed goes counter to what Aristotle says in a number of places, including his discussion of the "musical" arts in the *Politics* VIII 7. There, the theatrical forms are primarily for pleasure or intellectual enjoyment for adults, not for education, even if the latter is discussed earlier in VIII regarding the types of music and dance that are appropriate for training children.[11]

Therefore, in 2003 in another article, "Purging the *Poetics*,"[12] which is reprinted as Chapter 5 in *ADMC*, I extended and corrected the work of Petruševski, who, again, had argued that Aristotle could not have written *katharsis* in the definition of tragedy. I cover the detailed reasons in the appropriate chapters, especially Chapter 6, but give now some

---

11   Cf. *ADMC*, Chapter 4, and especially pp. 302-23.
12   Gregory Scott, "Purging the Poetics," *Oxford Studies in Ancient Philosophy*, Vol. 25 (Winter 2003) 233-264.

of the evidence. First, Aristotle never explains or discusses the word further even though he covers in much greater detail all of the other essential conditions in the definition. Indeed, the term *katharsis* only occurs one other time in the whole treatise, as "purification" in Chapter 17, when Orestes is said to go through the purificatory rites for having murdered his mother, Clytaemnestra. However, no specialist to my knowledge accepts now that "purification" can be meant by *katharsis* in the definition in the way that is relevant to Orestes, which entails that the second and final occurrence of *katharsis* in the treatise is irrelevant to the issue at hand.[13] For this and other grounds,

---

13   Kenny, *op. cit.*, 2013, returns to the Italian custom of the 1500's and to Gotthold Lessing (1729-1781) by translating *katharsis* as "purification." However, he hardly grapples with the resulting dilemmas, perhaps because he is not truly a specialist of the work, in spite of his late interest in it. As his bibliography attests, he limits his research of the secondary literature to some of the more popular recent British commentators. He does not, e.g., explain why pure pity is good nor why pure pity would allow a mixed fear, and he ultimately cashes out the issue the same way the Italians and Lessing did, who offered mere minor variations on the same theme (and in *ADMC*'s history in the Appendix we see, for example, how Jacob Bernays demolished Lessing's arguments that *katharsis* in the definition of tragedy, or at least in the *Politics*, can be "purification" or "cleansing").

Ironically and unwittingly, Kenny arrives at the same conclusion as I do in general, namely, that pleasure for Aristotle throughout the treatise is really the goal of tragedy, apart from the corrupt *katharsis*-clause. Kenny writes:
> Surely, one of the ways in which drama achieves the purification of emotions is that it allows us to experience even the most negative emotions without the pain that accompanies them in real life—we actually *enjoy* being frightened by what we see on the stage, and the tears we weep over tragic victims are an expression of a grief that is positively *sweet*. *It is the pleasure that we take* in feeling these normally depressing emotions that is *the pleasure peculiar to tragedy* [my italics] (p. xxvi).

Yet, how can pity and fear be sweet when Aristotle says in a number of places (some of which Kenny recognizes) that they are painful? Even Stephen Halliwell, whom Kenny praises, recognizes that catharsis and pleasure cannot be the same for Aristotle (proof of which is in *Politics* VIII 7; cf. *ADMC*, pp. 360-1; 363-5; 390-1; 402-5; 438; and espec. 440 and Ch. 7). Besides, given Aristo-

Introduction

Petruševski denies that catharsis is the goal of all tragedies for Aristotle, which means Aristotle could not have included it in the definition. Petruševski's arguments, therefore, obviate any need to determine the exact translation of *katharsis* in that particular location.

However, *ADMC* demonstrates in its own Chapter 6 more rigorously than either Petruševski's work or "Purging the *Poetics*" that Aristotle could not have written the *whole* catharsis, pity and fear clause in the definition. As we see in this *Primer*, although again in much less detail as befits an introduction to the treatise, Aristotle defines tragedy by what is called "biological division," collecting in his own Chapter 6 the elements that had been introduced in the first five chapters. Catharsis, pity and fear are never even mentioned in those five chapters. Moreover, when Aristotle develops all of the other necessary elements of tragedy in Chapters 6-7, he does not even allude to any of these three ostensibly essential conditions, much less develop them, whereas he does begin to develop *all* the other necessary ones. If that is not enough, and as just noted, he does not even mention catharsis again in the rest of the treatise in a germane way, when all of the other necessary conditions are examined to greater or lesser extent. Most challenging for the traditional reading, when Aristotle discusses or mentions the goal of tragedy in various places throughout the whole treatise, he ignores catharsis! Typically, the goal is (a proper) pleasure, as one of Plato's characters, Callicles, in the dialogue ironically named *Gorgias* says is common for the Greeks in general. Aristotle in effect confirms all of this when he compares in Chapter 23 the goal of epic with that of tragedy, saying that *they each produce their proper pleasure.*

---

tle's theory of definition, were Kenny right then pleasure rather than catharsis should have been in the definition of tragedy (cf. *ADMC*, pp. 354-7).
    Immediately before publication, I discovered another scholar who recently accepts "purification" as the meaning of *katharsis*, Gene Fendt. I discuss his view in detail in Chapter 6, when we get to *katharsis,* but to give a hint now, he ends by *explaining* it as purgation or transformation, not purification.

By keeping *katharsis* in the definition of tragedy, we miss the real goal of tragedy for Aristotle, which means we continue to distort his theory. Thus, to reveal his real view, we must suppress the wrongful interpolation, which is my retort to any scholar who insists in the name of conservatism that we must protect the manuscripts and a couple of words (instead of Aristotle's theory and the integrity of many chapters). In short, the real goal of tragedy is a kind of proper pleasure, as the reader will notice in various spots while reading the treatise.[14]

Chapters 5 and 6 of *ADMC* also demonstrate similarly why pity and fear are not possible essential conditions for all or even most types of tragedy, given Aristotle's own theory of definition and what he explicitly says throughout the treatise about various types of tragedy not having pity. Therefore, I explain how utterly foolish he would have been to include the two emotions in any definition of tragedy. His theory of definition requires that the two emotions apply to all instances of tragedy (leaving aside possibly some few rare exceptions that prove the rule). They are "essential conditions," just as "rational animal" for the definition of "man," used in the Greek sense of "human being," involves the essential condition "animal" necessarily applying to all individuals.[15]

---

14   Pleasure has different sorts for Aristotle, be they, for instance, sexual, gustatory or intellectual. The type of pleasure associated with tragedy is not only intellectual but can be aesthetical and emotional. I cover in *ADMC* Chapter 7 the places where pleasure is mentioned in the treatise, but, as just mentioned, the reader will notice them throughout the *Dramatics* from Chapter 4 onwards. Cláudio William Veloso shows how consistent this is with Aristotle in the *Politics* having *diagōgē* (intellectual enjoyment, delight, entertainment) as the best end of "musical" arts (*Pourquoi la Poétique d'Aristote?: DIAGOGE,* Paris: Vrin, 2018, with a Preface by Marwan Rashed).

15   Thus, Diotima, the wise woman who in Plato's *Symposium* teaches Socrates and who is obviously greatly respected as a thinker, is a "man" in the colloquial sense, as a figure of speech. To obviate feminists invoking the caricature of Aristotle who treats women always as second-class citizens or inferior beings because of some of the comparisons he makes between them and men, note that he also says that they learn faster, have better memories, and are the

Introduction

Pity and fear, however, are legitimately discussed in the middle chapters of the *Dramatics*, which is the main reason commentators have taken them to be authentically in the definition. Yet not only does Aristotle say in Chapter 13 when ranking plot-types that a plot with a virtuous person going from good to bad fortune *has neither pity nor fear* because it is *miaron* ("shocking" or "disgusting") but he notes explicitly a number of other plot-types in Chapters 2-18 that have no pity! Thus, including pity and fear in the definition of tragedy is like including "blonde-haired" (or "blonde-haired and pony-tailed") in the definition of human beings. The conditions clearly cause the definition to be much too restrictive, and although my blonde-haired sister teasingly might not object, my black-haired cousin certainly would.

Moreover, three times throughout his treatise Aristotle states that the protagonists in tragedy can go from fortune to misfortune *or misfortune to fortune*. Because, in addition, in Chapter 14 the best tragedies, those like *Cresphontes* and *Iphigenia (in Tauris)*, end happily for him, clearly we moderns too often foist anachronistically our own sense of "tragedy" on the Greek word *tragōidia*.[16] We will see that it really only means for the most part "serious drama" for Aristotle and for the Greeks in general and that, to underscore, it need not end badly even if it sometimes, or often, does. Hence, it becomes easy to understand in those cases of happy endings that pity does not occur. According to Chapter 13, pity accrues when a protagonist suffers serious harm without deserving it. Just as in basketball—"No harm, no foul"—so in drama: No harm, no pity. From this point forward, then, when I use

---

same in species as men (cf. *Metaphysics* X 9). For a very good treatment of Aristotle's views on women, without the typically distorted prisms, see Marguerite Deslauriers, "Aristotle on the Virtues of Slaves and Women," *Oxford Studies in Ancient Philosophy*, Vol. 25 (Winter 2003) 213-31.

16   I cover more of the issues when discussing Chapters 13 and 14, but have published the fullest details in Gregory Scott, *Aristotle's Favorite Tragedy: OEDIPUS or CRESPHONTES?*, 2nd edition (New York: ExistencePS Press, 2018); first published 2016. *ADMC* includes a summary of the issues.

"tragedy," the reader should understand it in a technical sense for Aristotle and with no *necessary* suggestion that it ends unhappily (and the same, by the way, holds for Plato, as Susan Sauvé Meyer, a professor of ancient Greek philosophy at the University of Pennsylvania, has recently shown[17]).

In Tandem with a Translation of the Greek

Let us turn now to the details of the second reason for this *Primer*. It is to be used in tandem with the ancient Greek or, as for almost all students, with any reasonable translation (and by "reasonable" I mean any of the commonly used translations coming from the academic publishing houses, in whichever language the reader prefers). Much of the literary interpretation of the *Dramatics* can stay untouched by my new insights, and I usually leave untouched interpretations of minor points, even if they have been debated by scholars. For example, to return to a major issue, as long as one understands what a *poiētēs* is, it will not matter whether one reads at times the anachronistic "poet" or the correct "dramatic composer" in this context for Aristotle. Since ancient Greek dramatists wrote their scripts in verse, they too have a talent for language in meter as a part of drama. By using synecdoche—calling a whole by a part, like "the arms hit the ball" in lieu of "the man hit the ball"—one can sometimes refer without confusion to a dramatist therefore as a "poet." One, however, should not make the further, illegitimate inference that the dramatist is *only* a poet for Aristotle. Similarly, when the Northern Greek discusses, say, the difference between *poiēsis* ("poetry" in the translations) and history, one should not take this to mean anything other than the difference between a *part* of *poiēsis* and history, and his discussion will still be clear.[18]

---

17   Cf. *ADMC*, p. 372, footnote 541.

18   Theatrical presentations by the Greeks were occasionally used in a way as history, like documentary film for us. An infamous early historical tragedy was by a rival of Aeschylus, Phrynichus, who with the *Fall of Miletus* in approximately 494 BCE was fined because he made the Athenians recall a

Introduction

When in Chapter 15 Aristotle says that characters should be as good as possible, appropriate, life-like and consistent, this could apply to characters on stage as much as to characters in epic, which was performed by rhapsodes in the 4th century BCE primarily with narrative and with some impersonation or gesturing, without the choral elements of tragedy. (The rhapsodes usually accompanied themselves with an instrument, like our minstrels or buskers, or sang the words or both). Using good characters as much as possible might also apply for Aristotle to purely literary tragedies that was just starting about his time, an example being by Chaeremon in *Dramatics* 1. Finally, the principles examined in Aristotle's discussion of "discoveries" in Chapter 16 (for example, how one character discovers who another character really is and whether the person might be a lost family member) also might apply to epic or to literature, although I emphasize "might." *ADMC* Chapter 9 explains the danger of extending principles of one art to another without due caution, given Aristotle's explicit warning in *Dramatics* 25 that different arts have different principles. We can easily see that *literary tragedy* actually functions more like *epic* in some important ways than like performed, dramatic tragedy involving a dancing chorus.

The point for the moment, though, is that once we have a correct understanding of Aristotle's terms and his goals, the traditional translations can often be read with "automatic correction" of the concepts normally given, and appropriate adjustments can be easily made. The final example is "rhythm" (for *rhuthmos*). When reading that word in a traditional translation of the *Dramatics* (or of *Politics* VIII 7), one

---

devastating and very painful episode in their history, the recent defeat and massacre of their allies by the Persians. Subsequently, the Athenians apparently passed a law that forbade such types of extremely painful historical representation. The issues admittedly get complicated if history is used merely as a skeleton for creating the secondary episodes and dialogue that themselves are not known to have existed but that might be plausible. In that case we may have a mixture of documentary and art, and sometimes it is difficult to tell when one begins and the other ends.

will realize that Aristotle really means "dance," and one can apply the thrust of the passage to dance rather than to a mere musical "rhythm" *qua* temporal ordering.

Because my corrections of Aristotle's treatise only touch seven of his core concepts, I do not attempt another translation of the work that has triggered hundreds, if not thousands, of translations around the world over the centuries, the most recent one to my knowledge being in Maltese.[19] With this *Primer*, one can make use of any of them, especially the well-received ones that go into subtleties concerning the non-foundational matters that I do not even begin to touch here or in *ADMC* and that classicists who specialize in drama cover much better anyway.

There are two other reasons why for the moment I do not offer another translation. It would probably be unethical to give students just learning the *Poetics/Dramatics* only a radically different view from what has been transmitted without question for over 465 years. The students would be at a severe disadvantage later when coming across the historical discussions in publications on literary theory and criticism, drama, ancient Greek philosophy, classics, and aesthetics, all of which presupposed the view that tragedy is literature with catharsis its goal. Although my approach requires a little more work, understanding *both* the old view and the new view, the advantage is that students will be able handle the mountains of related discussions in various domains of Western thought. Finally, my strength is as a philosopher, not as a literary stylist, and there are many scholars who can write a much more elegant translation of the correctly understood Greek text as a whole than I. As Socrates said, "Know thyself," and by implication, know thy limitations. If need be, depending on demand, I will present in the next few years an adapted translation of one of the most

---

19   *Aristotli, Dwar L-Arti Tal-Poezija*, trans. Karmenu Serracino (Malta: BDL Publishing/Malta Classics Association, 2012).

Introduction

acclaimed ones in the public domain, changing only what is necessary, but I wait to see the reaction to this book (and to *ADMC*) first.

Footnotes here will often refer to the (free) text on the web's Perseus Project, knowing full well that web sites can change because their funding is withdrawn or because of any other reason. Nevertheless, to reiterate, these prefatory sections and my *Overview* and *Comments* for each chapter would generally apply to any other commonly known translation. Thus, providing a primer that explains the seven core Greek terms correctly and that guides the reader especially through the ten heretofore badly misconstrued chapters—1, 4, 6, 13, 14, 18, 19, 23, 24 and 26–will suffice, I trust, to solve the major fundamental problems for the near future. Also, those already with translations can just re-use them.

To summarize: The two major misconceptions pertaining to Aristotle's treatise are explained in great detail in *ADMC*, and objections by specialists are handled there. However, as a result, *ADMC* is much too dense and complex for the student being first exposed to Aristotle's work, itself the foundation of Western dramatic theory and the *alleged* but mistaken foundation of Western literary theory, if by "foundation of literary theory" one means that Aristotle intended the principles throughout the treatise to apply directly to literature. In length, in prerequisites (which include readers having already worked their way through the *Dramatics*), and in content (which often includes evaluations of competing arguments of ancient Greek specialists who have spent 20 years of their lives examining Aristotle's work), *ADMC* is simply inappropriate as an introduction to this historically important work. Hence, the need for this *Primer*, which is less than one-third the length of *ADMC*. Nevertheless, for skeptical classicists reading this *Primer* who wish to see the more detailed reasons and evidence for any particular topic, I often refer here in the footnotes to the relevant pages in *ADMC*, as I have started doing already.

A Primer on Aristotle's Dramatics

How to Use This Book

I do not presume that the reader understands ancient Greek and thus explain all Greek terms.

There are four obvious ways to use this book, each having its advantages and disadvantages, although each presupposes reading the rest of this *Introduction*. The *Dramatics* is only about 42 pages, with each "chapter" not even 2 pages average. The chapter-breaks were created in the Renaissance for ease of reading,[20] and except for the renowned French translator André Dacier (1651–1722), who broke Chapter 14 into two chapters and who thus had 27 chapters, all translations to my knowledge have 26 chapters.

The first way of reading this book: After the preliminary material and starting with Chapter 1, begin with the *Overview* of each chapter, followed by its *Comments*, before reading that single chapter, say on the Perseus Project: http://www.perseus.tufts.edu/hopper/text?doc=Perseus%3atext%3a1999.01.0056

The disadvantage of this approach is that the chapters will not be read fresh, in the typical way that Aristotle would have expected. However, he would have expected readers to peruse the treatise in Greek, not in translation, *and to understand the terms as used in the Lyceum.*

Optionally, read a traditional translation of a chapter first (or the ancient Greek), then the *Overview* and *Comments*. If need be, re-read the chapter with the corrections in mind. The disadvantage of this approach, obviously, is that the particular chapter will need to be read twice.

---

[20]   *ADMC*, pp. 291-2, footnote 423.

If one has a photographic memory, naturally one can read a whole traditional translation (or the whole ancient Greek text) and then simply read the *Overviews* and *Comments* without break.

Finally, one could read the *Overviews* first, then the traditional translation (or ancient Greek), and *then* the *Comments*. This may or may not involve having to read the translation again after the *Comments*, depending on the complexity of the issues in each chapter. A student-tester, who used a draft of this book in conjunction with the web before publication, ended up choosing a paperback translation, for reasons immediately following, but in general found it best to read the *Overview* first, then the translation, then the *Comments* and then the translation again for the ten *misconstrued* chapters. The chapters that are typically non-problematic (as indicated in the respective *Overviews*) only needed the one reading, before or after the *Comments*.

Unfortunately, some of the translations, especially on the web, do not have line numbering (originally by Bekker), although the numbers usually exist in any reproduced ancient Greek version. The lack of numbering in a translation can make for some difficulty in locating a passage that is identified here by the Bekker number, e.g., 1448b20-22. Reading an *unnumbered* translation first, then, before the *Comments,* and then re-reading the translation might be best because the reader will have a good sense of where in the chapter any idea or passage is.

The translations on paper are usually better for the Bekker numbers. In case you wish to read the translation on paper, below are the English versions that I have consulted most. However, a plethora of others are available, and the following is not intended as a ranking or as an implication that other translations are sub-par. All assume that Aristotle is presenting literary theory and is authentically giving *katharsis* as the goal of tragedy, no matter how they interpret it (Gerald Else being one of the most creative in regards to *katharsis*). For fullest

How to Use This Book

details, see the Bibliography.

- S.H. Butcher, *Aristotle's Theory of Poetry and Fine Art*, 1st ed. 1895, reprinted 1923. In some ways, this is out of date, but Butcher often has a remarkable understanding of ancient Greek aesthetics, with valuable insights.

- Ingram Bywater, *Aristotle on the Art of Poetry*, originally published 1909; also, in *The Complete Works of Aristotle*, ed. Jonathan Barnes, 1984. A very faithful translation, which gives the standard traditional interpretations of the core Greek terms but without the commentary in the edition by Barnes. However, for example, in that edition Bywater without warning omits in his translation words like *kai melos* ("and melody" or "and music" or "and music-dance") in the definition of tragedy. Bywater, though, is not the only one who operates like this. Hence, unless students use an edition that scholars require, which gives the various words from the different manuscripts for any questionable sentence and which specifies the preferred one(s), they will have no clue that a translation changes drastically the ancient Greek text.

- Gerald Else, *Aristotle's Poetics: The Argument*, 1957. Available in the public domain at:
https://babel.hathitrust.org/cgi/pt?id=mdp.39015001819286;view=1up;seq=10
One of the great American classicists of the 20th century, Else has an idiosyncratic view of catharsis in Aristotelian tragedy, which is not an effect on the audience but a part of the structure of the play. On the other hand, he offers at times excellent accounts of other topics in the treatise and related Greek thought. The book is probably most relevant to those in graduate seminars but adventurous undergraduates may find it not too challenging.

- Richard Janko, *Aristotle: Poetics, with the Tractatus Coisilianus*,

Reconstruction of Poetics II, and the Fragments of the On Poets, 1987. Perhaps the most commonly used translation and commentary nowadays, having the advantage of additional fragments from Aristotle's earlier, similar "exoteric" work, from one of the very good, no-nonsense and no-frill publishers, Hackett. It also has a commendable, 30-page Glossary, although some of the basic terms continue to mislead (however, one can use the *Corrective Glossary* at the end of this book to ameliorate Janko not recognizing, for instance, that *poiēsis* for Aristotle follows Diotima's narrow sense).

- For a good sample, but a mere sample, of other translations from a variety of languages, see the "Translations" section at: https://monoskop.org/Aristotle/Poetics/Kassel

For those who read ancient Greek, the apparatus of Rudolf Kassel of 1965, which was reprinted in large part by D.W. Lucas in 1968, has been recently supplanted by Leonardo Tarán and Dimitri Gutas in their impressive *Aristotle Poetics: Editio Maior of the Greek Text with Historical Introduction and Philological Commentaries* (2012). However, given how weighty their book has been, and will be, for professionals (and almost solely professionals, because Tarán and Gutas do not translate the ancient Greek, Latin and German), a caution is necessary, after a sincere expression of gratitude.

Generations of scholars will be justifiably grateful to them for their remarkable achievement, at least with respect to the paleography and most of the philology. However, as this *Primer* and *ADMC* demonstrate, we should not accept all of their philological, nor many of their philosophical, interpretations, especially for the "musical" terms or even for such fundamental terms as *poiēsis* that they rigorously show existed, or probably existed, in the manuscripts and especially in what they call the "archetype." This archetype need not have been the original (and almost certainly was not the original by Aristotle) but was the source of all subsequent extant manuscripts.[21] To reiterate for newcomers to these issues, the archetype does *not* survive. Tarán and Gutas deduce what it probably contained in part by examining in microscopic detail the four "witnesses," the earliest or most authentic manuscripts that do survive in the four distinct branches. The two paleographers, however, do not even recognize, much less argue against, the possible relevance of Diotima's sense of *poiēsis* that resolves a number of the perennial philosophical dilemmas. As we see in more detail in the *Comments* of Chapter 6, Tarán and Gutas also do not even acknowledge, much less try to resolve, the philosophical inconsistencies between, say, catharsis in the definition of tragedy and Aristotle's theory of definition. Instead, they rely in this instance only on the (undisputed) fact that the word exists in all four primary witnesses to the archetype, which, however, *on their own grounds* itself was created, that is, presumably copied, 700-900 years after Aristotle.[22]

In short, paleographic ability, which Tarán and Gutas undoubtedly have to the extreme, does not automatically convert into philosophical excellence, nor does it even guarantee philological perfection (and I would be the first to admit that the reverse is also true). In brief, as this *Primer* and *ADMC* demonstrate, the two paleographers sometimes badly misinterpret some crucial Greek words that *they themselves argue powerfully are the best ones in the manuscripts*, again,

---

21 Unfortunately, their assumptions seemingly leave aside the possibility that the original was corrupted, then restored imperfectly, and then copied at least twice afterwards. The corrupted original and the identical copies take independent "trajectories" but all of them disappear except one or two, which become the sources, the "archetypes," of the subsequent four branches. That is, there could have been two identical (sources of the) "archetypes." I cover the related issues in Appendix 2.

22 Moreover, although unlikely, the version that Tarán and Gutas are calling the archetype could have been created by a scribe merging two slightly different previous manuscripts that were themselves lost afterwards with no other influence on the tradition. Again, this whole topic gets covered more in Appendix 2.

poiēsis being a case in point and *rhuthmos* being a second.[23]

---

[23] Cf. *ADMC*, pp. 12; 377; 386; 409; 445-6; 448; and espec. 452-3.

The Fundamental Revisions to the Tradition

Contrary to the received tradition, drama in general for Aristotle is a species of the *independent* art of performed theatrical art and not of literature. Drama in the 5th and 4th centuries BCE includes tragedy, comedy and the satyr play. We ourselves have opera, so-called "straight plays" (those without music), and musical theater, whether done on or off Broadway. They all make use of language but are not necessarily categorized correctly under literature (at least with respect to opera, for some nowadays would even categorize musical theater under literature because some consider the language to be the most important element). However, ancient drama and even some modern variation like pantomime could be performed without any language or with only a little language. The ancient drama could, and in its very early stages did according to *Dramatics* 4, essentially involve pantomime or dance, similar to our story ballets, which are done without language or with a little language. Yet they still convey a plot (*muthos*), Aristotle's so-called "soul" of tragedy.

Plot is the Northern Greek's most important part of the six necessary ones that all tragedies have, according to Chapter 6, which in his final ranking are: plot, character, "reasoning" (or thought), speech (or language), music-dance, and spectacle. Principles in the *Dramatics* may or may not be applicable to literature, for reasons Aristotle sometimes gives. If the principles are applicable to literature, though, it is because language is one *necessary part* of tragedy, *not because tragedy should be categorized under literature*. As we will see, tragedy can exist for Aristotle even without character, which is his second most important necessary part (and here "character" means one's ethical compass and not necessarily, or at least not primarily, what role an actor plays). Language is only the fourth most important part, and thus *a fortiori* plot and tragedy could exist without language. (The third-ranked necessary part is *dianoia*, "thought" or "reasoning.")

These are merely some of the reasons that tragedy as defined in *Dramatics* 6 cannot be a species of literature.[24]

Poiēsis is for Aristotle a technical term, as I stated. To emphasize, he follows Plato-Diotima in thinking of it as "(the making of) music-dance-verse," which he calls his three "means of mimesis." However, from the outset he presupposes something else that was probably explained or commonly known in the Lyceum and that can be clearly

---

24   Consider the typical thought-process when this is told to a scholar, in this case Leon Surette who gave a paper entitled "Is Art Worth More than the Truth?" to the Canadian Society for Aesthetics Meetings, Ottawa, May, 1993, which was then published in the *Journal of Value Inquiry* 28 (1994) 181-92, available at:
https://www.researchgate.net/profile/Leon_Surette/publication/226505450_Is_art_worth_more_than_the_truth/links/5678225c08ae125516ee760a

As Surette prints:

On hearing this paper Greg Scott reminded me that Aristotle placed diction fourth, and thought third—after plot and character—in the *Poetics,* and therefore could not be said to value the word as highly as I assert. I do not deny the justness of these observations, but *by placing plot or mythos first, Aristotle can still be said to have placed poetry or literature first, for the heart of literature is story or myth* (Endnote 6; my italics).

First, I never said Aristotle placed "diction" fourth; I would only have said language or speech, for reasons I give in detail with respect to Chapters 6, 19 and 20. Also, as I explain rigorously in *ADMC* in Chapter 3, *muthos* is explicitly said by Aristotle to be "the structure of actions," *not* "the structure of actions *in words."* Thus, as his comments about dance and the origins of tragedy in Chapters 1, 2 and 4 reveal, plot indeed can be given for him with miming or dance. Scholars simply assume that *muthos* has to entail language, but the Greek texts demonstrate that they are wrong and are blinded by traditional literary hegemony

Finally, specialists usually interrupt me at this point to say that at the end of Chapter 6 Aristotle says the effect of tragedy can be given without the performance and actors, as if this can overrule an essential condition in the definition of tragedy, allowing tragedy to be mere language. I easily handle this point at the proper time, and with the better translation, in Chapter 6.

deduced from his usage of *poiēsis* in the treatise, starting with the very first sentence: Plot is a fourth condition, to go along with the three means of mimesis. These four conditions reveal why only three "dramatic" art forms—tragedy, comedy, and epic—are analyzed in depth in the whole treatise. Aristotle expressly considers the last, epic, to be a subset and precursor of tragedy. These are the art forms that have music, dance (in the Greek sense), verse and plot. In other words, this meaning of *poiēsis* easily resolves the unsolved dilemma: Why are most of the poetic Greek forms not even mentioned, much less discussed, in a treatise called the *Poetics*? The answer is that the treatise is only about dramatic arts involving a plot, and Aristotle in no way intends to cover literature or poetry *per se*, or, as a few have thought, artistic principles in general that are best exemplified by the arts of literature. Thus, scholars who for generations have been banging their heads on walls, trying to figure out why poetic forms are not even mentioned, much less examined, in a *"Poetics"* can now sit back, relax, have a glass of wine, and focus on other matters.

I also explain at the appropriate level below how other Greek words, for instance, *harmonia kai rhuthmos*, *mimēsis*, and *mousikē*, have meanings that are different from the standard translations. The words are very ambiguous and have meanings that, like our "play," have to be determined within the particular context. "Mauricio plays King Creon tonight in the play *Antigone* while his wife Simone plays tennis; at the same time their daughter Sophi plays the violin for her year-end recital." Neither "play" nor the Greek words are univocal ("have a single meaning"). Rather they are richly equivocal but the English sentence is perfectly clear because, for instance, the direct object of the verb reflects the precise meaning. We will find that Greek speakers were equally capable of switching meanings in a nanosecond and we should realize that words are like universes. As Einstein said, "I have deep faith that the principle of the universe will be beautiful and simple," and we should strive, when possible, to find a single meaning for a word, whether English or Greek. Yet, more wisely, Einstein said ""Everything should be made as simple as possible, *but not simpler.*"

To underscore, I also provide the arguments in *ADMC* why Aristotle could not have written the clause with the words catharsis, pity and fear in the definition of tragedy. This solves one of the ongoing perennial dilemmas of the treatise. If *katharsis* was not written by Aristotle himself, obviously we need not concern ourselves with its meaning and translation *there*. One question then becomes: What is the real goal of tragedy for the Northern Greek? In this *Primer*, we get a mere summary of the many details and of the overwhelming evidence presented in *ADMC*. Pleasure or a certain type of pleasure is given throughout the treatise as the goal. As we saw, Plato claims via Callicles that pleasure is the goal of theatrical performances for the public. Plato himself disagreed and thought that the goal should involve instruction for the citizens, or thought it should make them better, as it should for Aristophanes in his comedy *The Frogs*, ll. 1009-1010. However, Aristophanes' view never gets discussed by Plato because the philosopher wants to ban tragedy and comedy from the ideal republic and because he hates comedy so much that even in his last book, the *Laws*, he will not cite Aristophanes favorably even concerning the one value they share. We will see precisely how Aristotle agrees and disagrees with them both.

Related to the topic of catharsis, pity and fear is another paradox in *Dramatics* 13 and 14 that no one before my findings had been able to solve to the satisfaction of the profession. In Chapter 13, *Oedipus* is presented as an example of the best type of tragedy that ends unhappily and that has pity and fear. Yet its type is only second-best in Chapter 14, behind the plays *that end happily*, like Euripides' *Cresphontes*! Without the mistaken requirement of catharsis, pity and fear, the heretofore assumed ultimate and penultimate goals, respectively, of *all* tragedy, we can easily resolve this paradox. As we see in the *Overview* and *Comments*, Chapter 14 gives the ranking of tragedies *in general* for Aristotle. Chapter 13, however, only gives the ranking of one,

Two Fundamental Revisions

or a mixture of a few, of the four *sub-types* of tragedy categorized in Chapter 18: tragedy of suffering, tragedy of character, complex tragedy, and simple/spectacular tragedy. (The first two sub-types are never even mentioned elsewhere in the treatise.) One or even a combination of two sub-types had pity and fear as their intermediate goal, but which sub-types are relevant would have to be demonstrated. Not one scholar to my knowledge has even begun addressing this topic in spite of the influence of Aristotle's treatise in Western culture.[25]

Catharsis is a separate issue from the different rankings of the best kinds of tragedies, and Aristotle in Chapter 14 only mentions the *pleasure* through pity and fear, not the catharsis through pity and fear. *ADMC* and this *Primer* show not only that Aristotle means what he says in Chapter 14 about the best tragedies ending happily but that "tragedy" (*tragōidia*) in the 4th century BCE really only meant serious drama, which could end happily (or not). This meaning changed in the Renaissance, especially with the Italian scholar Julius Caesar Scaliger. In the late 16th century, while using Aristotle's views as a foil for his own theory, he indicated that tragedy *must* end unhappily.[26] Unfortunately, this is the meaning that theatrical tragedy also acquired in English for hundreds of years, which causes great distortion in the understanding of the *Dramatics* when "tragedy" is employed as the translation for *tragōidia*. The term apparently only meant originally something like "goat-song" (the exact derivation is one of those perennially debated issues), perhaps because a goat was first given as a prize. However, just because a play ended happily, the Greeks would not have considered it necessarily a comedy. Rather if it dealt seriously with noble men and women, it would still be a *tragōidia*. Comedy dealt with vulgar or unbecoming or ridiculously irrational people, however a comic play ended, as Aristotle explains in Chapters 4-5. I continue to use "tragedy" in this book because it is so common, but

---

25   *ADMC*, pp. 376; 422-5.
26   *ADMC*, pp. 506-7; 548-51.

the reader should always be aware that I treat it as a technical term. Tragedy *for Aristotle* need not be tragic and often was not.

While examining "music (in the Greek sense)" in *Politics* VIII 7, Aristotle mentions that catharsis is *explained* in a treatise on *poiēsis*. His precise word is *(peri) poiētikēs,* which has lent legitimacy to the word *katharsis* in *Dramatics* 6, because *peri poiētikēs,* that is, "on the art of poetry" (if one takes the Gorgian sense) or "on the art of music, dance, verse, and plot" (if one takes Aristotle's technical sense) are the two words that begin the *Dramatics*. However, absolutely no explanation of catharsis exists in the extant *Dramatics*. Moreover, once we examine the issues more systematically and notice passages from Aristotle's *Rhetoric* that use the same phrase *peri poiētikēs* in referring to the treatise that has Aristotle's examination of jests, we can safely conclude that catharsis was probably explained in the theory of comedy in the so-called lost second book.[27]

Because, however, this *Primer* focusses on the extant "first book," which only covers tragedy and epic, I do not delve into the issues of comedy here. However, the reader might find the last two chapters of *ADMC* perfectly accessible in this regard. Since so little is written on the particular issue of comedy in the *Dramatics* and how catharsis might be applicable to it, the chapters merely introduce the topics and issues, and leave the matter for future exploration. The conclusion in *ADMC* is that, for Aristotle, catharsis is much more relevant for comedy than for tragedy, even were one able to deduce the way in which catharsis *might* be relevant to some *sub-types* of tragedy, which will not be an easy task for the reasons provided in *ADMC* and supplemented in Appendix 1 below.

---

27   The lost manuscript on comedy is the subject of the well-known film and thriller, *The Name of the Rose* (1986), with Sean Connery, based on the book by Umberto Eco.

Two Fundamental Revisions

Now that we know in more detail what this *Primer* fundamentally corrects, let us cover some more background of Aristotle's treatise and the related issues before starting with its individual chapters.

A Primer on Aristotle's Dramatics

The Manuscript Tradition

Naturally, some readers will be very curious about the manuscript tradition, because, after all, that is where we achieve our primary understanding of Aristotle's thought. Other evidence, including vase paintings, architecture or inscriptions on stone walls or columns or the like, can help us comprehend how the Greeks in general thought of drama and the other arts.[28] In other circumstances and concerning other books of Aristotle, we might avail ourselves of other texts from writers who commented on his works, but, again, there was no commentary on the *Dramatics* from antiquity or Byzantine times. It is as if the treatise had no value for the Greeks and Romans, and it is remarkable that the book which has become a, if not the, major part of the foundation of Western aesthetics and of dramatic-literary theory drew no excitement from the ancients themselves. Hence, at least a few remarks on the manuscript tradition of the treatise, and a preliminary remark about manuscripts in general from Aristotle's time, are called for.

Manuscripts were typically created in the form of scrolls, usually from the papyrus plant in Egypt. Another option was the more expensive and durable parchment, including vellum, that came from animal hides. Presumably to save space and money, the Greek writing, which involved all upper-case characters and no punctuation, had no spaces between the words. To get a sense of what you would read were you perusing an ancient Greek manuscript, try out these two equivalents:

---

28   An excellent example of how the surviving visual evidence, in this case from "dedications" in ancient Athens, help us understand ancient drama more, and for a bibliography leading to further resources on some of these issues, see Eric Csapo, "Choregic Dedications and What They Tell Us About Comic Performance in the Fourth Century BC," *Logeion: A Journal of Ancient Theatre*, 6 (2016) 252-284.

WELCOMEDEARREADERTO
ABOOKONARISTOTLESDRA
MATICSIHOPEYOUFINDITIL
LUMINATING

PATRICIASDAUGHTERTOO
KANAMERICANAIRLINESF
LIGHTTOPARISINORDERT
OPAINTSOMEOFTHEBRID
GESBEFORESHEVISITEDH
EROWNHUSBANDANDCH
ILDRENINTHESOUTHOFF
RANCEAFTERWARDSTHE
YALLFLEWTOROMETOSE
ETHEFAMOUSSCULPTURE
SOFBERNINILOCATEDATT
HEGALLERIABORGHESE

As you see, the words are also randomly broken at the end of the line. There were no rules similar to what we have for breaking a word at a natural syllable, using a hyphen. Over the centuries, lower-case letters, spaces and punctuation were introduced, as was the book form called the codex, flat sheets typically bound on one edge. It would not be, though, until about the 4th-5th century CE that codices supplanted the rolled forms.

We know of four branches of manuscripts of the *Dramatics* that were sometimes copied and then re-copied, manually, of course, and presumably when a manuscript was perishing or when demand occurred for another copy.[29] We simply do not know, however, when Aristotle's original was first copied. As discussed in great detail here in Ap-

---

29   *ADMC*, p. 527. For the most up-to-date discussion of the manuscripts, see Leonardo Tarán and Dimitri Gutas, *Aristotle Poetics: Editio Maior of the Greek Text with Historical Introduction and Philological Commentaries*. (Leiden and Boston: Brill, 2012). Still very valuable is E. Lobel, *The Greek Manuscripts of Aristotle's* Poetics (Oxford: Oxford University Press, 1933).

pendix 2, an ancient tradition attested by Strabo the geographer (c. 64-24 BCE) and Plutarch the biographer (46-120 CE), who was also an essayist and priest at Delphi, reports that Aristotle's library was bequeathed to Theophrastus, Aristotle's successor, and then to a student of Theophrastus, Neleus, who transferred it to Scepsis (a town in what is now Northwestern Turkey that had produced some Socratic philosophers). His descendants stored the library underground to hide it from the book-acquiring kings of Pergamum, the nearby capital.[30] The manuscripts were corrupted by moisture and bugs and, when recovered, were restored quickly to be sold in the Athenian and Roman marketplaces by those, the ancients say, more in love with book-selling than with philosophy. In other words, the restorers sometimes filled gaps in the manuscripts with words that were not accurate. Some gaps still exist in all copies, entailing that the so-called "archetype" of the *Dramatics,* which, again, is not necessarily the original but the source from which other extant manuscripts stem, had gaps that were too large for the restorer to fill. To reiterate, Tarán and Gutas place the creation of the archetype as late as 700-900 years after Aristotle's death.[31]

About 31 Greek manuscript copies exist, almost all in the first branch. They come from the best preserved and most complete copy called "A" (*Parisinus Graecus* 1741, circa tenth century). Curiously, "A" has, for example, the word *mathēmatōn* ("learnings") in the definition of tragedy alongside *katharsis*. The second branch has one definite copy called "B" (*Riccardianus* 46, circa twelfth-to-fourteenth century), which is very mangled and very incomplete. It has *pathēmatōn* ("experiences" or "emotions" or "sufferings") instead of *mathēmatōn* alongside *katharsis*. *Pathēmatōn* is the reading of the word in the *katharsis* clause that is standard now. Thus, the typical translation is "the catharsis (of such) emotions" rather than "the catharsis (of such)

---

30   ADMC, pp. 366; 408-9; and 433.

31   ADMC, pp. 445-6; 448; 452; and 592.

learnings." The third branch, which Avicenna and Averroes used, stems from an Arabic translation by Abū Bishr Mattā (circa 932 CE) of a Syriac translation of a lost Greek manuscript that itself apparently was created before, or around, 700 CE. (It also has *pathēmatōn* instead of *mathēmatōn*, which is one reason the *mathēmatōn* of the much greater number of copies is ignored.) The resulting mishmash of this third branch of translations formed the basis of Hermannus Alemannus's ("Herman the German's") Latin version from the 13th century. No one nowadays uses this version, for obvious reasons, except perhaps to determine whether a word might have existed that could resolve a conflict between manuscripts A and B and the copies descending from A. The fourth and final branch is acknowledged to be a very good translation by William of Moerbeke (1215–1286) from the Greek into Latin, which to this day has never been translated into another language, to my knowledge. The work seems to have been virtually unknown in the late Middle Ages and has had no, or extremely little impact, on the debates over the centuries.[32]

---

32 *ADMC*: pp. 377; 451; 530; 537; 540-2; 547; and 600.

The Reception of Aristotle's *Dramatics*

I save the understanding of drama at Aristotle's time until the end of the prefatory remarks but before the overall blueprint (and before the individual chapter *Overviews* and *Comments*), so that readers have a basic understanding of Greek drama fresh on their mind when they begin perusing the treatise, as would have been the case with Aristotle's expected readership. Now I cover briefly the way in which the *Dramatics* itself was translated and understood historically.

As emphasized, the *Poetics* or *On the Art of Poetry*—the standard previous translations of the first two words (*peri poiētikēs*) of a manuscript that did not begin with an official title, following normal Greek custom—is nowadays for professional aestheticians usually the most important work of dramatic, literary and artistic theory in Western culture. Not until the Muslim Avicenna offered the first commentary in the eleventh century, though, do we begin to see readers' reactions to it, and this was by an Arabic culture that was in no way familiar with the drama performed in amphitheaters in ancient Greece. Avicenna lived in Persia, within which there were apparently not even the remnants of ancient amphitheaters.[33] However, even non-Muslim Europeans for hundreds of years had not been privy to the experience of drama performed in an amphitheater, because, as alluded to, Justinian, the emperor based in Constantinople, in 528 CE banned public drama as part of his brutal implementation of very strict Christian values throughout the empire. He banned, too, the schools of philosophy, which must make us wonder what happened to anyone

---

33 In what is an ironic role reversal compared to modern times, Avicenna was greatly concerned with science. He was also one of the greatest philosophers and medical doctors of the Middle Ages, whereas Western culture at the time was much less scientifically-oriented. For instance, neither Copernicus nor Galileo would even be born for hundreds of years to come.

owning a pagan text and to the texts themselves. Let us postpone this topic, however, until Appendix 2, when we see that the Christians acted more like the Taliban regarding, for instance, the great library at Alexandria than the ideal gentle and tolerant Jesus.

When Averroes, in what is now Andalucia (Spain), followed Avicenna in the twelfth century with his own commentary, he tried to explain the Aristotelian precepts by incorporating verses from the Koran as examples (about twenty pages in the eighty-one-page commentary!). There is not one example of ancient Greek poetry in the Gorgian sense in the treatise, and Averroes was filling in what he thought was lost or omitted, given his comment on the matter. Since drama had not been directly experienced by *anyone* in Europe for more than 600 years, obviously neither he nor anyone else was in a position to comprehend fully the treatise. As mentioned, Averroes was influenced by Avicenna and also took Aristotle to mean speech by *poiēsis*, whether in prose or in verse. Yet, the latter is the meaning whose origin is attributed to the sophist Gorgias in approximately 415 BCE, about thirty years before Aristotle's birth, in *The Encomium to Helen*. Averroes, like Avicenna, never acknowledges Diotima's explanation of the term. One cannot help but wonder whether they had read the *Symposium*. However, this would only have been possible had the dialogue been translated into Arabic, and I know of no such history. I leave, however, any definitive claim in this regard to the specialists in this period or to the experts in the transmission of Plato's corpus.[34]

From Avicenna and Averroes on, the assumption that Aristotle was

---

34   A specialist, Peter Simpson, of the City University of New York says "Apparently most knowledge of Plato came to the Arabs from Galen's summaries of the dialogues" (private correspondence, 10/29/18). As I show in my Appendix in *ADMC*, it may be that Avicenna and Averroes knew in that case of the view of love given in the *Symposium* but in any event they made no use of any Diotiman sense of *poiēsis*. See, for example:
https://plato.stanford.edu/entries/arabic-islamic-greek/index.html#ref-28

employing the Gorgian sense was never questioned by any recorded scholar, whether or not the scholars knew of Gorgias's work, in any of the hundreds of translations and commentaries that I have seen, read about, or heard discussed (and confirmation is given in the very detailed Appendix of *ADMC*, where I report the views of the well-known commentators going back to Avicenna). As deserves more attention now, this is all despite there being two other attested meanings of *poiēsis* at Aristotle's time. Let us start again from the basics.

Diotima, who may or may not have been a real figure, gives the two meanings in Plato's *Symposium* at 205c. As noted, she indicates that *poiēsis* has a general meaning, "making" (or "producing"). Yet, she adds, the word is more properly used—in fact only properly used in its short form!—to refer to "*mousikē kai metra*" ("music [in the Greek sense]" and verses). Likewise, the "maker of *mousikē kai metra*" himself is a *poiētēs*, usually poorly translated there as "poet" because "poet" clearly means for us someone composing only verse. This all seems to allude to the related custom of the Greeks to add instead a cognate of *poiētēs* such as "*-poios/-poious/-poioi*" to the end of a maker's name (or to the group name), rather than to call that person simply a *poiētēs*.[35] Thus, to extend the examples I gave already, a spectacle maker is a *skeuopoios*; elegiac (verse) makers are *elegeiopoious*; epic (song-verse) makers *epopoious*; (comic) mime actors *gelotopoioi*; lyric or choral (music & dance) makers *melopoioi*; and comedy makers *kōmōdopoiois*. In summary, the short form *poiētēs* is *not* used by itself for *pure verse-making*. Rather it is "-maker" (*-poios*) added onto the particular verse-form that gives a composer the relevant label, with the two examples just given being elegiac-makers *elegeiopoious* and epic-makers (who used hexameter verse for the song) *epopoious*.

---

35   *ADMC*, pp. 117; 218; 224; 226; and 235. Throughout his corpus, Plato also uses the verb *poieō* in Diotima's broad sense of "doing" or "making" but he adds an object to make clear what the making specifically is.

Given how important Diotima's passage is, and how ignored it has been, even by modern day feminist scholars who concentrate on the *Dramatics*,[36] I repeat it here:

Diotima (Plato, *Symposium*, 205c):

"Take the following: you know that making or composition (*poiēsis*) is more than a single thing. For of anything whatever that passes from not being into being the whole cause is making (*poiēsis*); so that the productions of all arts (*technais*) are kinds of making (*poiēseis*), and their craftsmen are all "makers" (*poiētai*)... But still, as you are aware," said she, **"they are not called "makers" (poiētai): they have other names,** *while a single section disparted from the whole of making (poiēseōs)— merely the business* **of music-dance (mousikē) and meters (metra)**—*is entitled with the name of the whole.* **This and no more is called "music-dance-verse making" (poiēsis); those only who possess this branch of the art (poiēseōs) are "'musical' composers" (poiētai).**"[37]

---

36   I have yet to read any female scholar of the *Dramatics* discuss Diotima in this context. Nor have I read any male scholar discuss her meaning of *poiēsis* in significant detail, but that is much less surprising given the historical pattern. I present more of the unfair treatment of Diotima in speaking of Scaliger, who makes a strange bedfellow for modern-day feminists.

37   My translation, following *Plato in Twelve Volumes*, Vol. 9, trans. Harold N. Fowler (Cambridge, MA: Harvard University Press; London: William Heinemann Ltd., 1925). All previous translations to my knowledge, with one exception, translate *poiēsis* as "poetry" here. The exception renders also as "poetry," but puts the word in quotations, of which more below. See, e.g., Fowler's translation on the Internet: http://www.perseus.tufts.edu/hopper/text?doc=Perseus%3Atext%3A1999.01.0174%3Atext%3DSym.%3Asection%3D205c

The specialist considered most knowledgeable about the *Symposium* in modern times, Sir Kenneth Dover, only gives the Greek and a commentary on select phrases, rendering *mousikē kai metra* as "music and verse" and not specifying what he thinks *poiēsis* means in English (*Plato: Symposium*, ed. Kenneth Dover, Cambridge: Cambridge University Press, 1980, p. 146). However, it is practically impossible that he would reject "poetry," the typical

Reception of the *Dramatics*

As remarked, *mousikē* is ambiguous, but two of the three meanings, "music" as a purely aural art and "arts of the Muses," make no sense whatsoever. The last meaning is "music and dance," and this is in effect the meaning that Plato gives *mousikē* in his final large work, the *Laws* II (655a) and in the *Alcibiades* (108c) when he says it is singing, playing the kithara (a small lyre) and "stepping rightly." Amazingly, and to underscore what I stated, despite Aristotle's association with Plato and in spite of music being included in the definition of tragedy in the *Dramatics*, not one known commentator in history ever even hypothesized that Aristotle was following his mentor if only to prove that the Northern Greek was using the Gorgian sense of *poiēsis*. Once we interpret the word correctly for Plato, though, as "(the making of) music, dance, and verse," and once we see that Aristotle restricts the scope further by requiring plot, we dissolve a number of seemingly

---

translation of the word here, given that he offers no alternative. Benjamin Jowett, for instance, one of the great classicists and translators of the late 19th and early 20th century, writes "...music and metre; and this is what is called poetry, and they who possess this kind of poetry are called poets" (*The Symposium of Plato*, B. Jowett, Boston: International Pocket Library, 4th printing 1983, p. 72; with no date given for the previous three printings, only the number of copies printed, e.g., "First Printing, 5,000 copies.") Needless to say, *we do not think "poetry" involves music.*

The best treatment of the whole passage, or at least, of *poiēsis* that I have seen, and the exception just referred to, by Alexander Nehamas and Paul Woodruff, has "poetry" in quotation marks, or "scare-quotes," as philosophers sometimes call them, for *poiēsis*. They obviously find it odd to translate the word simply as "poetry" and warn the reader that the term is being used in an unusual way. Indeed, they wisely explain the passage in a footnote, saying "Greeks used the word *poiētēs*, however, mainly for poets—*for writers of metrical verses that were actually set to music* [my italics]" (*Plato: Symposium*, trans. with Introduction and Notes, by Alexander Nehamas and Paul Woodruff, Indianapolis & Cambridge: Hackett Publishing Company, 1989, p. 51; also reproduced in *Plato: Complete Works*, ed. John Cooper, *op. cit.*, 1997). Presumably, given the absolutely universal tradition of everyone using "poetry" they could not bring themselves to use "song-writer" or "song-composer" or the like, even with their roughly correct explanation. Alternatively, because of their explanation, they reasonably assume that readers would understand "poet" is used as a synecdoche, referring to the whole via a part.

intractable dilemmas in the *Dramatics*. Likewise, as alluded to, the same holds with some related and secondary terms like *harmonia kai rhuthmos*. This phrase is always translated as "harmony (or melody) *and rhythm*" but, when translated more properly in the context of orchestral art for both Plato and Aristotle as "music (or melody) and dance," helps us easily resolve other perennial dilemmas.

Drama at Aristotle's time (4th century BCE)

Musical drama, that is, a plot performed (usually in a theater) with language, music, dance and spectacle, was an ancient Greek invention that first occurred in the 6th century BCE in Athens and in Sicily. The latter is where the comedic plots were first done, according to Aristotle in Chapter 5. We need only concentrate here on the three dramatic or proto-dramatic art forms that the Northern Greek examines in his treatise: tragedy, comedy, and epic.

He in no way cares about various non-dramatic types of poetry or songs, such as epinicians (victory odes), paeans, encomia, hymns, and love songs (especially by Sappho, whom even philosophers admired). He does not even mention, much less analyze, them.[38] Epic is seemingly the origin of tragedy for Aristotle, as we will see in *Dramatics 4* on one of his accounts. Dithyramb, which was typically a performance of dance with music in honor of Dionysus, the god of wine, and the satyr play, which even had somewhat sophisticated plots as it evolved, are given later in the chapter as other origins. Scholars perennially debate the soundness of Aristotle's whole history or the relation between the accounts. Did dithyramb somehow get inspired by epic and evolve from it? It is hard, though, to imagine the riotous performance type coming from epic when Aristotle explicitly discusses two branches of composition from Homer, epic with noble characters and comedy with vulgar personages. Was tragedy instead a *combination* of epic and dithyramb, with the plot from epic and the full enactment including the choral performance from dithyramb? I discuss this

---

38 For a category of poems around the time of Plato, cf. Nagy and *ADMC*, pp. 209-10. See especially footnote 333 on p. 210 for why Nagy persuasively considers early works by, e.g., Sappho to be "songs" and not "poetry." See also J.W. Fitton, "Greek Dance," *Classical Quarterly*, New Series, Vol. 23, No. 2, (November 1973) 254-274, for how speech, music and dance in the theater were usually done together in earlier Hellenistic culture (and cf. *ADMC*, pp. 85; 113; and 196).

more in Chapter 4.

The paradigm of epic was Homer's *Iliad* and *Odyssey*,[39] and Aristotle and Plato both indicate that Homer was the first tragedian. We will see that epic is a kind of youthful tragedy, with the "singer" (as the epic reciters were originally called before the 4th century BCE[40]) either singing or playing an instrument or both and acting dramatically at times (that is, mixing some impersonation with narration). Thus, epic has the four necessary and sufficient conditions for "dramatic composition" of the Aristotelian *poiēsis*: plot, language, music and "dance" or what dance was in those days "ordered body movement" according to Plato,[41] *which could simply be gesturing and posturing, as long as it was done in an ordered manner.*

Dance for the Greeks naturally could be done stepping to music, as it is for folk dancers today and as it has been in many or all different cultures. However, in ancient Greece, dance could be, and was, done on one's head (like break dancing today!) or while sitting or while being in one place on a dais, as the rhapsodes of the late 5th century and 4th century BCE were, according to Plato's dialogue *Ion*.[42] It is still debated whether epic around the time of Plato and Aristotle involved music or whether the rhapsodes simply expressed various compositions like the *Odyssey* and *Iliad* as poets nowadays do, without singing. However, we will see that, just as tragedy was being composed only to be read around Aristotle's time, which is not the type of tragedy analyzed

---

39   Some scholars dispute that Homer really existed, or at least that he fully composed the two epics attributed to him. One option is that he created the core part of each, and subsequent bards embellished them.

40   Cf. Notomi, *op. cit.*, pp. 300-4; also, *ADMC* pp. 115ff.

41   *Laws* II, 665a. For the arguments and evidence from the rest of *Laws* II and elsewhere why "ordered body movement" is dance for Plato, see Chapter 1 of *ADMC*. For how Aristotle follows suit, see Chapter 2.

42   *Ion* 530a; 5352d; 535b. *Laws* II, 665a; Cf. *ADMC*, Chapter 1, and espec. pp. 111-3 and 465.

in the *Dramatics*, so it may have been that some epic compositions were being written not to be sung. I know of no solid evidence for this one way or the other.[43] Nevertheless, the Northern Greek himself in Chapter 26 follows Plato in assuming that the rhapsodes gesticulate because he complains that they sometimes do it too much. Whether this means that he recognizes Homeric readings without music of any kind, be it chanting or self-accompaniment, and whether he would give it as much praise as musical epic, we cannot say from the extant texts. In the *Laws* II, Plato himself, however, definitely denigrates the new-fangled approach of using words without tune (in the context of art) and shows that he prefers the older styles in which the music and words were combined.[44] I discuss this more when examining Chapter 26.

In any event, the Northern Greek does not care nearly as much for epic in the *Dramatics* as he does for tragedy. In the *Dramatics,* epic is considered mostly the early form of the more honorable tragedy. Aristotle also says that epic is a subset of tragedy and that whoever knows the principles of tragedy knows epic. As he emphasizes in Chapter 23, epic should be composed *in a dramatic manner*, even though it is primarily narrated and not *fully* impersonated, the latter style involving spectacle and a chorus (and locomoting actors). Epic,

---

43   Nagy suggests that purely linguistic epic was recited, but I believe the passages he looks at can suggest the rhapsodes were chanting, almost like rappers today, and although chanting is not like opera or pop singing, it still can qualify as music; cf. *ADMC*, pp. 207-8; 341-2; and 465-6. The passages from Plato's *Ion* are conclusive, in that they show that at least sometimes the rhapsodes still used music, gesture, and language. *Dramatics* 26 confirms that Sosistratus, the rhapsode, gesticulated too much, and if Aristotle assumes Plato's view, then as a rhapsode Sosistratus was singing too, in some fashion. Also, epic might have had different performance types, some with mere recitation that had no music and others which did. Finally, perhaps some epic was being composed to be read, rather than performed, just as we will see some tragedy was beginning to be composed only as literature, but I know of no classicist exploring this possibility as such.

44   669d-e; *ADMC*, pp. 120 ff.

though, for Aristotle has an advantage that tragedy does not have, the latter being constrained to the one action in the theater. Epic (like literature or film for us) can move around in time, as it were, and be more amazing. Another reason that the Northern Greek includes epic is that he wants to reject Plato's ranking, in which epic is placed above tragedy.[45] In Chapter 26 he articulates the reasons why tragedy is better. Aristotle in no way, though, suggests that epic should be discontinued in Greek culture. One might guess that if a dramatist, song-writer or wordsmith did not have the massive resources to stage a tragedy, then epic (and of course merely literary tragedy) would be a legitimate option. Hence, if only for diversity, epic should continue. That epic has its own place–just as radio continues to have a place in Western culture even after being usurped by television and film–is shown by Aristotle's love of Homer. Not only is Aristotle reputed to have given an illustrious copy of Homer's work to Alexander the Great, his student, but he wrote a treatise defending Homer, perhaps against Plato, who himself wanted in the ideal republic to censor all, or almost all, art forms like tragedy, comedy and epic. Aristotle's treatise, called *Homeric Problems*, is lost, although some scholars believe that Chapter 25 of the *Dramatics* is actually an interpolation of part of that work (and in my view it probably is).

Before focusing on tragedy, I should underscore that drama *per se*, as plays done in the theater, had three forms at Aristotle's time: tragedy, comedy, and the satyr play, the latter of which involved not only satyrs that were half-man and half-beast with erect phalluses, but more serious protagonists, in a mixture of serious themes, ribald jokes and outrageous behavior. However, Aristotle pays only passing attention to the satyr play in his history of drama, which is an utter mystery that is hardly ever acknowledged. Indeed, given the ramifications of my research and the Diotiman based-notion of *poiēsis*, it is one of the great unanswered questions of the treatise and is surely a topic for

---

45   658d; *ADMC*, p. 165. Also cf. *Republic* 394c, 397d and 398d.

future research.[46]

Unless more texts are discovered, though, anyone trying to resolve the mystery of the nature and role of the satyr play will sadly be working with scant evidence. Aeschylus' *Net Fishers* was highly regarded but is lost. We have fragments of Sophocles' *Ichneutai* (*The Trackers*), but the only extant satyr play is *Cyclops* by Euripides.[47] However, Aristotle could have no more been ignorant of these plays than a philosopher of science nowadays could be ignorant of Louis Pasteur.

One possible answer why Aristotle omits the satyr play in his treatise pertains to it being no longer required (or even permitted) when the annual competition went from a tetralogy (three tragedies finishing with a satyr play) to a trilogy of "mere" tragedies, in 340/39 BCE, when Aristotle was in the middle of his absence from Athens for about 13 years. When he returned at the age of about 49, there were no longer satyr plays in the competitions involving tragedy, and, if we assume that the *Dramatics* was finished late in his life, as at least almost all specialists believe, then Aristotle had good reason to ignore satyr plays

---

46   *ADMC*, pp. 373 (footnote 541); 442-3; 492-5, and especially footnote 729 on p. 495 and footnote 732 on p. 497.

47   Immediately before publication of this book, a review appeared of Carl Shaw, *Euripides: Cyclops. A Satyr Play* (Companions to Greek and Roman Tragedy, 2018). Not being able to get Shaw's work in time for my purposes here, I mention only that Ian Storey speaks in the review of Euripides' *Alcestis*. Storey recounts that it was "produced in the fourth position, after the three tragedies performed in the competition at the City Dionysia...in 438, [and] has no satyrs for its chorus... It is a curious play, set more in the world of traditional folk-tale than in that of the Olympians" (*Bryn Mawr Classical Review* 2018.10.24, available at:
http://www.bmcreview.org/2018/10/20181024.html, as of 10/15/18).

   This strikes me as the kind of oddity that Aristotle would note in a history of tragedy, although he would need a lot more space than he has in our *Dramatics* 4 and 5. Perhaps the passages are lost or perhaps he wrote about more precise developments like these in the other books that he wrote on tragedy or drama, of which more below.

in the *Dramatics*. However, it is still baffling why he does not discuss the evolution of the tetralogy and trilogy in his history of drama in Chapter 4, unless the discussion is lost. Another option that explains the omission in Chapter 4 is that Aristotle considered the satyr play to be a sub-species of comedy, or a genre closely allied to comic drama, and that he discussed it in the lost book on comedy, the topic to which I now turn (although, of course, he could have both discussed it in detail in the lost book and merely introduced it in Chapter 4 in a passage that is also lost).

As alluded to, I will not say much about comic drama here because of the absence of the relevant manuscript, again, the so-called lost second "book" of the *Dramatics* (on some accounts it was originally written on a different scroll). Aristotle does recount in Chapters 4-5 the basics of the history of comedy and a few of its features in giving the origins of drama, as well as the commonalities and differences with tragedy. He also, for example, praises comedy in Chapter 9 (1451b11ff) because the comic composers began creating universal themes with characters that were not real-life butts of satire, so-called invective or "iambs." The last were sometimes done in the Greek theater and even Aristophanes occasionally incorporates invective in some of his comedies, mocking not only political figures but the renowned Socrates. As Aristotle stresses with approval, the comedians created the universal characters even before the tragedians themselves. Instead, originally the tragedians habitually presented historical episodes on stage or stories about well-known families and myths that would hardly be considered "universal characters" (which for Aristotle had to be believable, and thus mythological figures like Hercules or Prometheus, like our Superman and Spiderman, would not count).

We know also from his *Politics* and *Rhetoric* that the Northern Greek discussed jests and catharsis in a treatise on *poiēsis*. It stands to reason that catharsis was discussed in the lost section on comedy, since the promised explanation exists nowhere in our extant treatise (assuming that another lost treatise did not contain the discussion). It also stands to reason, therefore, that catharsis may have been very relevant, indeed more relevant, to comedy than to tragedy. However, this is a topic that must be left for future scholarship, as shocking as it is to traditional sensibilities who have supposed for hundreds of years that all tragedy for Aristotle is supposed to have catharsis through pity and fear. The aforementioned influential Renaissance literary theorist Julius Caesar Scaliger and the famous French tragedians Racine and Corneille, among others, rejected Aristotle's goal of catharsis (correctly) as unempirical, a rather severe insult to one of the great empiricists of all times. Yet, neither Scaliger, Racine or Corneille questioned whether Aristotle actually wrote *katharsis* in the definition of tragedy. Petruševski was the first in that regard.[48] Ironically, then, in not holding catharsis to be the end of tragedy, Scaliger, Racine and Corneille were more Aristotelian in this regard than either they or anyone else knew.[49]

Let us now focus on Aristotle's account of tragedy. Even though the theory in the *Dramatics* is philosophical, it is not disconnected with the phenomena that Aristotle knew in real life, as is abundantly clear throughout the treatise. To reiterate, Aristotle was an empiricist. He also presents a theory of ethics in various treatises but does not thereby imagine a new kind of human being, with no body and only a soul that is completely separable. His ethics is of "hylomorphic" individuals, corporal entities with particular souls. (The term for soul, which

---

[48] A German-American specialist of Aristotle who perished in a Nazi concentration camp, Alfred Gudeman, and a Croatian scholar, Anton Smerdel, deserve some credit for claiming that the attempts to determine the meaning of catharsis in the definition of tragedy would never succeed, given not only the history of the attempts to solve the problem but the inconsistencies or outright contradictions with the rest of Aristotle's theories. They influenced Petruševski and gave him some of the insights and courage to start cutting this Gordian Knot. Cf. *ADMC*, Chapters 5-6.

[49] See the Appendix in *ADMC* for Scaliger's views. Scaliger actually held the view that comedy, as he defines it, is more admirable than tragedy!

for Aristotle does not survive death, is *psyche*, the root of "psychology"). As Gene Fendt puts it: "...the final cause [of happiness] neither is *nor is in* either the soul or the body, rather the final cause is the excellent functioning *of the composite*."[50] The individuals have emotions, needs and ideals, are part of the world, and realize the importance of living with others. "One man, no man," the Greeks and Aristotle would say.

Likewise, with tragedy: Aristotle places it in a biological and cultural context during his history of Chapters 4-5, ignoring, perhaps surprisingly, the political aspects while concentrating on the artistic aspects. However, this is one reason that Aristotle's work has resonated for so long. His account is not disproportionately subject to the vagaries of different epochs and nations. He does not care as much as Plato about the seeming influence that tragedy has on a particular audience and whether some tragedies might corrupt the audience (Plato's reason for wanting censorship), although Aristotle, too, has some definite concern in that regard in the *Politics*. Rather, at least initially in the *Dramatics*, he is more concerned about examining the natural aspects or "parts" of tragedy, including any "power" or "potential" (*dunamis*) of a particular part, giving us the type of understanding of art that in other circumstances is called "scientific knowledge" (*epistēmē*) without suggesting the modern notion that implies carrying out experiments. "Systematic empirical knowledge," then, might be a better description for 21st century readers. In the *Overview* and *Comments* for Chapter 1, we observe Aristotle starting off his treatise with his goal to provide this kind of knowledge of the activity known as *poiēsis*, following to some extent the way Plato conceived of "scientific knowledge." The debt to his mentor surfaces yet another time.

---

50 Gene Fendt, *Love Song for the Life of the Mind: An Essay on the Purpose of Comedy* (Washington D.C.: Catholic University of America Press, 2011) p. 35; my italics. For Aristotle, happiness is, or is caused by, the excellent functioning of the individual in life, as explained in the *Nicomachean Ethics*.

This desire for "scientific knowledge" should not be surprising, given Aristotle's concern throughout most of his life for biology, which can include psychology. Thus, I would categorize his ground breaking *De Anima* or *On the Soul* as a biological treatise. Even though Aristotle was an astute political and ethical theorist, the founder of logic, and one of the greatest metaphysicians who ever lived—"metaphysics" meaning simply the book of (first) philosophy that was written "after" (*meta*) his *Physics* (*phusica*)—he was also the son of the physician who ministered to the court of King Philip of Macedonia, Alexander the Great's father. It should not be too surprising, then, that Alexander, who was Aristotle's pupil, sent unusual biological specimens back to Aristotle during Alexander's conquests on the way to India and that Aristotle is arguably the most admired biologist of all time according to no mean biologist himself, Charles Darwin. Much of Aristotle's dramatic theory has biological frameworks or analogies, and, indeed, the origin of tragedy (and of dramatic composition in general) for Aristotle follows suit, as we see in Chapter 4.

For the moment we are focusing on drama at Aristotle's time, especially the origins that Aristotle provides in his Chapters 4-5. From the natural, biological disposition to impersonate, sing, and dance, and from the dancing and singing chorus, he says, the tragedy of his day was born and evolved. He does not say in the extant treatise that a seminal development was, as is commonly accepted, Peisistratos, the enlightened ruler or "tyrant" (*tyrannos*) of Athens, starting the annual competitions in tragedy in 534 BCE (although some classicists now place the date at around 508 BCE). Nor does Aristotle in the surviving text say that, as other authors recount, Thespis separated himself from the chorus and began speaking to it, of course for the benefit of the audience. (This is why the art of acting is called "Thespian.") Ultimately, the acting, discourse, song, and dance were for the audience, but the Greek actors, like us, seemingly imagined the so-called "fourth wall."

After discussing in Chapter 4 not only the biological disposition for singing, dancing and impersonating but the early choruses, Aristotle writes that Aeschylus increased the number of actors to two and then Sophocles increased them to three and added scene-painting. Aeschylus also made language the primary feature (but not the *only* feature) because before him, Aristotle says, the speech was "laughable" (but not comic because Aristotle is discussing tragedy and not comedy). In addition, Aristotle quips, the plots were trivial. However, according to the Greek rhetorician Themistius (fourth century CE), Aristotle said that tragedy was entirely choral until Thespis introduced the prologue and the internal speeches:

> As Themistius says in *Oration 26 (On Speaking)*, 316A-D: "Do we not pay attention to Aristotle, <when he says> that at first the chorus entered and sang to the god, Thespis invented a prologue and speech, Aeschylus (invented) actors and a stage..."[51]

Chapter 4 is the only place in the *Dramatics* where this topic is relevant, and it fills the gap where Aristotle jumps from the choral beginnings to Aeschylus increasing the number of actors to two. This helps prove that we are missing at least one passage from the extant treatise, and the reader will discover other ellipses that no one has been able to fill in sensibly (usually represented in translations with three dots "..."). This is presumably because of the damage done to the original manuscript, as chronicled by Strabo. It may well have been that in lost passages Aristotle also gave the political origins when Peisistratos started the annual competitions. Without more manuscripts or fragments being discovered, we will never know.

In any event, the whole history of tragedy by Aristotle is of a *fully performed theatrical art*, with language, music, dance and spectacle, exactly what the Athenians experienced and what Aristotle defines

---

51   Richard Janko, *Philodemus: The Aesthetic Works. Vol. I/3: Philodemus, On Poems Books 3–4, with the Fragments of Aristotle, On Poets* (Oxford: Oxford University Press, 2011) 434-5.

in Chapter 6.[52] Aristotle's description, and theory, of tragedy is in effect no different from his description, and theory, of animals. Both phenomena are natural even if the term artifact or artificial (as man-made) is often contrasted with nature in *one* of its senses (as "not man-made"). However, men and women *naturally* make artifacts, sing and dance, according to Aristotle, and here "naturally" means in line with "laws of nature." Greek words are often ambiguous, as are English words, and one has to pay attention to the exact context to determine their meaning. Similarly, Aristotle reports what he sees or what he deduces to be the functions or powers of different parts of tragedy, just as in his biology and zoology he theorizes about the functions of different parts of animals or plants. The function of a leaf on a tree, for example, is either to protect the fruit from the sun or to collect water (we might say to carry out photosynthesis). Although Aristotle does not say the following, because it is obvious or very strongly implied in his plan as given in Chapter 1, the totality of the powers (or capacities) is what is in tragedy as a whole, and we see in the individual chapters him discussing the powers of the individual parts.

To understand for the moment more how artifacts like tragedy are "natural," let us finish with one passage from outside the *Dramatics*.

---

[52] Stephen Halliwell, one of the renowned commentators of the *Dramatics*, recognizes that Aristotle reports this, but says that theoretically the type of tragedy that Aristotle examines could be done without spectacle, which would occur in our imagination ("Aristotelianism and anti-Aristotelianism in Attitudes to Theatre," in *Attitudes To Theatre From Plato to Milton*, ed. Elena Theodorakopoulos, Nottingham Classical Literature Studies, Vol. 7, Bari: Levante Editori, 2003: 57-75). Halliwell believes we can make a distinction for Aristotle between the plays that Aristotle himself always saw and the theoretical plays that could be done, which he alleges Aristotle is trying to cover in his chapter on definition. I explain how this view is contradicted, to give just one reason now, by Aristotle's necessary conditions of tragedy and his theory of definition, even if the view could apply in other, *modified* circumstances to merely written tragedy; cf. *ADMC*, pp. 285-89. Again, partly for reasons already given, merely literary tragedy is more like epic and is not the focus of Aristotle's examination in the *Dramatics*; cf. *AMDC*, Chapters 2, 3, and 9.

Within the larger context of discussing chance, necessity and whether nature is some type of cause and in explaining how things with an end in nature follow similar principles in art, Aristotle says:

> ...where there is an end, all the preceding steps are for the sake of that... *If a house, e.g., had been a thing made by nature, it would have been made in the same way as it is now by art*; and if things made by nature were made not only by nature but also by art, they would come to be in the same way as by nature... **Generally, art in some cases completes what nature cannot bring to a finish, and in others imitates nature.** If, therefore, artificial products are for the sake of an end, so clearly also are natural products. *The relation of the later to the earlier items is the same in both.* This is most obvious in the animals other than man: they make things neither by art nor after inquiry or deliberation. That is why people wonder whether it is by intelligence or by some other faculty that these creatures work,—spiders, ants, and the like... (*Physics* II 8, 199a19-24; my italics and bolding).[53]

If art *completes* sometimes what nature does not, clearly the completion has to be of the same type as the natural process. Thus, even though Aristotle makes a superficial distinction a sentence later between "nature" and "artificial," still the principles are the same for each, and in other places in the *Physics* he says that the most distinctive principle of nature is motion. Actors and singers move their mouths to speak and sing; dancers move their bodies to express; sculptors move their hands and tools to create; and theorists and composers move their brain cells to imagine (and all artists use their intelligence along with their bodies). Obviously, art also has to be natural in the latter sense of "nature" or "natural," characterized by motion.

---

53   Transl. by R.P. Hardie and R.K. Gaye, *The Complete Works of Aristotle*, ed. Jonathan Barnes, 2 vols. (Princeton: Princeton University Press, 1984). For other illuminating thoughts on this passage, cf. Fendt, *op. cit.*, 2011, p. 21, footnote 13.

Drama at Aristotle's Time

To finish the origin of tragedy: Starting from a biological foundation, Aristotle gives a short history of tragedy as a genre in Chapters 4-5. However, during this history, he does not name tragedians after Sophocles, who died in 406 BCE at the age of 90, nor does he present any new developments, suggesting that tragedy had matured and then stayed the same in terms of general considerations for the whole 4th century BCE. He discusses at length no tragedian of that century in the treatise, at the most mentioning a few like Theodectes or giving a short remark. In Chapter 18 he denigrates Agathon, one of the most famous dramatists, who died at the beginning of the 4th century very soon after Sophocles, because Agathon wrote musical interludes that were not integrated with the relevant play and could be moved to another play without difference. Clearly, then, for Aristotle tragedy in the 4th century BCE was *essentially* like that of the end of the 5th century, even if there might have been many *minor* differences.

It might be helpful to note how tragedy changed after Aristotle's day. Subtly at times and not so subtly at other times, this change affects how modern individuals through their own lens view ancient tragedy (and I already gave an indication of how *tragōidia* for Aristotle has been conceived for over 400 years as tragedy in our sense, *always* ending badly, whereas this was clearly not his meaning, given how the best "tragedies" in Chapter 14 end happily). Roman pantomime (from the Greek *pantos*, all, and *mime*, impersonator) became very well known subsequently and was actually more like musical drama of the 4th century BCE than our own pantomime, with Marcel Marceau being a prime example for 20th century viewers. See one of the most famous and beloved French films of all time, *The Children of Paradise (Les Enfants du Paradis)*, to get a better idea of what pantomime may well have been like in Roman times, when the pantomimes became as famous as rock stars today and as the mime Baptiste Debureau was in the 1840's (the setting of *Children of Paradise*).[54] Roman pantomime

---

54   Just as *Gone with the Wind* is usually voted the favorite film of all

had music and a story or plot, with characterization.[55] If anything, the mimes of the time danced even more than modern pantomimes, because they were called dancers rather than mimes, even though their dancing was extremely mimetic.

As we saw, Justinian brutally closed theaters and schools of philosophy about 528 CE in the name of Christian values, helping usher in the Middle Ages. It would not be for 1000 years that drama gets performed in public again in the West. This coincides with the time that the first book of Aristotle's treatise in its original language was "rediscovered" and studied at universities in Italy, over 400 years after the Arabic commentator Avicenna first attempted in print to make sense of the treatise.

After the Medieval religious pageants and morality plays, sometimes done on "pageant-wagons" that toured from village to city to countryside, Aristotelian-type drama with a chorus and spectacle began making a comeback around the mid-1500's. (Perhaps I should have mentioned earlier that the ancient Greeks like Thespis also reportedly toured around the country with their own pageant-wagons. Plato presumably alludes to this custom in the *Laws* VII, 817c, when, in arguing for the censorship of comedy, tragedy, music, and choral dances, he has the Athenian Stranger say, according to the translation of Trevor Saunders: "don't...[have] the idea that we shall ever...allow you ["musical" composers (*poiētai*)] to set up stage in the market-place.") The first "permanent" English theater, the Red Lion, opened in 1567 but

---

time in America, so *Children of Paradise* is usually voted the all-time favorite in France. On pantomime: The United Kingdom calls a type of musical comedy, especially targeted at children and families, "pantomime" or "panto." However, it has as much language as drama and should not be confused with non-speaking pantomime (also, I gather that "panto" does not usually, or ever, have a plot in Aristote's sense).

55   Cf. Ismene Lada-Richards, *Silent Eloquence: Lucian and Pantomime Dancing* (London: Duckworth, 2007).   Also cf. *ADMC*, pp. 307-8 and 578-9.

closed not long after, and Shakespeare (1565-1616) was part of the first generation of Elizabethan dramatists that also included George Peele and Christopher Marlowe, who were creating and often acting in their own plays starting in the late 1500's. As alluded to, about 1570, Julius Caesar Scaliger articulates in print (posthumously) a very influential definition of tragedy that must end unhappily while he examines Aristotle's own work and uses it to advance his own theories.[56] Scaliger, however, tries to dissuade readers from examining Plato's *Phaedrus* and *Symposium*, calling the two dialogues "monstrous," for reasons he does not state.[57] One might speculate that it was because male homosexuality is discussed frankly and with no opprobrium in both dialogues. Whatever the reason, the *Symposium* is where, of course, Diotima teaches us how the Greeks use the term *poiēsis*, and Scaliger must take part, but only part, of the responsibility for no one until my "*Poetics* of Performance" in 1999 (p. 18) trying to apply the Diotiman meaning of the term to the *Dramatics*.

---

56   J.C. Scaliger should not be confused with his son Joseph Scaliger, who became a famous classicist. Joseph's interpretation of Parmenides' famous philosophical poem has been very influential in the field, although not without its just critics, as Alexander Mourelatos, a Professor of Philosophy at the University of Texas, Austin, once explained to me because Mourelatos published a refutation of Scaliger's interpretation of one part of the poem.

57   Cf. *ADMC*, pp. 507-8 and espec. 549.

A Primer on Aristotle's Dramatics

Misunderstood Core Greek Terms

In this section, I merely introduce the heretofore misconstrued core terms in the order in which they appear in the *Dramatics*. They get explained more in the *Comments* to each chapter.

Poiēsis, whose cognate *poiētikēs* occurs in the first sentence of the treatise, has five meanings around the time of Plato and Aristotle: making in general; making music and verse; making music, dance and verse; making verse; and Aristotle's technical sense, unknown until now: making music, dance, verse and plot. Unfortunately, *poiēsis* has always been assumed to have the Gorgian meaning (making verse) in the *Dramatics*. Rather, as I demonstrate rigorously in *ADMC* and have explained here in a few ways already, in the *Dramatics* it has fundamentally the Diotiman narrow meaning (making music, dance and verse) with Aristotle adding a fourth condition, plot, to make the word a technical term in the Lyceum.

Mimēsis, often just transliterated and used as "mimesis" in English, is shown to be "impersonation," "representation," "expression," or "imitation" at times, with the context making one sense reasonable and the other senses absurd. One simply cannot take a rich word like *mimēsis*, and give it a univocal meaning, just as one cannot give *logos* a single meaning for all contexts. *Logos* itself primarily means language, speech, prose, proportion or ratio, to give just a few options, and the Greek lexicons reveal two full pages of different meanings for the term. In the *Dramatics* it generally means speech or language, and occasionally prose. That the Greeks were as capable as modern English speakers of disambiguating the correct meaning in any context will be shown to some extent below, although the plethora of reasons and details, along with a history of *mimesis*, must be left to *ADMC* (Chapter 3). Suffice it to say that the direct object or the activity being spoken of determines the meaning in the Greek, grasped by readers in a nanosecond, just as you and other readers immediately grasped the difference in "play," when you read the example above, where "play" was used in three different senses in one and the same complex sentence. You had no problem realizing immediately that "play" for tennis meant compete or engage in a game, whereas "play" Hamlet meant impersonate (an imaginary prince) on stage, and "play" the piano meant make music with that instrument. Again, the direct object or the context of the activity gave the meaning of the verb, and if someone (especially 2000 years from now) tried to understand "play" in a univocal sense in the cases above, it would make the other cases nonsense.

The next two crucial, and previously misunderstood words, are *harmonia kai rhuthmos*, most often translated as "harmony and rhythm." They are two of the three so-called "means of mimesis" that Aristotle introduces in Chapter 1, the third being speech or language (*logos*). Because there was no such thing in ancient Greece as musical harmony in our sense of the word (a chord or progression that itself presupposes a chord), *harmonia* should not be translated as "harmony." Rather, as at least a few commentators have long recognized, it means "melody" (as a synecdoche) or just "music," given that Greek music was always done as a single melodic line, at least for Plato and Aristotle. Yet it is then redundant in a high-level philosophical treatment to say "and rhythm," when melodies and music *always* had their own tonal rhythms. Rather, as I show in the *Comments* for Chapters 1, 4 and 6, Aristotle follows Plato in the usage of *rhuthmos*, even if he disagrees at times with his mentor with respect to some aspects of "musical" or dramatic practice. *When done in the theater or in the context of the orchestral arts, rhuthmos* primarily means for both "ordered body movement" or dance. This is the sense of the term that Plato explicitly gives in the *Laws*, in the so-called second book, at 665a, when he discusses children putting order into their chaotic jumping, saying that *rhuthmos* is the name of "ordered body movement." There *harmonia* is also said to be "song" or "music," that is, the ordering of the wild pitches that children would initially just shout. Plato immediately adds via his stand-in, the character Socrates, that the combination of the two (*harmonia kai rhuthmos*) is the choral art (*choreia*) and in *ADMC* (Chapter 1), I demonstrate in great detail how trying to read this phrase as anything but "music and dance" leads to grave absurdities.

Hence, for Plato a primary sense of *harmonia kai rhuthmos* is "music (or song) and dance"; likewise, Aristotle in the current treatise. Scholars have missed this in large part because Aristotle uses the terms in the *Rhetoric* with one of their other legitimate senses, and the scholars have wrongly assumed that, again, *rhuthmos* is univocal, no matter what the context. Aristotle says in the *Rhetoric*:

> ...it is the *numerical limitation of the form of a composition* that constitutes rhythm, of which metres are definite sections. *Prose, then, is to be rhythmical, but not metrical, or it will become not prose but verse.* It should not even have too precise a prose rhythm, *and therefore should only be rhythmical to a certain extent* (*Rhetoric* III 8) [my italics].[58]

Harmony is using tones loudly (or high-pitched), softly (or low-pitched), or in-between (*Rhetoric* III 1), but it is obvious that a single orator and his voice is being discussed. Thus, in the *Rhetoric* Aristotle is not following Plato's use of *harmonia kai rhuthmos* in *Laws* II as the blending of the high and low while *singing* or of *rhuthmos* as "ordered body movement," capturing the evolution of children wildly jumping into something more intelligible. No Greek would think Aristotle in the *Rhetoric* is using *harmonia* in the sense of singing, or *rhuthmos* in the sense of dance, given the context of a single orator speaking to the law courts or political public assemblies (for Aristotle the setting of the relevant, rhetorical speaking[59]), just as no English speaker would

---

[58]   1408b28-32, *op. cit.*, *Complete Works*, ed. J. Barnes, Vol. 2, trans. by W. Rhys Roberts, as are all other passages from the *Rhetoric*, unless stated.

[59]   Aristotle is concerned with what we would call persuasive speaking

think that playing a violin means trying to score against an opponent with that instrument by using it to hit a ball (although the image of a tennis player serving with a violin rather than a racket is rather amusing). Unfortunately, as we see in detail in Chapter 1 and as you would see in any of the dozens of traditional translations, commentators have simply assumed that *rhuthmos* in the *Dramatics* means "rhythm," the numerical limitation of the form of a composition, or a temporal order, similar to how it is used in English. However, this usage is mostly anachronistic and triggers major paradoxes. What they are, above and beyond the ones noted above, will be covered in the *Comments*.[60]

Metron generally means "meter." It can also mean "verse" (because the language is in meter), as it does at the end of Chapter 1. There, Aristotle combines *metron* with music and dance, to recapitulate the three means of mimesis introduced earlier, where *logos* was the word first used for language or speech. *Metron* in this case must be the substitute for *logos* and thus must mean verse. Again, we need to use the context to help determine the meaning of a word, and even then it may be difficult, as we will observe, for example, in Chapter 4 with *metron*.

Lexis is even more ambiguous and can mean speech, language, diction, and style, to note just four connotations. In the *Dramatics*, it typically

---

in legal or political matters. Contrast this narrow scope with a modern definition of rhetoric, which is about all kinds of writing in general: "*All books* about writing are concerned with rhetoric, whether they make their concern explicit or not. *Rhetoric is the study of effective writing...* [my italics]" (Robert H. Moore, *Effective Writing*, 4th ed., New York: Holt, Rinehart and Winston, Inc., 1971, p. 4; first printing 1955).

60 For the rigorous arguments and evidence, including the meaning of *rhuthmos* before Plato and Aristotle, see *ADMC*, pp. 28-105. This, along with Chapter 4 that involves dance in the *Politics,* is the part of *ADMC* that is most useful for dance historians, putting dance back into the treatise after it had been omitted for centuries because of distorted translations of the "musical" terms.

means speech or language, but is too often translated wrongly as diction or style, causing significant confusion for the careful reader.

Melos likewise exudes ambiguity. Its primary meaning in ancient Greek is limb, that is, arm or leg. Yet in the context of the *Dramatics* it is typically translated as "melody." However, as at least one musicologist has shown,[61] and as the independent reasons of Chapter 6 demonstrate, it can also mean "music-dance," or the music going along with a dancing performer (which probably helped cause the term to be used for melody, perhaps because the length of a musical phrase coincided with a certain movement, or a sequence of movements, of a limb or limbs). The etymology was probably analogous to "foot" in poetry, as Fitton and others have shown, which associated often the steps of the chorus with a particular syllable or sequence of syllabi.[62] A similar word to *melos* in archaic Greek, and perhaps its predecessor, is *melpō*, a song-dance, with the associated verb *melpesthai* meaning "to sing and dance in a tragedy," for which we obviously have no single English word.[63] Melpomene is a Muse and songstress in Hesiod (who flourished around 700 BCE), and then later the Muse of tragedy, obviously reflecting the importance of song and dance in this art form for the Greeks, given the meaning of *melpō*. The reader new to Greek can easily guess, then, the meaning of another common word we find in the *Dramatics*, *melopoiia*, given, we saw, how cognates of *poiēsis* like "-*poios*" were added to the end of the primary word. Yes, it is the "making of the *melos*."

---

61   Thomas J. Mathiesen, *Apollo's Lyre: Greek Music and Music Theory in Antiquity and the Middle Ages* (Lincoln, NE and London: University of Nebraska Press, 1999). *ADMC*, pp. 67 and 106-8.

62   Cf. Fitton, *op. cit.*, and Christopher C. Marchetti, *Aristoxenus "Elements of Rhythm": Text, translation, and commentary with a translation and commentary on POxy 2687* (Ph.D. diss., Rutgers University, NJ, 2009); *ADMC* pp. 85; 195-6.

63   *ADMC*, p. 59.

Mousikē is used by Aristotle only occasionally, and invariably translated before me as "music," implying simply an aural experience, not only in *Dramatics* 26 but in the *Politics* VIII 7. As we saw, however, for Plato it can also mean "music-dance," like *melos*, and indeed by usually taking it this way, even if music is more important than dance, a number of other perennial dilemmas in the ancient Greek treatises can be resolved. Aristotle defines *mousikē* succinctly as *harmonia kai rhuthmos* in VIII 7, and similarly to the reasons already given, the two terms there must be not the inappropriate "harmony and rhythm," but "music and dance."[64] Again, we see Aristotle using terms often in the exact same way as Plato, in this case following the meaning of *mousikē* as given in the *Alcibiades* and *Laws*.

---

64 Cf. Chapter 4 of *ADMC* for the in-depth reasons. I demonstrate that *Politics* Book VIII is much more understandable if the three equivocal musical terms—*mousikē, harmonia* and *rhuthmos*—are usually rendered the way I suggest.

Blueprint of Aristotle's *Dramatics*

Along with understanding correctly the core Greek terms, the key to grasping rightly the whole treatise comes at the beginning, assuming we understand Aristotle's famous doctrine of the four causes. They are explanatory causes or what one scholar calls the "be-causes": material, formal, efficient, and final. The material cause is the matter, bronze in the case of a statue. The formal cause is the shape or the definition, so in the case of an individual statue, woman or lion, and in the generic case it might be, *qua* definition, "three-dimensional shape," in contrast to painting, which might be "two-dimensional colored shape." The efficient cause moved the thing or caused it to come into existence, sculptor in the case of the statue. The final cause is "that for the sake of which," money, fame, beauty, self-satisfaction or whatever else motivated the sculptor to create the statue. Aristotle uses health as the final cause of someone running with the clarification that it is the desire for health that, in terms of antecedent causality, makes the person get dressed and go through the pain of jogging on any particular day (because one cannot travel back in time for Aristotle).

Keeping the four causes in mind, we need to recognize also that Aristotle proceeds in important ways in the *Dramatics* with biological paradigms, which can be gleaned from the *History of Animals* I 6 (491a7ff). There, he says, we can get a relatively clear notion of a subject by determining the differences and common properties with similar things and by covering the "causes." Getting a "relatively clear notion" of drama, that is, tragedy, comedy, and to some extent of epic, is accomplished by Aristotle following this pattern in Chapters 1-6. He articulates the differences and common properties of the three art forms and their material causes in the first three chapters; then he recounts the birth of tragedy and comedy, along with differences from epic, in Chapters 4 and 5. The birth—namely, tragedy's genesis and history—is a discussion of the "efficient cause,"[65] and the definition of tragedy in Chapter 6 is the formal cause. The final cause of tragedy has been wrongly taken for centuries to be catharsis, because of the interpolated phrase in that definition, as we see in Chapter 6. However, a close reading of the whole treatise repeatedly shows the final cause to be instead (a proper) pleasure, starting in Chapter 4. Thus, we may surmise, Aristotle is indeed following the procedure recommended in the *History of Animals*. Alternatively, the procedure there is a result of his reflecting on the plan he first used in writing the first drafts of the *Dramatics*, if, as some believe, he slowly wrote the treatise over his professional career and modified it to arrive at the final version, late in life.[66]

In conjunction with the above, we may view Aristotle's outline for the treatise as following Plato's method for achieving scientific knowledge of an object or a practice. Plato reports the following in the *Phaedrus* at 270dff, which I dissect with numbered curly brackets:

I suggest that the way to reflect about the nature of any-

---

65   That the history of something—in this case tragedy as a kind of *poiēsis*—can be an efficient cause is confirmed by the *Posterior Analytics* II 11, where Aristotle uses "the Athenians raiding Sardis" as the efficient cause of the Persian war (94a35ff). Since something's history is the series of events leading up to it or causing it, the history of tragedy will presumably be an account of (at least one of) its efficient causes. I stress that this is the cause of the genre, not of any particular instance. The efficient cause of the latter is presumably the individual dramatist and the actors, dancers, musicians, and scene-makers assisting in creating it.

Aristotle also says in the *Politics* I 2, 1252a24: "He who thus considers things in their first growth and origin, whether a state or anything else, will obtain the clearest view of them" (transl. B. Jowett, in *The Complete Works of Aristotle*, ed. J. Barnes, *op. cit.*). As it stands, without qualification, this might suggest a *merely* historical approach, where we present only the genesis, and so would not be the procedure Aristotle is using in the *Dramatics*. However, in the *Politics* he is only addressing the benefit of understanding the efficient cause, without ruling out the importance of the other causes.

66   In particular, Stephen Halliwell; cf. *ADMC*, p. 491.

thing is as follows: first, to decide whether the object in respect of which we desire to have scientific knowledge, and to be able to impart it to others, {1} *is simple or complex*; secondly, if it is simple, to inquire {2} *what natural capacity it has* of acting upon another thing, and through what means; or by what other thing, and through what means, it can be acted upon; or, if it is complex, {3} *to enumerate its parts* and {4} *observe in respect of each what we observe in the case of the simple object, to wit what its natural capacity, active or passive, consists in* (R. Hackforth translation).

Take now what Aristotle says in his first sentences of the *Dramatics*. I also interpolate numbered curly brackets:

Our topic is "dramatic musical composition" (*poiētikēs*) {1} *in itself and its kinds*, {2} *and what capacity (dunamis) each has*; how plots should be constructed if the composition is to turn out well; also, {3} *from how many parts it is [constituted]*, and {4} *of what sort they are*; and likewise all other aspects of the same enquiry. Let us first begin, following the natural [order], from first [principles] (my translation, following Janko).[67]

As the numbered points illustrate, a correspondence holds between Plato's method and Aristotle's. In brief, the method is to determine if something is simple or complex; if simple, determine the active and passive capacities; if complex, proceed recursively in the same manner for each of the parts. Aristotle appears, then, to be also following Plato's plan in the *Phaedrus* for attaining the best kind of understanding of dramatic "musical" composition. Contrary to the accepted tradition, he is *not* promising, for instance, to present a taxonomy of the forms of poetry, even if his scientific method results secondarily in some occasional type of minor classification of the various arts. S.H. Butcher also reminds us of the similarity between Aristotle's approach as outlined in the *History of Animals* and Plato's in this regard, leaving aside that Butcher asserts that the *Dramatics* is about "poetic crit-

---

67   1445a8ff.

icism" instead of "musical" dramatic theory:

> **The idea of an organism** evidently underlies all Aristotle's rules about unity; it is tacitly assumed as a first principle of art, and in one passage is expressly mentioned as that from which the rule of epic unity is deduced. [Here Butcher gives the quasi-definition of epic in Chapter 23:] '**The plot must, as in a tragedy, be dramatically constructed**; it must have for its subject a single action, whole and complete, with a beginning, a middle, and an end. *It will thus resemble a single and coherent organism* and produce the pleasure proper to it'.

> Plato in the *Phaedrus* had insisted that every artistic composition, whether in prose or verse, should have an **organic unity**. 'You will allow that every discourse ought to be constructed like a **living organism, having its own body and head and feet**; it must have middle and extremities, drawn in a manner agreeable to one another and to the whole [264c]'. Aristotle took up the hint; **the passage above quoted from the *Poetics* is a remarkable echo of the words of the *Phaedrus***; and indeed the idea may be said to be at the basis of his whole poetic criticism.[68]

In short, the overall blueprint that Aristotle follows seems to be either the one articulated in the *History of Animals* or in Plato's *Phaedrus* or a combination of the two, and the following indicates that the last option is best. If this combination is not enough, we will see later how Aristotle also uses "biological division" in defining tragedy. One of the reasons that the complex blueprint of the *Dramatics* has not been recognized clearly is that Aristotle follows three interwoven methodologies, at least in the first six chapters, with the recursive methodology (showing the capacities of the various parts) predominating for the rest of the treatise. However, given that Bach composed and per-

---

[68]   S.H. Butcher, *Aristotle's Theory of Poetry and Fine Art* (London: Macmillan and Co. Ltd., 1923) 187-189; 1st edition 1895; Butcher's italics, but my bolding and comment in brackets.

formed five-part fugues, it should not be surprising that one of the most brilliant thinkers, if not the most brilliant, in history could easily proceed with three criteria simultaneously or at least start with one set of criteria and, when revising, later incorporate additional criteria.

I now present fuller details of the blueprint of the whole treatise. Again, it was not written to provide a systematic classification of the arts (for many arts are never touched), nor to provide a taxonomy of the poetic arts (because, again, not one poem exists in the book and almost none of the Greek purely poetic types are even mentioned). Rather, immediately after the opening passages about the capacities of the various parts of "dramatic musical composition" and about the importance of plots, Aristotle introduces the concept of *mimēsis* (impersonation, representation, imitation or expression[69]). Instead of the form-content distinction that Plato gives in *Republic* III, Aristotle introduces the three modes of mimesis that become his first analytical tool for achieving scientific knowledge of drama: the means (music, dance, language); the objects (admirable individuals versus vulgar ones); and the manners (fully impersonated expression or fully narrated expression or a combination of the two).

While explaining "musical" drama in general, in a fugue-like way Aristotle also begins explaining tragedy. The modes of mimesis in effect present the *material cause* of tragedy, "what it is made of." The means get explained in Chapter 1; the objects in Chapter 2; and the manners in Chapter 3. Then, as noted, we have the *efficient cause*, the history of drama and of tragedy in Chapters 4-5. Starting also in Chapter 4 we get the (legitimate) *final cause* as pleasure interwoven in passages throughout the treatise. In Chapter 6 we find the *formal cause* of tragedy, namely, its definition (and, if one accepts the authenticity of the catharsis-clause, the *final cause* as *katharsis*). Because trag-

---

69   Again, for the history of *mimesis*, and why the concept is absolutely not univocal, similar to "play" in English, see *ADMC*, pp. 250-265.

edy is complex, with six necessary parts, and because of Aristotle's desire to follow Plato and examine recursively the capacities of each of the parts, the Northern Greek discusses plot in Chapters 7-11 (and then in Chapters 13, 14, 16, 17, and 18). The other five parts also get examined, or are explicitly stated as being covered in other treatises, through Chapter 22. The second kind of dramatic "musical" composition, epic, along with the debate whether it is better than tragedy, is then covered from Chapter 23 until the end of Chapter 26, which concludes our surviving text. The treatment of comedy, which would have been Chapter 27 onwards, is lost. The final cause of both tragedy and epic is said in Chapters 23-26 to be a "proper pleasure," and in the original manuscript this legitimate *final cause* might well have been in the definition of tragedy where the impostor catharsis-clause now resides. Certainly, Aristotle refers to pleasure in different places as the goal of drama, as readers will see for themselves and as gets discussed more in the various *Comments*. All of this, then, reflects Aristotle admirably following his own recommended methodologies, with one of them being inspired by Plato's *Phaedrus*.

In summary, following the *History of Animals*, Aristotle attempts to get a relatively clear notion of "musical" drama by determining the differences and common properties with similar things and by discussing the causes. He also applies the concerns of scientific knowledge from the *Phaedrus*. That is, because drama is complex, he must examine recursively its parts and their capacities. The focus on dramatic "musical" composition explains in and of itself why Aristotle examines only three art forms in depth in the *Dramatics*. We know that he wrote a section on comedy for a number of reasons, one of which is articulated at the beginning of Chapter 6, when he states that he will examine the hexameter-type of composition (that is, epic), comedy and tragedy. No other art is mentioned.

This blueprint also explains why art forms like poetry (as pure language in meter), dithyramb, nomes (singing to harp) and mimes (a purely literary and representational form mentioned in *Dramatics* 1) are not examined in any depth whatsoever. They do not have all four of the necessary and sufficient conditions to be *poiēsis* in Aristotle's technical sense, namely, music, dance, verse, and plot. Poetry of course is missing music and dance, and only has plot on occasion. Mime in the literary sense may have plots but did not have music and dance. Nomes only had singing and seemingly gesticulation of the face and body but no plot. Dithyramb has song and dance but also no plot in the proper sense, that is, something with a beginning, middle, and end, with a complication leading to a dénouement, conditions which Aristotle gives in Chapters 6 and later. The one mystery from this high-level perspective is why the satyr play, which had all four necessary and sufficient conditions of *poiēsis*, does not get examined in the extant treatise, but one answer is that its discussion may have been in the lost section on comedy.

In short, just as one would not to expect a discussion of novels in a book on song-writing (even though language is part of song), one should not expect to find a discussion of purely literary forms in a book on *poiēsis qua* music, dance, verse and plot,—although a *relevant* treatment of verse would be expected.

We need only cover one final issue while discussing Aristotle's overall blueprint. In the *Rhetoric*, after claiming at III 1 (1403b23) that the dramatists acted in earlier times in their own productions, Aristotle declares in III 12 the following:

> The style of written compositions is most precise, that of debate is most suitable for delivery. Of the latter, there are two kinds, ethical and emotional; this is why actors are always running after plays of this character, and poets after suitable actors. However, poets whose works are only meant for reading are also popular, as Chaeremon, who is as precise as a writer of speeches, and Licymnius among dithyrambic poets. When compared, the speeches

of writers appear meagre in public debates, while those of the rhetoricians, however well delivered, are amateurish when read. The reason is that they are only suitable to public debates.[70]

As a literary theorist might initially be happy to see, Aristotle appears to recognize two genres of plays, one to be performed and another to be read.[71] Does this mean, however, that he treats both genres in the extant *Dramatics?* The answer is absolutely not. The basic reasons are these: As is obvious from *Dramatics* 1, in which tragedy and comedy are said to use not only language but music and dance, Aristotle deals exclusively with the first genre in the *Dramatics.* Second, music is a necessary condition in the definition of tragedy in Chapter 6. Moreover, as is implied in the passage above from the *Rhetoric*—when Aristotle says that the speeches of professional writers sound meager in actual contests and that the speeches are thus unsuitable there—he would refrain from applying the principles of merely written drama to performed drama, and vice versa, at least without grave qualifications. This obviously entails that he would not treat both genres as substitutable in any context.[72] Because Aristotle illustrates his points in *Dramatics* 3 and elsewhere with the older dramatic composers and not with those composing the relatively new type of tragedy designed only to be read, he concentrates on the traditional, performed sort of tragedy in the treatise.[73]

---

70   1413b9ff, trans. J. H. Freese, *Aristotle: The Art of Rhetoric* (London: W. Heinemann, 1926).

71   Eric Csapo has questioned (privately) in discussion whether the Greek can mean that plays were written only to be read silently (as opposed to being recited in public but not performed with a chorus), and I am attracted to his view. Nevertheless, to play Devil's Advocate, I accept Freese's translation.

72   I show the absurd consequences of not following this guideline in *ADMC*, Chapter 9.

73   Readers perhaps should remind themselves that the Greeks were still becoming a literate culture in the days of Plato and Aristotle. Previously, as with all other cultures, very few people owned manuscripts. The oral tradition was paramount, and it would have made no sense to try to write a treatise

or drama for general purchase, as authors now sell books (although private purchase was a different matter, as we see in Appendix 2). Only a few would have been able to afford a copy of the manuscript and there were no public libraries. Memorization or learning from those who themselves had learned from either original sources or descendants of the original creators were crucial. Cf. Fitton, *op. cit.*, on this phenomenon. The initial scripts for plays, some of which had musical markings, and it appears, even brief comments for the dancing chorus, were probably for the dramatists and anyone reconstructing their plays. Cf. *Music, Text, and Culture in Ancient Greece,* edited by Tom Phillips and Armand D'Angour (Oxford: Oxford University Press, 2018) and https://www.heritagedaily.com/2018/07/ancient-greek-music-now-we-finally-know-what-it-sounded-like/121236

As I discuss in Chapter 1, with Chaeremon and others like him, all this was starting to change, but one should not assume his approach was the typical one of the era, despite what Susan Feagin says:

> The earliest known reference to reading a play for pleasure occurs in Aristophanes' *Frogs*, first presented in 405 BCE, where Dionysus says that he was sitting on the deck of a ship one day, "reading once more that dear *Andromeda*," a (now lost) play by Euripides. *Assuming that what he was doing was not unusual at the time, we can conclude that people have been reading plays for at least 2,400 years.* Indeed, public demand from readers has long driven the publication of script—legitimate and pirated—in the Western world (Susan L. Feagin, "Reading Plays as Literature," *The Routledge Companion to Philosophy of Literature,* eds. Noël Carroll and John Gibson, New York and London: Routledge, 2016, p. 107; my italics).

However, *pace* Feagin, Dionysus *was* doing something unusual (leaving aside that the description comes from a comedy instead of a historical record that aims at truth). To my knowledge, there is no evidence that the scripts were sold to the general public, as opposed to being made available only to a select few, who, again, probably had professional reasons for having them. Of course, this changed over time but it is an interesting question exactly when. Perhaps the closest similar modern phenomenon is the tradition of learning ballet roles and choreography from the 18th to 19th centuries into the 20th century, given the lack of any effective notation or video (although difficult-to-master notations were sometimes used, like Labanotation or Benesh in the 20th century). Dancers learned from others who had danced the roles, going back to the dancers who originally had the choreography set on them. The Greeks in the 5th century BCE and even into at least the 4th century BCE, unlike us, were simply used to the oral, performative traditions being more prevalent

Furthermore, Chaeremon is mentioned in *Dramatics* 1 when Aristotle discusses language and what a *poiētēs* (whether "poet," "composer" or "'musical' dramatist") is, within the context of discussing how *other* people use the term. Nevertheless, the passage has caused generations to think that Aristotle himself uses the Gorgian sense of *poiēsis* throughout the treatise. For additional, precise reasons, though, that we examine in Chapter 1, Aristotle focusses primarily, if not exclusively, on the traditional performed type of tragedy, even if he recognizes in the *Rhetoric* that new composers were writing plays only to be read. One absolutely conclusive piece of evidence for this is that the definition of tragedy in Chapter 6 has six *necessary* parts, including music and dance. One has to be careful when determining which type of tragedy Aristotle mentions or analyzes but starting at the end of Chapter 1 it will invariably be the performed, musical type.[74]

Another reason why the traditional literary view of tragedy has survived for so long is that Chapters 20-22 are on language, the fourth most important condition of tragedy as stated in Chapter 6. However, only a very short section, at the end of Chapter 22, is relevant particularly to drama, and many scholars including myself think that these chapters were interpolated from other Aristotelian texts, for reasons having to do, as mentioned, with Aristotle's library being hidden un-

---

than the recorded, literary one.

74   Feagin makes the distinction between "scripts," which are meant for performance, and "dramatic literature," and notes a few playwrights who tried to do both. Although she does not recognize, at least in the article cited, any of the dilemmas articulated in this book and in *ADMC*, she nevertheless understands the nature of Aristotelian drama well enough 17 years after my "The *Poetics* of Performance" to mention other considerations that cause her to conclude when dealing with the *"Poetics"*:

> In sum, Aristotle appears to have assumed that the tragic playwrights were writing for performance... [and she goes on to] caution [us] against generalizing to other types of theater or to contemporary drama as read to oneself on the basis of the claim he makes (Feagin, *op. cit.*, p. 110).

derground, damaged, badly re-assembled and then poorly edited in order to make it more valuable in the Athenian or Roman marketplace. As alluded to, some scholars also believe that Chapter 25 comes from *Homeric Problems*, and we will see other evidence that additional chapters were interpolated (e.g., Chapter 18) or that we are missing *massive* sections of text that would permit the treatise to be a unified whole.

A final remark on this last point, because the treatise was a puzzle to the Italians who had learned Greek in the 16th century and it is notoriously still difficult for modern readers, one reason being the problems just noted. Also, chaos reigns after Chapter 11. Because character is the second most important necessary condition in Chapter 6, we would expect to find it discussed after the chapters on plot, the most important necessary condition. Plot is logically examined immediately after the definitory remarks in Chapters 6-7, through Chapter 11. Yet Chapter 12 is on the chorus, which has led some to think as a result that the chapter is not legitimately in the original text because Aristotle returns to plot in Chapters 13-14. However, the inclusion of music in the definition of tragedy helps prove that the discussion of the (singing and dancing) chorus is perfectly legitimate, if out of order. Also, even though Chapters 13 and 14 return to plot, Aristotle presents there two different accounts of the best tragedy. Chapter 13 gives *Oedipus* but Chapter 14 gives the happily-ending plays like *Cresphontes* and *Iphigenia (in Tauris)* over the type that includes Sophocles' *Oedipus*, which is ranked only second. This ranking mimics, albeit unintentionally, the award Sophocles received when his play first premiered, losing to Philocles, the nephew of Aeschylus. I explain in the middle chapters how the perspective of tragedy as performed drama without the goal of catharsis, pity and fear allows us to resolve this conflict of the best plays of Chapters 13 and 14.

However, even with this solution, no one (including myself) can explain with certainty whether the chaotically-ordered chapters come from a much larger, unified book or whether they come from different treatments of tragedy by Aristotle. Chapter 15 introduces character, a logical sequence after the earlier discussions of plot (leaving aside Chapter 12), but then Chapters 16-18 return to plot, yet again out of sequence. Moreover, Chapter 18 introduces four types of tragedy—tragedy of suffering, tragedy of character, simple or spectacular tragedy (the text is corrupted), and complex tragedy—even though the first two types had never been discussed beforehand and never get mentioned again after this chapter. Chapter 19 covers "reasoning" and language, the former being the third necessary condition from the definition of tragedy, although for the most part Aristotle simply points us to the *Rhetoric*, where he covers this matter. The last part of Chapter 19 and Chapters 20-22 discuss language, the fourth necessary condition, in ways that are for the most part not really appropriate for this kind of philosophical treatise, being, for instance, basic grammar. It appears as if one of the Greek or Roman editors from the 1st-3rd centuries BCE interpolated at least Chapters 20-21, in an effort to fulfill the expectation that the fourth most important element, language, gets some treatment. However, realistically only the final part in Chapter 19, maybe the middle of Chapter 21, and the treatment of metaphor at the end of Chapter 22 seem particularly authentic for the *Dramatics* (even granting that they were written by Aristotle). The fifth and sixth, final conditions of tragedy—the arts of choral composition and scene-making—are covered in proportionate fashion. That is, since Aristotle ranks them as least important compared to the other elements, but still necessary, he spends only a little time on them in the whole treatise and also suggests that others should be responsible for the details. However, Chapter 12 is devoted to the choral elements throughout and other remarks on music or music-dance as well as scenery and performance and their importance are scattered throughout the treatise, as we see in the *Comments*.

In brief, in my opinion we would think better of the *Dramatics* as a collection of Aristotelian texts rather than as a single unified organic whole. Trying to make the chapters all cohere in their current shape (apart from Chapters 1-8, which appear to be a unit) leads to massive confusion, serious inconsistencies, and occasional outright contradiction. Thinking of the chapters as all Aristotelian but perhaps out of order, or with some of them interpolated, or with significant connecting passages missing allows us to appreciate better Aristotle's ideas. Indeed, many of his insights can still be applied to modern or future dramatic musical theater, as I cover in the last chapter of *ADMC*. I proffer only one point here: One of the sublime qualities of Aristotle's theory is that "musical" drama stems from human nature, as he states in Chapter 4, and not just from, say, a particular *polis* (city-state) in a particular culture. Hence, as long as we, like many other animals, imitate our parents or anyone or anything else, and as long as we are predisposed by biology to song and dance, we will be drawn to the performing arts. Unless human beings drastically change, that means for a very, very long time.

A Primer on Aristotle's Dramatics

Chapter Overviews & Comments

The emphasis from this point onwards is explaining correctly Chapters 1, 4, 6, 13, 14, 18, 19, 23, 24 and 26, for these are where the previous commentators have most significantly misconstrued Aristotle's intentions and meanings. Other chapters will be briefly discussed, but one can often find excellent translations and commentaries by philosophers or classicists on those units, upon which I cannot improve.

A Primer on Aristotle's Dramatics

Chapter 1

Overview

As Aristotle and the Greeks liked to say: "A good beginning is a job half done." This rings true for this chapter-by-chapter examination of the *Dramatics*. Aristotle formulates so many important concepts and plans in his opening chapter that we need to proceed carefully to make sure they are understood. The rest of the chapters, with a few exceptions, can then go much more speedily. What this means more precisely is that, unlike some of the other chapters that need only occasional microscopic examination of some words or phrases, I need to explain the one and a half pages of this chapter line by line.

Aristotle begins by indicating the structure of the whole treatise: He plans to examine *poiētikēs* (in his technical sense of "the art of dramatic 'musical' composition") and its types, and what makes good plots. He also plans to examine the parts of each type. I just discussed what these statements meant for Aristotle's blueprint, and I explain them more in the *Comments*. It bears repeating now that he then shows the importance of mimesis. He adds that mimesis has three modes—means, objects, and manner—and he finishes Chapter 1 by explaining the three *means*: music (*harmonia*), dance (*rhuthmos*), and language (*logos*). He explicitly states that he will examine them *either separately or in combination*. This statement is one of the most underappreciated statements in the whole treatise, and those who place little worth on it cannot fully understand the rest of Chapter 1.[75] Worse,

---

[75] For instance, the authors who recently present the highest quality paleography of the manuscript traditions, Leonardo Tarán, who focusses on the Greek, and Dimitri Gutas, who focusses on the Arabic, utterly downplay this statement, which helps them maintain the traditional literary interpretation of the whole treatise (*op. cit.*, 2012). Moreover, they do not even consider the Diotiman meaning of *poiēsis*, if only to reject it in favor of the Gorgian one. More on this below, and cf. *ADMC* pp. 217-8; 220-1; 229-30; 409; 445-6; 448;

they then muddle Aristotle's thought as a result, often contending that the ancient Northern Greek is presenting a taxonomy of arts and wondering why he omits so many art forms, especially poetic art forms. However, if we grasp that Aristotle is *only* concerned with explaining in the rest of Chapter 1 how the three means of mimesis—*harmonia* (music), *rhuthmos* (dance), and *logos* (language)—can be used *separately or in combination*, we gain a much better comprehension of the whole chapter and we do not start searching for taxonomies where none is intended.

Aristotle only gives examples of some arts to support the explanation of the means of mimesis, nothing more. He does not care to provide systematically *all* seven possible combinations despite his statement about examining the arts either separately or in combination:
1) Dance;
2) Music;
3) Language (or speech);
4) Dance and music;
5) Dance and speech;
6) Music and speech;
7) Dance, music and speech.
It suffices for Aristotle to cover only four cases, and in this order: music and dance together; dance by itself (as "ordered body movement"); language by itself; and then, at the very end of the chapter, the art forms that have *all* three means, in particular tragedy and comedy.

The following table not only summarizes all of this but prepares us for the rest of the very dense chapter and of the treatise, because the top four complex arts are the only ones the Northern Greek plans to examine, with the possible exception of the satyr play (although that type of drama might have been covered with comedy).

452-3; and 524.

Overview & Comments: Chapter 1

Table 1: Showing which (complex) arts have all four necessary and sufficient conditions of Aristotle's technical sense of *poiēsis*

	Music	Dance (in the Greek sense)	Language	Plot
Tragedy	X	X	X	X
Comedy	X	X	X	X
Epic (traditional forms)	X	X	X	X
Satyr play	X	X	X	X
Dithyramb	x	x	x	
Mime			x	x
Socratic dialogue			x	x
Lyric poetry (by, e.g., Pindar and Sappho)	x		x	? (but only on occasion, if ever)
Nome	x		x	
Visual art				
Poetry *per se*			x	? (but only on occasion, if ever)

Comments

In the first two sentences, Aristotle presents what I noted before is a Platonically-inspired plan, following the *Phaedrus*. He tells us, on the hypothesis that *poiēsis* has a technical meaning:

> Our topic is (the art of) dramatic "musical" composition (*poiētikēs*) in itself and its kinds (*eidōn*), and what power (or capacity) (*dunamin*) each has; how plots (*muthous*) should be constructed if the (dramatic "musical") composition (*poiēsis*) is to turn out well; also, from how many parts (*moriōn*) it is constituted, and of what sort they are; and likewise all other aspects of the same enquiry. Let us first begin, following the natural order, from first principles (1447a8-14; my translation, following Janko).

I examine the passage phrase by phrase.

Our topic is (the art of) dramatic "musical" composition (*poiētikēs*) in itself and its kinds (*eidōn*)
Since the only kinds of *poiēsis* to be discussed in detail in the whole treatise are epic, comedy and tragedy, these are presumably the (only) kinds of *poiēsis*, leaving aside for the moment the satyr play. This statement is an example of how one grasps the meaning of a Greek word by its behavior. Note an adage for interpreting ancient Greek philosophy (and indeed for translating any other lost language). If authors, in this case Aristotle, do not define a word, see how they use it, which may not be how the culture in general uses it, for in the case of technical terminology the denotation must be determined by its application.

Because in Chapter 18 (1455b33-56a3) Aristotle notes four sub-categories of tragedy—spectacular or simple[76] tragedy, complex tragedy,

---

[76] As noted earlier, the text is corrupt and could mean either. The major conclusions of this book, though, in no way depend on which reading one takes. Cf. *ADMC*, p. 211 and 376.

Overview & Comments: Chapter 1

tragedy of character, and tragedy of suffering—those also are meant, at least as sub-kinds. Strikingly, Aristotle says very plainly too that "epic must have the same kinds of tragedy, for [it must be] either (i) simple or (ii) complex, (iii) epic of character or (iv) one of suffering" (24.1459b8-10). This shows not only that the sub-kinds are equivalent to "kinds" (in the same way that "directories" and "sub-directories" on a computer mean often the same thing) but that epic sub-kinds have the same number as dramatic sub-kinds, although, paradoxically, no antecedent to the four kinds of tragedy can be found, as such, anywhere before or after Chapter 18. I discuss this more when we arrive at that chapter but the crucial point now is that Aristotle obviously fulfills his promise to treat the *kinds* of *poiēsis* in the treatise. Since the section on comedy vanished, we do not know if there were (sub-) kinds of comedy too for him, although it is very likely there were, given the sub-divisions above of tragedy and of epic and given the richness of ancient Greek comedy (for example, Old and New Comedy). I have also suggested that the satyr play may well have been considered a sub-type of comedy, or closely related to it, and discussed in the lost section. In any event, the three major kinds of *poiēsis*—tragedy, comedy and epic—comprise the high-level scope of the *Dramatics* and without question the sub-kinds of tragedy and epic exist.

... and what power (*dunamis*) each has

In *Dramatics* 1, the *dunamis* related to the playing of the oboe and *kithara* in combination with dancing is mentioned; likewise, the *dunamis* of the *melopoiia* (the making of the choral composition or "music-dance") that Aristotle says in Chapter 6 is so plain as to need no explanation. Even though these passages pertain only to parts of tragedy, they still help cover the general topic of *dunamis*, which surely is complex for tragedy as a whole and given by the totality of the parts. Aristotle uses the term *dunamis* again in Chapter 6, when he speaks of the similar power (*dunamis*) of verse and prose (1450b13-15), and yet another time when he presents a phrase that has caused people to believe wrongly that tragedy as analyzed in the *Dramatics* need only be written. Let us jump ahead for a moment to Chapter 6 to examine the passage, where Aristotle pens the following in order to rank spectacle at the bottom of the six *necessary* elements of tragedy (but not to exclude it, especially because spectacle is stated to be a necessary condition a few times in the chapter).

> Spectacle (*opsis*) is something enthralling, but is very artless and least particular to the art of musical drama composition, because the **power (*dunamis*)** of tragedy exists even without a competition and the [very competent] actors; besides, the designer's art is more important for the accomplishment of spectacular effects than is the dramatist's (my translation and boldfacing, following Janko, 1450b18-20).

The important point for the moment is that the *dunamis* of tragedy *simpliciter* (related perhaps to its soul, plot) is obviously being referenced, whatever *dunamis* means, whether power, potential, or capacity. Commentators sometimes take the power here to mean the emotional consequence or the intellectual pleasure one can have in contemplating a play. This interpretation strikes me as correct in general if not in all the specifics, and I suggest a different import for the rest of the passage (covered in Chapter 6). The commentators, though, shockingly think that with this one ambiguous passage Aristotle gives up the plainly stated *necessary* conditions of music-dance and spectacle and allows tragedy to be purely literary, in spite of his theory of definition that entails the contrary.[77]

---

[77] The only other four scholars I know who emphasize that Aristotle defines tragedy following his own strictures of definition—Anton Smerdel, Gerald Else, M.P. Battin, and Richard McKirahan—nevertheless just accept the tradition on the *dunamis* of tragedy in this passage, a tradition that goes back to Avicenna and Averroes. As noted, the Arabic scholars themselves did not even understand what spectacle meant (cf. *ADMC* and their history) but thought that, whatever it meant, it was optional. After the Arabic scholars, even the Italians in the *cinquecentro* who did know that *opsis* meant the scenery, masks, and costumes, still misinterpreted the passage, and every commentator to a person afterwards followed suit. It took my Ph.D. dissertation in 1992 to prove they erred, with an important subset published as "The *Poet-*

To return to the Northern Greek's promise to examine *dunamis* in the rest of the treatise: The final noteworthy occurrence of the *dunamis* of tragedy pertains to its plot. In *Dramatics* 9, Aristotle compares episodic plots with simple plots in general and says that dramatists extend the episodic plot "beyond its potential (*dunamis*)" when they compose in order to accommodate actors during the competitions. Whatever this means—and I imagine it suggests that the plot is made illogical or unconvincing merely to showcase the talents of a particular celebrity-actor, a phenomenon that we ourselves see on stage, cinema and TV—obviously Aristotle carries out his promise of Chapter 1 to focus on the *dunamis* of at least one form of *poiēsis*, namely, tragedy. However, because epic is essentially a subset of tragedy, the *dunamis* of parts of epic are given as well by implication. Moreover, we see in Chapter 24 (1460a12ff) that epic is said to have the power to create more amazement than tragedy, illustrating yet again that Aristotle fulfills his promise to show the power of each type of *poiēsis*.

how plots should be constructed if the (dramatic "musical") composition is to turn out well

The obvious chapters that carry out this part of the agenda are Chapters 7 through 18, except for Chapter 12 on the chorus and Chapter 15 on character. With good reason, Else, one of the most prestigious commentators of the *Dramatics* in the 20th century, claimed that at least Chapter 16 came from a different text because Aristotle had already switched to the second most important element of tragedy, character, in Chapter 15. Still the *Dramatics* might have been just rearranged by a later editor, and the discussion of Chapter 16 might also have been in the original text, were the text much larger; likewise, with Chapter 17 and parts of Chapter 18, which also cover issues of plot.[78] Whether

---

ics of Performance," *op. cit.*, revised and included in Chapter 2 of *ADMC*.

78   As Else and others like Daniel de Montmollin, who have produced equally magisterial treatments of the *Dramatics,* have emphasized, the whole treatise seems to be an amalgamation of different texts. Cf. *ADMC* pp. 213-4; 425; 433; and 588. See also Appendix 2 for newer arguments not in *ADMC*

Else is correct will be discussed when we examine those chapters.

In spite of the obvious treatment of plot in the treatise, this phrase from the first sentence is actually very surprising on reflection and very rarely acknowledged as such. However, in another way, the lack of acknowledgement is unsurprising because no one previously even considered whether Aristotle follows Diotima's meaning of *poiēsis* or whether he modifies her meaning by adding plot as the fourth and final necessary condition. If Aristotle, however, is following Diotima's notion at least fundamentally, then why is he not concerned in detail with art forms like the dithyramb, which itself has music, dance, and speech? Moreover, even leaving aside the Diotiman meaning of *poiēsis*, why is plot even mentioned in the first sentence, as if all forms of *poiēsis* in ancient Greece have it? I examine the latter question shortly, when examining the view of Tarán, who is astutely one of the very few to call attention to this oddity (in fact, he is the only commentator noting this in writing that I can recall).

For the moment, though, let us focus on the first question, pertaining to the dithyramb and other arts. According to Diotima, any work combining music, dance and verse should properly be called *poiēsis*. We should not be surprised, therefore, that poems and other literary art forms like prose mimes and Socratic dialogues, instrumental music, dance, painting and sculpture are *not* analyzed even in any superficial way in the *Dramatics* in spite of being at least mentioned by Aristotle.[79] They do not integrate all three means of mimesis. However, what

---

supporting this conclusion. In the interest of full disclosure, I should acknowledge that I had the pleasure of studying under de Montmollin at the University of Toronto.

79   This helps show why Kenny unjustifiably says:
      What English term, then, covers all and only the things that Aristotle calls *poiesis*? "Imaginative writing" and "creative writing" come close, but one expression is too clumsy and the other too academic for regular use. The closest modern equivalent in Aristotle's word is the German *Dichtung*, which covers prose fic-

Overview & Comments: Chapter 1

about dithyramb and nome? They certainly have the three means, and therefore presumably are two other forms of *poiēsis* on Diotima's account. In fact, dithyramb is mentioned not only by Plato in the *Gorgias* 501-502, when he notes examples of *poiēsis* that are almost identical to the ones at the beginning of *Dramatics* 1, but also by Aristotle twice in Chapter 1, once at the beginning and once at the end.

It is very intriguing, therefore, that Aristotle excludes dithyrambs and nomes for analysis in the treatise, even though he gives a reason why they are both different from the quintessential dramatic forms, tragedy and comedy, at the end of *Dramatics* 1. They use the three means of mimesis *concomitantly*, whereas tragedy uses them *sequentially*. That is, dithyrambs and nomes will involve the music, dance [in the Greek sense] and verse happening together throughout the performance. Tragedy, though, may involve a speech all by itself, by a lead actor, and then the chorus dancing for a period of time with no words, even if at some point for certain sections they may sing words and dance simultaneously. Then an actor may speak again, and so forth.

We will see in Chapter 3 that Aristotle follows Plato, alluding to dithyramb as having only pure narration, which is why, strictly speaking, it is not dramatic at all and thus drops out of the rest of the treatise. Nevertheless, the dithyramb still has speech, music, and dance. The solution to this conundrum is that Aristotle does not think of dithy-

---

tion as well as verse (p. xi, *op. cit.*, 2013).
Yet, Aristotle only cares about prose in Chapter 1 to help explain the three means of mimesis, *harmonia*, *rhuthmos* and *logos* (speech/language), used "separately or in combination." Moreover, as we have also seen and will see many more times, he only cares about three dramatic-type forms in the whole treatise: tragedy, comedy and epic. These forms always used verse in his day, and the Northern Greek has absolutely no intent to examine prose forms in any detail. That is, after mentioning the prose forms in passing in Chapter 1, mimes and Socratics dialogues in passing, he drops them and all similar examples for the rest of the treatise.

rambs and nomes as having a plot (*muthos*) in his sense as defined in Chapter 6 at 1450a2-3, as the "arrangement of incidents," either in the primary sense involving the incidents shown on stage or, as we will see with epic, even in a secondary mixed-narrative sense of plot that must apply to that art form. In epic, most of the incidents of the plot are imagined by the audience, as when reading a novel, rather than enacted on stage, even if the incidents are expressed partially with gestures by the rhapsode, who might mimick grief with the face. The incidents *qua* plot will have a beginning, middle and end, along with, for instance, a climax. Because of the lack of a proper plot, dithyrambs and nomes are excluded from any in-depth treatment in the *Dramatics*. To emphasize, Aristotle restricts Diotima's notion of *poiēsis* to the "musical" forms *that, in addition, have plot*, so that in this way—and only in this way—he uses the term in a different way from Diotima. The reason, we see in *Dramatics* 6, is that plot is the soul of tragedy and is the most crucial aspect of the whole enterprise of "musical" drama in general (and "musical" drama was apparently the most important art form in Athens, given the money, time and attention devoted to it and given Plato's comment in the *Laws* that the "musical" arts were the most important because the most talked about[80]).

Because Aristotle indicates in Chapter 4 that *by nature* we engage in those exact three means of mimesis; because of the inclusion of "music" in the essential conditions of tragedy in Chapter 6; and because of the importance of "music (in the Greek sense)" in Chapter 26 to help rank tragedy over epic, the latter being Plato's most esteemed art, Aristotle obviously keeps the Diotiman notion of *poiēsis* throughout the whole book. The focus on tragedy and epic until the end of Chapter 26 also demonstrate that he continues always to care about the art forms that have plot, the condition that completes his technical notion of *poiēsis*.

---

80   II 669b.

Overview & Comments: Chapter 1

I have now covered the basic reasons why tragedy, comedy and epic are the only arts to be discussed in depth in the whole treatise. Why Aristotle could have expected readers of the treatise to know all of this, and why he therefore did not have to explain *poiēsis* more, may be fascinating questions, but they have no impact on my argument here. Whether the *Dramatics* was a book in a larger collection where the term was explained; whether Aristotle explicated it during lecture or it was simply and commonly understood this way in the Lyceum; or whether the term was used by others in Greek culture, I cannot and need not determine. Suffice it to say that by taking *poiēsis* in the particular Diotiman way with the additional condition of plot and by thereby easily resolving a host of perpetual dilemmas, we can be confident that Aristotle truly uses the term in this manner.

As a result of these insights, we can now easily ascertain where Tarán has enlightened us further but missed the real import of Aristotle's first paragraph. Tarán observes in his *Notes* as he painstakingly proceeds sentence by sentence and sometimes clause by clause or word by word:

> ... *not only is the plot mentioned early but it is also the only qualitative part mentioned explicitly in 1447a8-13 at all*. It is therefore clearly implied that each species of poetry has its own power to affect the audience, not that each species of poetry has several such powers. Thus the function of Tragedy is to raise in the audience the feelings of Pity and Fear (cf. chs. 6ff.). In ll. 8-10, Aristotle is implying that *the plot is the essential element **of each species of poetry***. As he himself says in 6, 1450a38-39: *archē men oun kai hoion psyche ho muthos tēs tragōdias*. ["On the one hand, the plot, therefore, is the first principle and, as it were, the soul of tragedy" with the *men* signaling a series of *de* clauses that begin to give the second through the sixth necessary conditions of tragedy in Chapter 6;[81]

---

81 The Greek *men* with one or more *de* clauses is like our "on the one hand" and "on the other hand" (or "additionally").

my translation of the Greek, because Tarán leaves it untranslated, and also my comment here, along with the italics and bolding.][82]

Let us examine this full remark. Tarán astutely observes that not only does plot arise in the very first sentence of the treatise but that it is "qualitatively" unique in that way. The qualitative parts of tragedy are explained in Chapter 6 (with plot being the most important) and the "quantitative" parts in Chapter 12. On my account, because *poiēsis* is being used *fundamentally* in the Diotiman sense, comprising the three means of mimesis—language, music and dance—Aristotle adds plot immediately in the first sentence of the treatise to restrict *poiēsis* to the three art forms to be discussed in the whole book. This amply explains the seeming oddity that Tarán notes.

Tarán's subsequent claims are all false except the citation of plot (*psyche*) being the soul of tragedy. First, as we just saw to some extent and as will be clearer shortly, tragedy also has multiple powers because it is made of multiple parts, each having its own power(s). Then comes Tarán's stunning, and one might say perverse, claim that "Aristotle is implying that *the plot is the essential element **of each species of poetry**.*" For a classicist as capable as Tarán[83] to claim, or at least strongly imply, that the many diverse kinds of Greek poetry (didactic, Sapphic, paeanic, etc.) all have plots for Aristotle is staggering. Tarán has seemingly fixated on the Gorgian interpretation of a Greek word and is drawing out its logical conclusion, no matter how implausible the outcome. As alluded to and as we see in significant detail in Chapters 6-18, plot for Aristotle has a beginning, middle and end, with a certain, substantial magnitude, along with complications

---

82   Tarán and Gutas, *op. cit.*, p. 224. Since their book is addressed to classicists, they often leave Greek passages untranslated, and nothing should be inferred from my translations other than to make the passages understandable for the non-Greek reader.

83   He was the Chairman of the Classics Department at Columbia University when I was pursuing my M.A. in philosophy there.

Overview & Comments: Chapter 1

and a dénouement. Most ancient Greek poetry or "song" does not have those features or even come close to having them. Take but two examples of Simonides (c. 556-468 BCE), the second of which shows the Greeks having as much love for their pets as some moderns (with Simonides writing an epitaph for the grave of a dog):

> Being a man you cannot tell what might befall when tomorrow comes
> Nor yet how long one who appears blessed will remain that way,
> So soon our fortunes change even the long-winged fly
> Turns around less suddenly.[84]

[and]

> Huntress, your bleached bones buried here
> still frighten the beasts! Great
> Pelion, conspicuous Ossa and Cithaeron's high
> Pastures now your excellence.[85]

These poems no more have a plot in Aristotle's sense than the Greek island of Samos has the Empire State Building. Rather, again, plot enters in Chapter 1 to restrict the Diotiman notion of *poiēsis* and this immediately telegraphs Aristotle's intention to cover only the arts of tragedy and comedy, with epic included as a secondary, "proto-dramatic" art.

This takes us to Tarán's final claim about the function of tragedy being "to raise in the audience the feelings of Pity and Fear." I must address this claim later, because in Chapter 6 we will see that catharsis (through pity and fear) cannot be the goal of tragedy in general for Aristotle, even though Tarán follows almost the whole tradition on

---

84   Simonides 521 *PMG*, Stobaeus 4.41, in David A. Campbell, *Greek Lyric Poetry* (London: Bloomsbury/Bristol Classical Press, 1982) 90.

85   *Early Greek Lyric Poetry*, trans. with an Introduction and Commentary by David Mulroy (Ann Arbor, MI: The University of Michigan Press/Ann Arbor Paperbacks, 1999) 143.

this matter, Petruševski and his supporters excepted. Indeed, because Tarán cites Petruševski, Tarán should have known that the modern Macedonian athetized *katharsis*—that is, bracketed the word as illegitimate, whether as a product of bad copying or editing—and yet Tarán rejects the Macedonian's view for merely paleographic reasons. That is, because all four branches of manuscripts have the word, Tarán believes *katharsis must* be legitimate. However, all four branches of manuscripts having *katharsis* does not handle the case that the earlier "archetype" itself had been using a wrongly interpolated word to begin with (to reiterate, the archetype could have been a perfect or imperfect copy of the true original). Other cases can be found in which the only manuscript reading in the texts has been demonstrated to be impossible, and the paleography, although crucial and primary, does not always settle the subsequent philosophical interpretation.[86]

also, from how many parts (*moriōn*) it is constituted, and of what sort they are;

The number and nature of the "parts" is, with respect to tragedy, surely the six necessary parts enumerated and explained in *Dramatics* 6, especially given Aristotle's use of the same word *moriōn* there (at 1449b26) with the cognates *merē/meros*. Aristotle own words are: "**Necessarily then every tragedy** has six constituent **parts**

---

[86] Cf. Rashed (*Pourquoi, op. cit.,* p. 11), who gives some noteworthy examples. Tarán does not even follow his own paleographic strictures all of the time, claiming, for instance, that one important Greek word in Chapter 6 immediately preceding the definition of tragedy "does not yield the right meaning" (Tarán and Gutas, *op. cit.,* p. 246-7). He accepts an emendation, even though three of the manuscripts (the two Greek ones and the Arabic one) have the word he rejects! Thus, even for him at times, the sense of the passage is more crucial than the actual Greek word. He has doubts about Moerbeke's Latin version on this point, but cf. Veloso, *op. cit.,* 2018, p. 335-6 for why Tarán's doubts do not support his conjectures with respect to that final manuscript. In any event, the crucial consideration is that sometimes the sense of a text, as determined, for example, by the rest of the corpus, is more important than what is found in the manuscripts, and this principle will be very important when we discuss catharsis more in Chapter 6 and in Appendix 2.

Overview & Comments: Chapter 1

(*merē*), and on these its **quality** depends (*kath' ho poia tis estin*). These are plot, character, diction [speech for me], thought, spectacle, and song ['music-dance' for me]."[87] As mentioned, Chapter 12 has the *quantitative* parts (*merē ... **poson***) of tragedy. Epic has a brief, similar treatment in Chapter 23, examining the number and nature of its parts.

The reason why epic's definition is much shorter is that Aristotle says repeatedly that tragedy has everything that epic has and more, and that whoever knows tragedy then knows epic (Chapters 5, 24 and 26). Given that Aristotle has clarified the various parts already in detail for tragedy, he need not duplicate the task again for what epic has in common. Finally, comedy also had its parts delineated and elucidated, I venture to say, which we would find were we ever to discover the lost second book. Whether Aristotle only analyzes there, however, the parts not already examined in common with tragedy in *Dramatics* 1-5 is something we cannot determine without more texts. It may be that comedy also has six necessary parts for Aristotle but that the comic dramatist merely uses them differently, for example, to elicit laughter. Given the preliminary divisions and the origin of comedy in *Dramatics* 4-5, the definition of comedy may have been as short as the definition of epic, although the subsequent examination could have been, and was probably, long indeed.

---

[87]   1450a8-10. Aristotle. *Aristotle in 23 Volumes*, Vol. 23, trans. W.H. Fyfe (Cambridge, MA, Harvard University Press and London, William Heinemann Ltd., 1932). Available at the Perseus Project, Greek & Roman Materials: http://www.perseus.tufts.edu/hopper/text?doc=Perseus%3Atext%3A1999.01.0056%3Asection%3D1450a

Because it is freely available on the internet, I cite Fyfe's translation purposefully so that non-specialists can see the common but distorting use of "diction" and "song" in lieu of (i) speech/language and of (ii) "orchestral art"/music-dance. "Diction" only covers part of language, and song for *melos/melopoiia* not only redundantly implies language but omits dance, a very important part of the choral phenomenon of all tragedy until long past Aristotle's time. Cf. *ADMC*, pp. 123-7.

A Primer on Aristotle's Dramatics

and likewise all other aspects of the same enquiry.
This catch-all phrase could refer to the history of the three dramatic forms in Chapters 4 and 5 and to anything else related to the previously discussed blueprint. It need not detain us here, though, in my view.

By this point, the ancient Greek reader would have understood the scope of this treatise. It is to examine only the theatrical forms that present the full mixture of music, dance, verse and plot, similar to our Broadway musical theater. In the case of epic and its rhapsode, the treatise will usually involve a solo performer who typically sings and gesticulates in an ordered, "rhythmed" way while presenting a story that involves plot in Aristotle's sense, almost like a one-man show on Broadway.

Let us continue to the next sentence of Chapter 1.

> Epic-making and tragedy, comedy also and dithyramb-making (*dithyrambopoiētikē*), and most oboe-playing (*aulētikēs*)[88] and kithara-playing (*kitharistikēs*), are all, viewed in general, modes of representation (*mimēsis*) (1447a14-16; my transl.).

First, and I say this especially for musicians and music historians, some commentators have said or suggested that all music for Aristotle is mimetic.[89] Yet, he only says "most" of the oboe-playing and

---

88 As noted in the initial credit for the book cover, the *aulos* is too often translated as "flute," when it is actually a reed instrument, very similar to our oboe. However, it has two pipes with one mouthpiece, and some music historians claim one of the pipes often carried a single tone, almost like a Scottish bagpipe (cf. *ADMC*, pp. 29 and 176). It would be better to call it a double-oboe, but for brevity, and given this caveat, I call it an oboe for short.

89 D.S. Margoliouth, a noteworthy figure responsible for translating the *Dramatics* from the Arabic manuscripts, correctly says in part, "for we learn from Plato's *Laws* — **the primary source of the *Poetics*** — that **all** *mousike* ['music'] is *mimesis*" (my boldfacing; *op. cit.*, p. 118). *ADMC* confirms how important the *Laws* is for understanding the *Dramatics*, although we see here in Chapter 1 that Aristotle only says *some*, not *all* music, is mimetic.

These comments, along with the ones on the upcoming passage in

Overview & Comments: Chapter 1

kithara-playing is mimetic. Obviously, some oboe-playing and kithara-playing might be purely "formal," and, moreover, his statement leaves aside the many other instruments that the Greeks played. The oboe and kithara were the primary instruments used in the dramatic arts in the theater, which is why, we can deduce, Aristotle mentions them precisely rather than simply saying "music."[90]

Second, previous commentators have missed Aristotle's restriction of *poiēsis* to only the three "dramatic" forms first listed in this third sentence (as I did for years, until I wondered whether the Northern Greek might be using Diotima's notion). The reason is two-fold. The commentators have forgotten, ignored or never realized Diotima's narrow sense of *poiēsis* and they got easily distracted by the dithyramb and "most oboe-playing..." being immediately appended to those three dramatic forms, all of which muddies the scope of *poiēsis*. However, given the arguments above, Aristotle appends the non-dramatic art forms here simply to segue immediately from *poiēsis* into representation (*mimēsis*) and to begin explaining its three modes. For the ancients, or at least for the students in the Lyceum, who understood what *poiēsis* (and *poiētikēs*) and *mimēsis* really meant, the scope would not have been adversely muddied and the transition would have been much more apparent than it has been for modern scholars, especially if, as many commentators claim, the treatise was a series of lecture-notes and Aristotle augmented them with oral explanation. For modern scholars who inherited, and have grown up in, a literary rather than a performative tradition, the arts he lists get immediately jumbled together and the scope of *poiēsis* simply becomes indistin-

---

which dancers impersonate, and the related arguments in Chapter 2 of *ADMC* also show why, for instance, Noël Carroll and Sally Banes severely distort Aristotle's views of *mimesis* in their article "Dance, Imitation and Representation," in *Dance, Education and Philosophy*, ed. by Graham McFee, Chelsea School Research Centre Edition, Vol. 7 (Oxford: Meyer & Meyer Sport, UK, Ltd., 1999), especially pp. 14-20.

90   *ADMC*, pp. 145 and espec. 170-9.

guishable. Of course, the music of the oboe and kithara are part of tragedy and thus *part* of the *poiēsis*, so in one way the only art form that Aristotle adds that is not directly relevant to "musical" drama is dithyramb (although all of the listed arts are indeed relevant to mimesis). Another reason that Aristotle perhaps adds dithyramb and the music of the oboe and kithara is that Plato himself had called them forms of *poiēsis* in the *Gorgias*, at 501-2, where, as I noted, the other arts are almost identical to the ones that Aristotle here lists. I should emphasize that Plato, too, does not give one purely literary art in his list, so he must be using either the Diotiman sense of *poiēsis* himself or an older sense in which music is primary for the "making." His entire list is: the playing of the *aulos* and *kithara*, tragedy, dithyramb and "choral displays" (*hē tōn chorōn didaskalia*), whatever that phrase means for him above and beyond the implied singing and dancing.

In short, the non-dramatic arts in *Dramatics* 1 are only intended by Aristotle to be examples of representation (*mimēsis*)—not *poiēsis*! This is a very subtle but crucial distinction, especially given that one might think Aristotle completely follows Plato in categorizing dithyramb as *poiēsis* when he really only follows Plato in categorizing it as *mimēsis*. That is, Aristotle partially follows Plato in thinking of dithyramb as *poiēsis* in the Diotiman narrow sense, of making in music, dance, and verse. However, to re-iterate Aristotle adds plot as a fourth condition for *poiēsis*, which dithyramb does not have. *Mimēsis* is a much broader term than *poiēsis*, which Aristotle's later examples in Chapter 1 prove. For instance, painting is mimetic for Aristotle and yet is not *poiēsis* in either Diotima's or Aristotle's technical sense or in the sense that historically commentators have embraced, as "poetry." Of course, if one uses Diotima's *broad* sense of "doing/making," then painting, like candle-making, indeed could fall under *poiēsis*. However, then the word is being used equivocally in the same passage, which is possible but not likely given the rest of the treatise, in which Aristotle is not concerned even with the purely literary arts much less any other kind of production, be it of candles, saddles, or anything else.

Overview & Comments: Chapter 1

Table 2: The different senses of *poiēsis*[91]

Source	Meaning	Examples
Ancient Greek culture	Composition, production, creation, or making (Diotima's broad sense, *Symposium* 205)	Candle-making, house-building, saddle-making, and epic(song)-making (but generally with *-poios* added onto the name of the object or class to form the name of the maker *per se*, e.g. *eikonopoios* for "maker of image," that is, painter, or *epopoios*, "maker of epic-song [in hexameter]")
Ancient Greek culture	Making of music, dance, and verse (Diotima's narrow sense, *Symposium* 205)	Dithyramb, tragedy, and choral displays (Plato, *Gorgias* 501-2); the corresponding maker is *poiētēs*
Gorgias	Language and meter (i.e., verse or poetry)	Poems (without music)
Aristotle	Music, dance, and verse (from Diotima's narrow sense) plus plot	Tragedy, comedy, epic (if the rhapsode physically expresses in an ordered way), and satyr play

To return to *mimēsis,* Butcher had noticed that:

> "Imitation" as the common characteristic of the fine arts, including poetry, was not originated by Aristotle. In liter-

---

91 Cognates like *poiētikēs* (the art of composition) and *poiētēs* (composer) have similar richness and ambiguity.

> ature the phrase in this application first occurs in Plato...
> He [Aristotle] applies the term *mimēseis* only to poetry
> and music (*Poet 1*...), but the constant use of the verb
> *mimeîsthai* or of the adjective *mimētikós* in connexion
> with the other arts ... proves that all alike are counted arts
> of imitation (*op. cit.*, p. 121).

However, *contra* Butcher, *mimēsis*, like *logos*, is a rich word, and one translation like "imitation" across all contexts will lead to absurdities at times. Commentators often, if not always, ask: "What is the meaning of *mimēsis*"?, expecting that there would be one meaning, univocally, across the whole *Dramatics*. Again, this is an imprudent assumption, just as asking what *the* meaning of "play" is (when used with drama, tennis, and violins). The better question is what *meanings mimēsis* has and what precise sense applies in any particular passage.

Let me explain further by first asking an obvious question. What does "imitative music" imitate, when nothing in the real world exists to be imitated *per se*? If one says that other music is imitated (e.g., Prokofiev imitates a melody by Chopin, or Joan Baez and Boys II Men imitate the Beatles), that only pushes back the problem. What did the melody of Chopin imitate? Besides, where is chordal harmony found in nature? Does anger or a swift stream suggest even a minimal melody or, for example, does the latter not just emit random sounds? If you had never heard the titles of Beethoven's famous compositions, would you believe that one of them was imitating a rage over a lost penny? Even if one magically guessed that the subject is rage rather than excitement or the like, why not a lost florin or guinea or bottle of wine? However, since all or most students will have heard this work, probably it is better to take a relatively unfamiliar work, *Threnody to the Victims of Hiroshima*, by Krzysztof Penderecki. Play it for your friends, without giving the title, and ask them what it "imitates." See if anyone comes even remotely close to what Penderecki associates it with, whether one considers the title or not.

Overview & Comments: Chapter 1

In other words, given the saying that "imitation is the sincerest form of flattery," what is being "flattered" in the real world in the case of the (first unique creation of a work of) music, leaving aside any words that might be simultaneously sung and leaving aside the title? Does the *Blue Danube Waltz* really imitate the Danube while *Roses from the South* imitates roses (whether or not from the south), when often waltz dancers can hardly distinguish the difference between both compositions of Johann Strauss, Jr.? One might say, and scholars have said in order to justify that music is imitative, that a fast tempo imitates anger or a battle or a swiftly running stream. However, the better, more literal, account would be that *one aspect* of music imitates *one aspect* of those phenomena, not that music truly imitates them. In philosophy, we may use metaphors and images and other linguistic devices as aids in understanding but it is crucial ultimately to explain an issue literally.

Imitation, similar to copying (or cloning nowadays), suggests that many different aspects together are "imitated." If I imitate George Washington in a play, I look like him, try to speak like he spoke, walk like he was reported to have walked, etc. However, let us grant that imitation can be of one, or a few, salient characteristics. What is salient? Generally, a sufficient resemblance is considered crucial for x to imitate y. For example, when baby Joanne whines in 2018, we do not say she is imitating the American President at the time who is infamous for whining and complaining publicly on television that he is being unfairly investigated in a "witch hunt" for colluding with Russia in the Presidential election of 2016. There is not sufficient resemblance, even if both are whining and therefore sharing one characteristic (like the fast tempo and the fast-moving stream). However, when the television comedian Stephen Colbert speaks in such a way that he very much resembles the President whining and when we think, in merely hearing the voice from a different room, that it is the President himself speaking, we legitimately say that Colbert is imitating (or impersonating or mimicking) the President. The imitation in this case is of one individual's voice that is very much like another's. If an older woman were trying to simulate the President's voice and repeated the same words but was an octave or two higher, it is very questionable whether we would call this an imitation or merely an attempt (successfully or not) to imitate. In short, in the case of music, there is not enough resemblance between music and other phenomena, like a brook or a psychological phenomenon like anger, to have imitation, especially when the object being imitated, like anger or a dead victim of a nuclear bomb, does not even have sound.

With respect to *mimēsis* in music, then, "express" or "re-present (a musical *idea*)" is the better translation (which is one reason musical composers give titles, to suggest what their intent is). This leads to a similar issue even in drama for the Northern Greek. One reason that *mimēsis* has been confusing for commentators throughout the *Dramatics* and very hard, if not outright impossible, to understand and translate univocally, is that sometimes the characters that actors portray on stage never existed in reality. They are fictional constructs created in the imagination of the dramatist-playwright. Hence, it is odd then to say that the composers, whether in music or drama, are copying, imitating, or representing, which is another reason that some scholars think "expression" is a better translation at times. All of this is confirmed by looking at the background of the term *mimēsis* before Aristotle and seeing that its primary sense was to impersonate or to express and secondarily historically to imitate.[92]

Aristotle typically uses his words very precisely, even if they have rich meanings. I discuss the ramifications of this particular issue (and, for instance, of music not being able to *imitate* character) in *ADMC*, especially with respect to a notorious passage in the *Politics* that has been always interpreted (wrongly in my view) as Aristotle saying that

---

92 Cf. *ADMC*, Chapter 3, pp. 250-66 for the in-depth explanation of all of these issues pertaining to *mimēsis*.

aural music, in and of itself, is the most imitative of all of the arts![93] Suffice it to say here that mimetic music is music that is expressive of the type of things that actually can be expressed by it (perhaps certain moods that themselves are vague, like sadness or wistfulness). I venture to say that this is what individuals automatically interpret the phrase "imitative music" to mean, given the oddities at least subconsciously realized when the object being supposedly "imitated" is something completely unmusical. It is analogous to me saying in 1990 when I was a graduate student "My mentor Francis Sparshott is an ancient Greek philosopher." Since Sparshott lived in the 20th century, we know that he cannot really be an ancient Greek philosopher like Plato, and so we automatically interpret the phrase to function in lieu of "he is a *specialist of* ancient Greek philosophy." Similarly, "imitate" functions like "express." Thus, we need not take "imitate" literally in informal conversations. Again, though, the situation is different when we need to make precise and literal sense of a claim, such as in a philosophical analysis.

In the *Dramatics*, Aristotle sometimes explains a topic with back-to-back explanations of mimesis in painting and then in the dramatic "musical" arts, where the first meaning of mimesis means "imitate" (if the painter is painting a vegetable to look like the original) and the second "impersonate." The reason, as we see in detail in the Comments, is that Plato himself had used *mimēsis* in both domains, painting and "musical" drama, and Aristotle follows suit to cover the same topics, for the sake of rigor. If this is not complicated enough, at other times *mimēsis* may mean "express" if music is the topic.[94]

To recapitulate: My own view is that, just as it would be impossible to give "play" a univocal sense when it is used with drama, tennis and violins, it is probably impossible to give *mimēsis* a univocal sense

---

93   Chapter 4, notably pp. 316-18.

94   To emphasize, I discuss this whole issue in depth when dealing with

throughout the many different contexts in the *Dramatics*. If we do not want to be precise with each and every occurrence of the word, because often a general impression is good enough, it might be best to leave it untranslated and let the context dictate the meaning. Alternatively, write "re-presentation," with a hyphen, or "(re)presentation," with parentheses. This formulation signals that we are not necessarily copying or imitating something in the world and perhaps just (re)presenting or expressing something imagined. However, for simplicity, I use "representation," expecting the reader to bear in mind these *caveats*.

This all suffices for the introductory passage of the *Dramatics* and how Aristotle begins to switch focus to mimesis and its three modes. I capture the basics of the modes of mimesis in the following table.

Table 3: The modes of mimesis and the chapters explaining them

Mode	Type	Chapter
Means	Color/form, sound (in general), but especially music, dance, or language (separately or in combination)	1
Objects (or "subjects")	Good men (in action) versus vulgar men (in action)	2
Manner	Narration, full impersonation, or a mixture of both	3

---

the claim by previous commentators that "music" is the most imitative of the arts for Aristotle (*Politics* VIII 5). I demonstrate that he really speaks of the dance and the music that goes along with it, which not only makes perfect sense but meshes seamlessly with what he says in *Dramatics* 1-2, as I start discussing in the next few pages. Cf. *ADMC*, Chapter 4, espec. pp. 300-18.

Overview & Comments: Chapter 1

Aristotle now writes:

> But they [epic, tragedy, comedy, dithyramb, oboe-playing and kithara-playing] differ one from another in three ways: either in using different means or in representing different objects or in representing objects not in the same way but in a different manner. For just as by the use both of color and form people represent many objects, making likenesses of them—some having a knowledge of art and some working empirically—and just as others use the human voice; so is it also in the arts which we have mentioned, they [epic, tragedy, comedy, and dithyramb] all make their representations in dance (*rhuthmō*) and language (*logō*) and tune (*harmonia*), *using these means either separately or in combination*. For tune and dance (*rhuthmō*) alone are employed in oboe-playing and kithara-playing and in any other arts which have a similar function [*i.e., to be performed in the theater*], as, for example, panpipe-playing. Dance (*rhuthmō*) alone *without tune* is employed by the *corps de ballet* (*orchestōn*) in their representations, for by means of danced figures they represent even (*kai*) character and (*kai*) emotions and (*kai*) actions (my italics and translation, following Fyfe, with my bracketed explanations for "similar function" and the antecedent of "they").

Let us proceed from the top. As emphasized, the means of mimesis are given here in Chapter 1, and we now focus on them. After noting that people can represent with, e.g., color and voice, Aristotle says:

> so is it also in the arts which we have mentioned, **they all** make their representations in dance (*rhuthmō*) and language (*logō*) and tune (*harmonia*), *using these means either separately or in combination.*

Clearly, by "the arts which we have mentioned," Aristotle must mean those like tragedy and comedy and *not* painting, because it does not make its representation in *rhuthmō*, *logō* and *harmonia*. This shows that painting is introduced merely to help explain mimesis, not to help set forth a full classification of all arts in the treatise.

111

Regarding the rest of the passage, *logos* (or its inflection *logō*) is a very rich word, meaning language, speech, prose, ratio, proportion and so forth. However, here and usually in the treatise as a whole it clearly means language or speech. *Harmonia* conveys a "fitting together" (as of a ship's planks), or "harmony" in a social or personal sense, or the goddess Harmony, or melody/music. As indicated but as needs stressing, there was no harmony in our musical sense, however, in ancient Greece. Fyfe, like only a few other translators historically, recognizes this and translates "tune," although "music" would be arguably better, given the high level of examination at this point (an equivalent mistake would be translating *logos* here merely as sentence, when surely Aristotle means the whole of language and not just a part). Most other translators wrongly and too abstractly render *harmonia* as "harmony" when clearly the context is musical and theatrical. Again, Aristotle is speaking of the arts he had just delineated.

Rhuthmos also is an ambiguous word. It has been recognized to mean commonly in ancient Greece "shape" or "spatial order," "temporal order" (as in modern English), "measure" or "number." However, every previous translator to my knowledge, including Fyfe, renders it here as "rhythm," even if some explain in a footnote that it must convey dance. This is despite the incongruity that results from the previous translations. Given that *harmonia* must be melody or music, which always has its own inherent musical rhythms, it would be redundant and foolish for Aristotle to use *rhuthmos* as "rhythm," which for us means something like "temporal order." Rather, I have demonstrated that Plato uses *rhuthmos* at *Laws* II 665a as "ordered body movement" (with children's jumping as the context)[95] and that Aristotle simply follows suit.[96] Since the context is the theatrical arts, "dance" is the closest term we have for the phenomenon.

---

95   *ADMC*, Chapter 1, pp. 28ff.
96   *ADMC*, Chapters 2, pp. 144-7; 156-7; and 169ff.

Overview & Comments: Chapter 1

We come now to the phrase that I indicated has been perhaps the most under-appreciated one in Chapter 1: *"using these means either separately or in combination."* This phrase anticipates how the rest of the chapter is structured, and Aristotle proceeds *not* to set forth a taxonomy of arts, poetic or otherwise, but simply to describe how the means of mimesis can be used, separately or in combination. As noted, he only cares about four of the seven possible combinations, and they suffice not only to explain the different means of mimesis separately or in combination but to allow him to proceed in Chapter 2 to cover the next topic, the objects of mimesis.[97]

Next is another sentence that has always been badly misconstrued because the Arabic scholars 1000 years ago started misinterpreting them, and the literary theorists in the 15th and 16th centuries followed suit once the Greek texts became available to the nobility, clergy, and universities. Everyone afterwards continued to follow the well-trodden path, treating *rhuthmos* as mere "rhythm," even if they try to examine the statement afresh. As I translate more concretely:

> For music and dance (*rhuthmō*) alone are employed in oboe-playing and kithara-playing *and in any other arts*

---

97 Thus, I emphatically disagree with Tarán when he says, after merely noting the three means of mimesis in passing (*op. cit.*, pp. 224-5): "...the fact that he [Aristotle] mentions the employment of the three means separately or in combination does not imply that he is primarily interested in them as such" (*op. cit.* p. 229). First, in reply to Tarán, the *men-de-de* construction of the Greek shows the importance of Aristotle explaining the three means separately or in combination: Aristotle reports "on the one hand" (*men*) the musicians using both *harmonia kai rhuthmos*, then "on the other hand" (*de*) the *corps de ballet* (using) the *rhuthmos* by itself, and then "on the third hand" (*de*) at 1447a28 the composers (using) the language by itself. Why would he structure much of Chapter 1 around this *men-de-de* pattern, were explaining "separate" versus "in combination" unimportant? To reiterate, in my view, anyone who misses how crucial the three means of mimesis are for the bones of Aristotle's theory in *Dramatics* 1 will never get the muscles and flesh clear. This is a matter of philosophical interpretation and consistency, or of philology and philosophy, *not* of paleography.

> which have a similar function [i.e., to be performed in the theater], as, for example, panpipe-playing.

Commentators have taken this passage as if it were about musicians "glued to a chair," like in our symphonies. That is one reason, probably the primary one, that for centuries they have continued to translate *rhuthmos* as "rhythm," ignoring the redundancy that results (because music always has its own temporal rhythm). They foisted the anachronistic "harmony" onto *harmonia* in order to try to make some sense of the phrase, sometimes saying harmony is a set of "vertical" pitches whereas "rhythm" is "horizontal" timing, in spite of no clear textual evidence existing that *harmonia* was used in that very restricted way in ancient Greece musical theory before Aristotle, at least in the context of choral performance.[98] Worse, for reasons we see later, the reader cannot tell whether *rhuthmos* applies to language or music or both, or why it cannot be equally independent, as those two other means are.

However, the relevant musicians were more like rock-and-roll performers or strolling minstrels. They were the musicians of the chorus who played *while* "dancing," if only the "stepping rightly" that Plato includes under *mousikē* of *Alcibiades* 108. Note the front cover of this book, which is only part of one vase-painting among the many in the Louvre that show the *aulos*-players and the kithara-players locomoting while performing with their instruments.[99]

---

[98] Plato says at *Laws* 665a that *harmonia* is the blending of the high and low, which puts order (*taxis*) into the children's chaotic cries. However, this is not to convey our notion of "(musical) harmony," but to suggest song or music, and indeed Plato immediately says that this "song" and dance (*rhuthmos*) make up the choral art. It is two full practices that make up the choral art, not two mere "abstracted" aspects of the single art of music/song, namely, harmony and rhythm. The analogy would be saying scales and tempo make up a singing competition instead of music and language. Cf. *ADMC* Chapter 1, espec. pp. 28-65.

[99] One finds many other similar examples in the various museums of Europe and the USA that have collections of ancient Greek vases. I hasten to

Overview & Comments: Chapter 1

Aristotle's "similar function" refers, I gather, to a similar function in *theatrical choral composition*, because, after all, the treatise is about dramatic performed art, especially the types he is primarily concerned with *and the ones he had just mentioned*, including tragedy and comedy. Given, therefore, that those arts are the scope of the current discussion, it would be perfectly clear to readers or to an audience in lecture that the musicians (combining music and dance) are the ones in the chorus. The panpipes were the instruments often used in the satyr plays, with the satyrs playing them as they cavorted in front of the audience. This is one of the surviving indications that Aristotle is also interested in the satyr play, the fourth and final art form that satisfies his technical sense of *poiēsis*. Otherwise, Aristotle could have referred to many other musical instruments that were *not* used in the orchestral arts to make his point.

We now arrive at his next sentence:

> Dance (*rhuthmō*) alone without music (*harmonia*) is employed by the *corps de ballet* (*orchestōn*) in their representations, for by means of danced figures (*schēmatizomenōn rhuthmōn*) they represent even (*kai*) character and (*kai*) emotions and (*kai*) actions [my translation].

This is one of the most famous passages in history for dance theorists. It is also one of the most misunderstood because traditionally, even (Greek-speaking) classicists have not recognized that *rhuthmos* and *orchēsis* can both mean dance, albeit with different shadings (like our "dance" and "ballet"). Two possible exceptions are the dance theorists Claude-François Menestrier (1631-1705) and Carlo Blasis (1795-1878), who did not, however, focus on this particular passage but spoke only

---

add that the "comasts" on the front cover are revelers, and I do not claim that the picture of the two musicians playing while walking was of a tragic chorus. I only emphasize that *aulos*-players and *kithara*-players commonly played while walking or moving although they sometimes played, and are depicted, while sitting too. Think of the marching bands at halftime at football games now. For the Greeks, if done in the theater, they would be musicians dancing.

about *orchēsis* meaning complex or imitative dance for the ancients, including Plato and Aristotle.

Before beginning the analysis of *rhuthmos*, we should recognize that Aristotle feels the need to strip music away from the dance as he starts the sentence: *"Rhuthmos* **alone** *without music..."* He thereby switches from the combined music and dance that he had just been highlighting to the separate dance (again, following his plan to explain the means of mimesis separately or in combination). If the concrete means of music and dance are ignored as the translation, or not even recognized, as has been the case for centuries, and if "harmony (or melody)" and "rhythm" are rendered instead, then Aristotle is absurdly saying that only with rhythm (as a temporal ordering) does the *corps de ballet* represent. Yet this is as preposterous as claiming that only with rhythm do poets represent. Surely, poets need words, too, even more fundamentally, and the choral performers likewise need dance. In the chronicles of ancient Greek culture, there are many cases of ancient Greek dancers not moving rhythmically in our sense of rhythm (cf. *ADMC* Chapter 1). We ourselves have the same phenomenon in theatrical dance, which need not be like, and is often unlike, folk dance. The opening of Michael Fokine's *Petrouchka* and some improvisational dance has no rhythm or no perceptible rhythm, even if the dancers are ordered spatially (which is Plato's normal concern in the *Laws*, with never a worry about whether the dancers are temporally ordered or "on the beat"). Rhythm is often needed to keep groups together or is employed dance-wise to augment any associated music, but, if the latter is not a concern (like when a dance such as Jerome Robbins' *Moves* is done to silence) and if choreographers give sufficiently good rules to dancers ("Eric dances within *this* rectangle and creates angular movements whereas Florence dances within *that* remote circle and does curved movements"), then rhythm as "temporal ordering" can be, and occasionally is, dispensed with.

Orchēsis always means some kind of dance but often conveys more sophisticated, or orchestral, dance and sometimes complex, imitative dance. In contrast, dance *qua rhuthmos* was broader and as just "ordered body movement" could be done by children learning to order their chaotic jumping, as Plato explains at least a few times in the *Laws* II (for example, 653 and 665). However, just as the terms "ballet" and "dance" for us overlap and sometimes are used synonymously, but sometimes not, with ballet referring to a certain style involving significant training, so *orchēsis* and *rhuthmos* often overlap and are used synonymously at times for the ancient Greeks. The implied differences between *orchēsis* and *rhuthmos*, then, obviate any redundancy by Aristotle in the passage at hand.

I should add that *orchestōn* (the trained dancers) is not only related to *orchēsis* but to the verb "to dance," *orchesthai*. These words are also associated with *orchestra*, long appropriated by musicians. However, unlike its meaning now as "a group of musicians" or "the seats closest to stage at ground level," the *orchestra* is where the dancing (and singing or music) took place. The *corps de ballet* members, the *orchestōn*, even if not professional, were still much more capable than people dancing naturally. If *corps de ballet* seems too modern to you as a translation, render instead the Greek term as "chorus members" or "Terpsichorean performers."[100] The ancient Greeks were famous as dancers, and I only present one piece of evidence here in order not to turn this *Primer* into a tome, to support all of the above (we see direct evidence also in *Dramatics* 2, 4 and 26 and overwhelming evidence is given in *ADMC*, Chapters 1, 2 and 4). According to Athenaeus of Naucratis a Greek rhetorician of the 2nd-3rd centuries CE:

> Telesis, or Telestes, (whichever was his right name), the dancing-master, invented many figures, and taught men to use the action of their hands, so as to give expression to what they said.[101] Phillis the Delian, a musician, says

---

100 However, for a discussion of an example on a vase of one woman on *pointe*, fleetingly, without wearing modern *pointe* shoes, cf. *ADMC*, p. 122.
101 A modern form of this type of dance expression is Bournonville

> that the *ancient harp-players moved their countenances but little, but their feet very much, imitating the march of troops or the dancing of a chorus.* Accordingly Aristotle says, that Telestes the director of Aeschylus's choruses was so great a master of his art, that in managing the choruses of the *Seven Generals against Thebes*, he made all the transactions plain by dancing.[102]

I hasten to stress that, in the passage of *Dramatics* 1, Aristotle also indicates that the (pure) dance (of the *corps de ballet*) is done by the performers who *themselves* are not making the music. An implication presumably is that the dancers *better* convey passions, character and actions (in part because they were not encumbered by instruments). The accompanying musicians in the chorus typically provide the tunes, unless at times the dance is only to words or to silence (and what Aristotle says allows that at other times the choral dancers could sing, too, simultaneously). However, since the musicians often or always moved along with the more imitative dancers, the musicians also are part of the chorus, even if they are not part of the *corps de ballet*. Violinists and singers are still part of the modern orchestra even if they are not part of the brass section. Nevertheless, *Dramatics* 26 proves that the musicians sometimes were also physically mimetic while playing, like some of our modern musical performers on stage.

Aristotle now introduces the final art to be treated "separately" in Chapter 1, language, with neither *rhuthmos* nor *harmonia*. If we understand that Aristotle leaves aside dance and music, the long passage makes much more sense, although some ambiguities still creep in, which I need to explain. If we think, however, as so many have, that *rhuthmos* means "rhythm," as temporal order, and that Aristotle is implying that language can have rhythm in this passage, the possible

---

mime, as developed by August Bournonville in the mid- to late 1800's and carried on for generations at the Royal Danish Ballet.
102   *The Deipnosophists, or Banquet of The Learned of Athenaeus*, ed. C. D. Yonge (London: Henry G. Bohn, Covent Garden, 1854), i. 39; my italics.

Overview & Comments: Chapter 1

interpretations magnify and confusion occurs. It is not that language cannot have rhythm, as we see in a moment, it is simply that Aristotle does not care about this particular point now. One suggestion in the passage according to traditional translations is that *poiētēs* refers *only* to wordsmiths, which is to say, *poiētēs* in the Gorgian sense rather than the Diotiman one. We need, therefore, to inspect this passage very closely because it is perhaps the primary reason that scholars have mostly just assumed that Aristotle accepts the Gorgian sense and never questioned it.[103] To emphasize, Aristotle uses only language (*logos*) or verse (*metron*) in Chapter 1 when dealing with (pure) language, and he *never once* uses *rhuthmos* in describing or qualifying the different forms of language. This particular means of mimesis ("unaccompanied" language or verse) itself gets examined in Chapter 1 from 1447a29 to 1447b24, almost to the end. All of this is especial-

---

103   "The art that imitates by words, says Aristotle, is poetry" (M.A.R. Habib, *A History of Literary Criticism: From Plato to the Present,* Hoboken/ Oxford: Wiley-Blackwell Publishing, 2005, p. 51). Yet Habib never cites a passage, and this directly contradicts *Dramatics* 1 when, as we shall see, Aristotle speaks about the *nameless* mimetic art of words (whether or not in verse). Richard McKirahan also similarly says:
> Chapter 1 states that the medium, the objects, and the manner are the only differentia *of literary forms* (1447a16) ... Further, *Chapter 1 classifies literary forms by the medium in which they operate (rhythm, words and harmony)* [my italics; "The Place of the *Posterior Analytics* in Aristotle's Thought, with Particular Reference to the *Poetics*," *Apeiron* 43/2-3 (2010), 88].

In addition to the objections in the body of this book, one of which is that commentators mechanically apply *rhuthmos* in the *Rhetoric* to the different context of theatrical art, I must emphasize immediately that Chapter 1 never states that the medium, objects and manner are the differentiae *of literary forms*. Rather, as the explanation of pictures and music at 1447a19 make clear, Aristotle is saying that the three means are the differentiae of *mimesis*, not of "poetry" or of literary forms, a very important difference. McKirahan's account also contradicts the treatment of all three means of mimesis being equal for Aristotle.

On this last point, George Whalley perspicaciously says, "Aristotle's three 'in-what' differentiae are rhythm, melody and speech. In our way of thinking, these three are not at the same level: rhythm is radical to both melly easy to see if one realizes that in the context of the theatrical arts *rhuthmos* means "dance." This realization also explains in large part the confusion of Avicenna, Else and all other like-minded commentators regarding *rhuthmos* and language over many centuries, some of whom (like Else) were so baffled by the relationship of *rhuthmos* to language and to music that they wanted to excise *rhuthmos*. Others, like George Whalley, claimed *rhuthmos* was an unfortunate later addition.

Let us now work through the passage on language, pausing when necessary, in order to understand that *poiēsis* does not mean "word-smithing" or "poetry" in the Gorgian sense, at least for the Northern Greek. We need also to understand that, although he gives the *appearance* when mentioning Chaeremon of allowing a *poiētēs* to be someone who writes only with language, this is, at most a temporary secondary sense of the word or a meaning that *others* give, one that does not outweigh Aristotle's own primary, Diotiman-based sense of the term.

According to Janko, Aristotle says in explaining the third and final means of mimesis at 1447a28ff that:

The art of representation that uses *unaccompanied* words

---

ody and speech" (*Aristotle's Poetics: Translation and with a Commentary by George Whalley*, ed. by John Baxter and Patrick Atherton, Canada: Mc-Gill-Queen's University Press, 1997, p. 46). However, Whalley never resolves the problem, because he never even considered that *rhuthmos* could mean dance, which is on the same level as language and melody, being equally concrete. Although a few commentators have thought that *rhuthmos* was referring *indirectly* to dance, more than to the other two means of mimesis, they all assumed anachronistically that the Greeks before Aristoxenus, a student of Aristotle's, were (at least in this precise context) using *rhuthmos* to mean what we mean by it, "temporal order" or the like. Only a few seem to have realized that *rhuthmos* had at least six meanings in ancient Greece but no scholar recognized that it simply should be translated here in Chapter 1 always as "dance" (or "ordered body movement"). Margoliouth, whom I discuss later, came close; cf. *ADMC*, p. 145, footnote 212, for others like M.E. Hubbard and Andrew Bongiorno.

(logois psilois) or verses *(metrois)* (whether it mixes these together or uses one single class of verse-form) *has to the present day no name. For we have no common name for the mimes (mimous) of Sophron and Xenarchus and the Socratic dialogues, and would not have one even if someone were to compose the representation in [iambic] trimeters, elegiacs or some other such verse. But* **people attach the word "poet" (*to poiein*) to the verse-form, and name some "elegiac poets" (*elegeiopoious*) and others "epic poets" (*epopoious*)** terming them poets not according to [whether they compose a] representation but indiscriminately, according to [their use of] verse. Thus if someone brings out a work of medicine or natural science in verse, *they* normally call him a poet; but there is nothing in common between Homer and Empedocles except the verse-form. For this reason it is right to call the former a poet *(poiētēn)*, but the latter a natural scientist *(phusiologon)* rather than a poet. Likewise, if someone produced a representation by intermingling all the verse-forms, just as Chaeremon composed his *Centaur* (a recitation which mixes all the verse-forms), he must still be termed a poet *(poiētēn)* [my italics & bolding; Janko's own unbolded bracketed insertions].

Proceeding from the top: First, on the interpretation with which I am completely sympathetic, pure language (whether prose or verse) is "unaccompanied" because Aristotle is still explaining how the three means of mimesis can be used separately or together. He is now considering language *separately*, that is, "unaccompanied." This means language–*as either prose or meter/verse*–has neither of the other two means of mimesis, *harmonia* or *rhuthmos*. On another interpretation, the "unaccompanied" does not refer back to the means of mimesis being treated separately but instead suggests "*bare* language, namely prose," which is being contrasted to verse, with the implication that verses are most crucial and *(only) themselves* are accompanied by *rhuthmos qua* "rhythm."[104] It is crucial to see that in this passage

---

104   Tarán gives an excellent discussion of the Greek and the historical

Aristotle is considering language now, in *both* its prose and metrical forms, without *rhuthmos* as currently used, and this helps refute any suggestion by scholars that somehow *rhuthmos* (*qua* rhythm) in Chapter 1 is being applied by Aristotle to pure language. To begin with, Aristotle says that we would not have a name to categorize the prose forms of mime and Socratic dialogue *even if they were converted into verse*. This means the rhythm in verse is irrelevant, even if it is presupposed. That is, as we saw, in the *Rhetoric* III 8 Aristotle specifies that even prose can have "rhythm" but should not have too much, otherwise it becomes verse. Thus, just because language is in prose entails *nothing* about whether it has "rhythm" or not. Reading *rhuthmos* as "rhythm" does *not* cause prose to be "bare" and *only* verse to be "accompanied" (with rhythm). Thus, the second interpretation of this passage on "pure language" completely fails, and Aristotle must be considering language "separately" from both music and *rhuthmos qua* dance.

To reconcile the inconsistency with the *Rhetoric*: That treatise has a different scope, just as "play Hamlet" (within drama) has a different

---

interpretations on this particular point, which I believe should help settle the debate once and for all (2012, pp. 226-229), although we have seen where he has gone astray on some related points. However, he is wrong in thinking that language in *Dramatics* 1 includes *rhuthmos* as used in *this* chapter. In short, I agree with his account of Solmsen and Else, who claim that "meters [which in this context mean verses] alone" means "apart from the other two means of mimesis," but for different reasons than Tarán attributes to them. Tarán himself says "by 'meters alone' he [Aristotle] must refer to language plus the special kinds of rhythms that constitute the several kinds of Greek meters, but excluding music" (p. 299). Tarán then tries to support this by appealing without explanation to the difficult statement of Aristotle in *Dramatics* 4 that meters/verses are part of *rhuthmos* (p. 229). Yet we will examine that passage later, and it in no way supports his own position against Solmsen and Else. The arguments of this book and of *ADMC* should help permanently protect the assertion of the latter two scholars, namely, that "unaccompanied language and verse" means "language and verse *apart from the other two means of mimesis*."

Overview & Comments: Chapter 1

scope from "play tennis" (within sports). The *Rhetoric* has a different meaning of *rhuthmos*, and thinking that the word has the same meaning there that it has in the *Dramatics* is like thinking "play" has the same meaning in tennis (or in music) that it does in drama. To repeat, Aristotle never once uses the word *rhuthmos* in his analysis of language in Chapter 1. Although commentators have often applied the *rhuthmos* of the *Rhetoric* to the *Dramatics*, they have done it without paying enough attention to the redundancies and problems that result, some of which have been mentioned.

While on the topic of "unaccompanied" versus "accompanied" (that is, "separately and in combination"): Why Aristotle never discusses other possible combinations of the means of mimesis involving words—for example, "lyric poetry" (words with music) and "dance with words"— in Chapter 1 might give us pause. However, probably he does not mention these combinations because he has already given an example of two means of mimesis being combined (oboe-players using music and dance), and he would senselessly duplicate the explanation of how composers could mix two means of mimesis. Indeed, had Aristotle really wanted a full taxonomy, as so many have thought, he could and would have covered easily all seven, aforementioned permutations. Commentators like Else conceived of the different permutations and whether or not Aristotle dealt with them, and if so, how.[105] It hardly needs restating that the commentators never came to a solution because they never even considered that *rhuthmos* could mean "dance." They were thrown off by thinking *rhuthmos here* was some quality of language or of music, like "ordered temporality," that could *somehow* apply to language and music (leaving aside the puzzle that it then gets identified with dance in some kind of way for them, never sensibly explained).

Curiously, Aristotle expounds the art of pure language in much greater

---

105   Cf. Else, *op. cit.*, pp. 17-32.

detail than the other two means of mimesis. One must not assume, however, that the greater detail entails tragedians using only one means of mimesis, verse, evidence of which we will see after discussing Chaeremon. I should add that Aristotle does not remark in great detail in Chapter 1 on all three means of mimesis being used in combination because that is the default position of the whole book. He does state it, though, almost breezily, as befits a situation when the matter is completely obvious. He simply indicates at the end of the chapter that tragedy uses all three means.

Let us look more carefully now at the whole previous passage, starting at the top.

> The art of representation that uses unaccompanied words or verses ... has to the present day no name ... [and] we have no common name for the mimes ... and the Socratic dialogues, *and would not have one even if someone were to compose the representation in trimeters ... or some other such verse.*

Again, Aristotle denies that any Greek term means "language giving representation," *whether or not in verse.* Thus, the Greeks had no term like our "literature" or "novels," although one cannot help but wonder why the Gorgian sense does not qualify. Presumably, Aristotle chooses to ignore it because the Gorgian sense is not restricted enough and includes non-representational subjects, whereas Aristotle emphasizes the importance of representation, *which obviously is a pre-condition of a plot.* That is, much poetry in the Gorgian sense has no plot or no representation to speak of, expressing a mere wish or personal feeling or subjective impression or command or exhortation (say, to die bravely), as we saw before with the example of Simonides. Indeed, the Gorgian sense would actually include Empedocle's verse, which, however, Aristotle expressly excludes from *poiēsis*.

All of this may be, and on some traditional interpretations *was*, initially unsurprising because Aristotle includes prose examples like Soc-

Overview & Comments: Chapter 1

ratic dialogues. One might believe and scholars did believe, therefore, that the Northern Greek assumes *poiēsis* to be the Gorgian term for verse and is making the *further*, more crucial point that no *general* term exists for pure literary *mimesis* in *both* verse and prose. That is, one might think that Aristotle suggests no term exists like "literature" in English, which is broader of course than "novels" or "poetry." Yet, Aristotle never adds that the word *poiēsis* means only verse, and, in fact, undoubtedly he indicates that *even were the prose to be reformulated in verse* we still would not have a term, which rules out *poiēsis* as being the rubric for some variation of the Gorgian sense (perhaps as "representation in poetry").

Aristotle's formulation does not deny Gorgias the privilege *in Gorgias' own works* of calling *poiēsis* "language in meter." Instead, Aristotle's formulation only implies that this is not the relevant meaning *here*, which involves plot as a fourth condition and which therefore necessarily presupposes mimesis. *Neither does Aristotle deny that a name exists for (simple) "language in meter."* Obviously, Gorgias uses *poiēsis* in just this fashion. Rather, Aristotle more precisely says that no name (akin to our term "novel") exists *for the art of representation* (in his sense that can presumably entail a plot) *in pure language*, as his following explanation using literary plots of Sophron and Plato prove. This subtle difference is absolutely crucial.

Thus, poetry (*poiēsis*) in the Gorgian sense is definitely not used to cover the family of (representational) verse or of (representational) prose or of the combination of the two — nor, Aristotle adds, would it. He suggests, moreover, that he could not offer a suitable term, even were pure representational prose to be put into verse. Why? One answer is that *poiēsis* as the short, single word seems already habitually employed by the Greeks to denote another phenomenon, as Diotima had explained, either in its broad sense of "making" in general or in its narrow sense of making *mousikē* and verse. Indeed, confirmation that "unaccompanied" language even with a plot is excluded from any deep analysis in the *Dramatics* and that the *poiēsis* to be examined is the "musical" Diotiman type arises in Aristotle's continuing discussion in the passage we just saw, as I now explain further.

Aristotle explicitly gives mimes and Socratic dialogues as examples of pure (representational) prose. To start with an example of the latter, the *Symposium* is undoubtedly representational *with plot in a literary sense* (an arrangement of actions *in words*). Socrates attends a dinner party called a "symposium," debates the meaning of love, and then leaves without becoming too inebriated; likewise, with other Socratic dialogues (although they are not set in symposia). The plots are minimal, and the emphasis in the *Symposium* is on the speeches given by the interlocutors, but there is still a plot, and without question the story is mimetic, even if much philosophical dialogue is incorporated. Similarly, mimes are also literary representations, perhaps with plots in Aristotle's sense, and perhaps not. (By that I do not deny that they could also have been performed in a certain sense, at least by being read out loud, just as epic was performed by rhapsodes. Again, "performance" or reading out loud was much more the norm in Plato's and Aristotle's time than ours, even if the reading was in a private room, for oneself.)

One of the most famous composers of mimes is Sophron of Syracuse, an elder contemporary of Euripides, whom Aristotle cites in the passage above, and who

> composed in the Dorian dialect prose dialogues, partly serious, partly comic, which faithfully represented scenes of actual life, mostly in the lower classes, interspersed with numerous proverbs and colloquial forms of speech.[106]

Nevertheless, without question, the scope of the *Dramatics* is limited only to tragedy, comedy and epic (and probably to satyr play in

---

106   From the classics dictionary of the University of Pennsylvania: http://www.classics.upenn.edu/myth/php/tools/dictionary.php?regexp=SOPHRON&method=standard. Also, see J.H. Hordern, *Sophron's Mimes*.

lost sections), and neither Socratic dialogue or (literary) mime is ever again addressed after Chapter 1.

Table 4: How and when Aristotle explains the means of mimesis in Chapter 1 for the relevant arts, "used separately or in combination"

Separately: one by itself	Combination of two	Combination of all three
Dance (*rhuthmos*) (14457a26-5)	Music and dance: Oboe-playing and dance (*rhuthmos*); kithara-playing and dance (*rhuthmos*); and panpipe-playing and dance (*rhuthmos*) (1447a23-6)	Dance (*rhuthmos*), music (*melos*), and verse (*metron*): Dithyramb, nome, tragedy, and comedy (1447b24-8)1
Language (verse or prose; mimes and Socratic dialogues) (1447a28-b23)		

Thus, having *representational language and plot* is still not sufficient (even though it is necessary) to be included in the scope of the *Dramatics*, that is, to be part of *poiēsis* in the crucial sense. The mixture of "music [in the Greek sense]" and verse is still much more relevant for *poiēsis* for Aristotle than arts of mere language, when the context is the theater, just as "music" and language were for Plato in the *Laws*.[107]

Text, Translation, and Commentary (Oxford: Oxford University Press, 2004), and Rolando Ferri's review of it in the *Bryn Mawr Classical Review*, 2005.08.02.

It might be said that the dialogues of Sophron were not technically plots, in the sense of having a beginning, middle and end, with a complication and dénouement, but this gives even more reason why Aristotle would not examine the genre in a book for which plot is crucial.

[107] Cf. *ADMC*, pp. 118-25 for a discussion of the passage at *Laws* II 669d-e, where Plato denigrates composers who strip language of music.

Naturally, a book like the *Symposium* is a different issue. This kind of production is expected to be without music (or dance).

Let us examine now the next portion of the full passage at hand, which, again, is Janko's translation:.

> But **people attach the word "poet" (*to poieĩn*) to the verse-form, and name some "elegiac poets" (*elegeiopoious*) and others "epic poets" (*epopoious*)**, terming them poets not according to [whether they compose a] representation but indiscriminately, according to [their use of] verse. Thus if someone brings out a work of medicine or natural science in verse, *they* normally call him a poet; but there is nothing in common between Homer and Empedocles except the verse-form. For this reason it is right to call the former a poet (*poiētēn*), but the latter a natural scientist (*phusiologon*) rather than a poet.

Obviously, Aristotle remarks on what *other* people say, presumably because *poiēsis* in his own sense necessarily has music, dance, language and representation (*qua* plot). On traditional translations, he indicates that by attaching "poet" *onto the verse form* those people get the various designations, all of which still follows Diotima. As introduced before, the reason is that the names for the other kinds of creators were not the short form *poiētēs* but rather involved this type of "mixed" name, with *-poios* on the end. Aristotle gives the example of *elegeiopoious* for "makers of elegy," which presumably had no dance or music. Yet Aristotle uses not *poiētēs*, which itself is the normal, plain word for "poet," but the expression *to poieĩn*, which requires a discussion.

First, *to poieĩn* is an unusual, or abstract, formulation, involving the article *to* coupled with the infinitive *poieĩn* ("to make"). Literally, it is "the 'to make'", and different translators offer different renderings. Some like Heath say "poetry"; others like Janko say "poet," when Aristotle could have written the shorter *poiētēs* (and Janko telegraphs the

Overview & Comments: Chapter 1

unusual phrase by putting "poet" in quotation marks). Second, composers of elegiac and epic verse are not *elegeio***topoein** and *epoto-**poein**. No Greek would say such a thing, notwithstanding Aristotle's exact words. Rather, as we just saw, his formulations become "elegiac *makers*" *elegeio***poious** and "epic *makers*" *epo***poious**.

Now, leaving aside that "poets" here is anachronistic for Aristotle because epic makers composed songs, not poems as such, why would he use *to poiein* when he knows he will give *elegeiopoious* and *epopoious* to explain his point? I propose that *to poiein* in this discussion of "pure language" means "*-composer.*" There was no hyphen in ancient Greek, and Aristotle could not write "*-poious.*" It is not proper to use the short form *poiētēs* in this precise context, for reasons I give. Yet once the examples are provided, and the suggestion clearly made as a result, the short form immediately thereafter can just be elliptical for the proper designation being tacked onto a prefatory name.

Hence, since the Greeks of his time had no hyphen, I suggest that Aristotle uses *to poiein* to convey that the naming follows the approach just described. Rather than suggesting quotation marks, as Janko implies, which would result in *"maker"* or *"composer"* (leaving aside the anachronistic "poet"), *to poiein* suggests *-maker* or *-composer*.

In any event, for Aristotle, the type of composer is said *by others* to include *both* Homer and the scientist Empedocles because, as the Athenians would know, they both wrote in hexameters: "if someone brings out a work of medicine or natural science in verse, *they normally* call him a *poet.*" However, again, this statement appears to be elliptical, just as it was when Aristotle summarized a few words before how *"people"* refer to the cases of the *elegeiopoious* and the *epopoious*.

To summarize, Aristotle suggests that the short form *poiēsis* is not used by itself for pure verse-making. Rather it is "-making" (*-poios/-poious*) added *onto the particular verse-form*, and it is *other* people who are inclined to call each of them a *poiētēs* (as a single, short word). That is, even though Homer is said to be a *poiētēs,* this may be merely elliptical for him having *–poios* on the end of his label.

Actually, Aristotle can legitimately label Homer here with the short form *poiētēs*, for after all he was *both* an *epopoios* and a true *poiētēs*. That is, he was also a quasi-dramatist, and Plato calls him the first tragedian with Aristotle following suit, as I discuss more in Chapter 3. It was well known in ancient Greece that Homer was a musician, too, whom Aristotle praises for being the most dramatic, switching characters with the least amount of narration (because in Chapter 3 epic will be seen to have a combination of dramatic and narrative elements). I gather by changing quickly the tone of voice, demeanor and gesticulation (as ordered body movement), mode of language (first person to third person), etc., Homer could instantly change character (1460a9-12). Given that he therefore uses all three means of mimesis in the Diotiman sense (and also presents a plot using various techniques, with song and language admittedly primary in epic and the gesture or "ordered body movement" secondary), Homer qualifies for Aristotle's technical *poiētēs* (meaning "musical" composer who represents). Hence, because the issue is currently language (used "separately"), Aristotle calling him a *poiētēs* in this context does not mean Homer necessarily *only* composes in, or performs with, language or that *poiētēs* can mean in *all* contexts only a Gorgian creator. Rather it means that *insofar as* Homer composes in language *representationally*, he satisfies (at least some of) the conditions of being a true *poiētēs*.

All of this would no more cause confusion for the Greeks of Aristotle's day than me calling Babe Ruth a ball player in one breath among sports fans while also calling Stephen Curry a ball player in the next breath. Anyone knowing the basics of American sports would understand that Ruth is a base-ball player while Curry is a basket-ball player. Similarly, I could call both Laurence Olivier and Luciano Pavarotti great performers and anyone familiar with the arts would know that the first

Overview & Comments: Chapter 1

is a great TV and stage actor while the second is a great opera singer. We do not always spell out tediously every detail.

Aristotle leaves aside the other considerations pertaining to music and gesture-dance because they are irrelevant in this discussion of pure language. It is not because of Homer's versification or his other qualities in *this* context (of pure language) but the "representation" of a story that truly makes him an appropriate "-composer" (*poiētēs*). To underscore, "composer" here could be merely synecdochal from Aristotle's perspective, "epic composer" or "dramatic 'musical' composer." Moreover, even were a composer oddly to use music, dance, and verse in order to function like Empedocles, and to pass on, say, natural science, he would not be fulfilling the fourth condition — *of plot* (or what amounts to the same in this context, of representation). The prospect is so unworldly that Aristotle does not even care to acknowledge it, and in any event music and dance have already been dropped here to focus on pure language.

In reality, Aristotle does make a remark about this strange type of theoretical situation, saying in the *Rhetoric:* "Nobody uses fine language when teaching geometry."[108] Aristotle implies that much less would anyone use fine language and, *in addition*, music (and dance) to teach geometry, all of which reflects a difference with some education nowadays, when some teachers do use music to help students memorize. Hence, nothing so far in Chapter 1 commits Aristotle to the Gorgian sense of *poiēsis* (as "verse") for his treatise, even if he accepts that sense—or mentions *other people* accepting it—*for the sake of argument* in the passage on "unaccompanied language."

Let us examine now the final remark of the passage from above, again according to Janko:

Likewise, if someone produced a representation by in-

---

108   *Rhetoric* III 1, 1404a13. Trans. W. Rhys Roberts, in *The Complete*

termingling all the verse-forms, just as Chaeremon composed his *Centaur* (a recitation which mixes all the verse-forms), he must still be termed a poet (*poiētēn*).

Aristotle suggests now, perhaps again, that he himself would properly call someone only using language a *poiētēs* in the purely literary, Gorgian sense ("poet" or "literary composer"). What should we make of this, above and beyond recognizing that it is a statement that encouraged the literary view of the *Dramatics* for hundreds of years?

Chaeremon is, we know, a mere writer of verses according to the *Rhetoric*. In that treatise, while discussing works to be read[109] (a relatively new phenomenon) versus works to be performed in the theatre, Aristotle says: "However, poets (*poiētai*) whose works are only meant for reading are also popular, as Chaeremon" (*Rhetoric* III 12). On the surface, then, Aristotle arguably uses *poiētēs* as "poet" in the particular case of Chaeremon, not as Diotima does, but as a mere writer of verse, or, to be more precise, of multiple verse-forms that are combined. What are we to make of this seeming inconsistency? Does Aristotle really mean that *poiētēs* now in *Dramatics* 1 should have a new meaning, a writer of "unaccompanied" and *representational* language in verse, perhaps to change the tradition that he had just finished describing, namely, that no term for representational works of pure language exists even if versified and that we would not have a name even if the prose representation were put into meters? The answer is no, for the following reasons.

To begin with, we might best read the existing passage again as an

---

Works, Vol. 2, ed. J. Barnes, *op. cit.*

109   The distinction for the Greeks is between private "reading" (which was still usually done out loud) and public presentation, not whether the private reading itself is silent or voiced. The first recorded case of someone reading a scroll silently, to the shock of colleagues walking in on him, is seemingly of Ambrose in 384 CE, *almost 700 years after Aristotle*; cf. Augustine, *Confessions* Book 6, Chapter 3.

elliptical statement, where *poiētēs* really stands for *-composer*, that is, for adding "*-poios*" onto the relevant name of the composer. It is no different from Aristotle saying a sentence or two before that others call the verse writer *poiētēs* when they really call him a longer name, with "*–poios*" added to the verse, as Aristotle's examples prove. Again, given the lack of a hyphen in Greek, Aristotle really means the following (with my comments in brackets):

> For this reason it is right to call the former a "-composer [using representation]" (*poiētēn*) but the latter a natural scientist (*phusiologon*) rather than a "-composer [using representation]." Likewise, if someone produced a representation *by intermingling all the verse-forms* [when normally "composer" gets added to a *single* verse-form] just as Chaeremon composed his *Centaur* (a recitation which mixes all the verse-forms), he must still be termed a "[mixed verse]-composer."

In other words, even though Chaeremon is not like the traditional composers who only used a single verse form (hexameter for epic composers), he is also not like a *phusiologon* such as Empedocles because Chaeremon "represents" in the appropriate way (with plot). Therefore, Chaeremon still deserves the name "[mixed verse]-*composer*."

Aristotle's treatment here of others using *poiēsis* is analogous to students of dance saying "Yes" when, among backstage professionals, someone asks the students "Are you dancers?" They are not really implying that they are *professional* dancers, they just mean "Yes. We're *student* dancers." No one, unless the most finicky, quibbles about them perhaps suggesting (because they wish to be brief) that they are professional. No ancient Greek reader in the Lyceum would complain about Aristotle being elliptical for the sake of brevity in this long passage on pure language and using *poiētēs* rather than the long-winded "mixed-verse-composer." Indeed, the long-winded label apparently did not even exist then in ancient Greece.

One final aside: As noted, some teachers nowadays use music to aid in memorization but this was not apparently what the Greeks did for *scientific* purposes, even if they used music in our sense to aid in remembering the lyrics of very long epics *and* to give the enjoyment that music provides. They may well have employed rhythm or meter *in the literary sense* to aid in remembering the words of natural science (as was presumably the case with Empedocles). We cannot forget that the culture was primarily oral, even if slowly changing, and memorization, rather than having a written document, was usually still most important. Any technique, like verse, that allowed easier or better memorization was not to be sneezed at.

In any event, to return to our major concerns and to recapitulate, with respect to Chaeremon, *poiētēs* in this context seems to be elliptical for having "*-poios*" on the end of his label, *whatever that label would be. That* is what Aristotle means by saying Chaeremon should be called a *poiētēs*. In any event, whether or not he is speaking elliptically, Aristotle has been dealing with the issue from the standpoint of *others* (perhaps those like Gorgias using *poiētēs* to mean a writer of mere verse), and he is arguably suggesting that we should call Chaeremon a *poiētēs from that standpoint* even though Chaeremon breaks tradition and uses multiple types of verse.

One final option: Because the discussion at this point is simply of pure language, a clear shift in context for the reader, Aristotle may be using *poiētēs* temporarily with another, secondary meaning, namely, a writer of mere (representational) verse, akin to Sophron and Plato the dialogue-writer. As a secondary meaning, though, this does *not* contradict the *primary* Diotiman meaning of *poiētēs* as "dramatic composer (using language, music and dance)."

Why Aristotle does not spell this all out can be explained because he is far less concerned with maintaining his Diotiman sense of *poiētēs* for the moment–which the audience or reader would know very well anyway—than he is with making the point that it is *representation* (especially *qua* plot) that should determine any verbal part of the composition. Indeed, were Aristotle to insist on using the Diotiman version of *poiētēs*, he would arguably convolute unnecessarily the argument he is now trying to make, especially because medical or scientific verse was never done with music and dance, *and he could not continue easily with his discussion of "unaccompanied" language.* How could he discuss (representation in) pure language effectively in this context if he continues to adamantly insist on Diotima's sense of *poiēsis*? Recall that it took Diotima a paragraph to explain how people use *poiēsis/poiētēs* and the issue is probably now more complicated because the Gorgian notion is becoming more prevalent, causing the term to be even more over-loaded with equivocal meanings. By accepting others' use of *poiētēs* in a discussion of pure language (again, music and dance having been dropped for the moment), Aristotle can more effectively make his point about *representation* (and indirectly plot), not verse, being crucial.

To conclude our analysis of the passage on pure language, Aristotle clearly at times is speaking for other "people" and at least in one instance is speaking elliptically. Even if he ignores his earlier statement that there is no word for unadorned representational language, whether in verse or prose, at the worst for my themes in this book, he only shifts his meaning of *poiētēs* provisionally to make a point about the maker of representation over superficial verse-forms. Yet this meaning of *poiētēs* becomes then a secondary sense of the word, not the primary and preferred one.[110] Proof comes from what immediately follows, at the end of Chapter 1. After the passage on Chaeremon,

---

110 In Chapter 21, during the discussion of names (in pure language), Empedocles is spoken of at 1457b24 and suggested to be a poet (if only because of the later, indirect use of *poiētēs* at 1457b34). Yet, if anything, this suggests that Chapter 21 is from a different text, as many, including Else, have asserted. Empedocles is clearly ruled out in *Dramatics* 1 as being a *poiētēs* in the relevant sense.

Aristotle adds this passage to conclude the chapter:

> On this point the distinctions thus made may suffice. There are certain arts that employ all the means which I have mentioned, dance (*rhuthmō*) and music (*melei*) and verse (*metrō*)—dithyrambs and nomes[111] for example, and tragedy too and comedy. The difference here is that some [like the dithyramb] use all these [means] at once, others [like tragedy and comedy] use now one now another. These differences then in the various arts I call the means of mimesis.[112]

Clearly, tragedy in the primary sense, as confirmed in the rest of the treatise, is the traditional kind of performed, Diotiman-type "musical" drama. Therefore, the person who makes that kind of product, the composer *qua* dramatist or *qua* tragedian, cannot *primarily* mean one who creates *merely* in verse, no matter how one translates *rhuthmos*. Indubitably, as we saw earlier and as is confirmed now, the ancient Greek maker of tragedy uses at least *melos* (or its cognate *melei*) too, so in English would have to be *minimally* a "maker of music and verse." Diotima's sense of *poiētēs* is maintained.

Furthermore, why the kind of composer like Chaeremon who only writes verse is derivative or secondary gets shown also by the fact that no tragedy that has the six necessary conditions in Chapter 6—

---

111   As Fyfe says, "the Nome was a solo sung to a harp accompaniment in honor of Apollo" (*op. cit.*, in notes accompanying his translated passage). Others give different accounts, but what they all share is at least a singing. My interpretation shows that the solo nomic singer must have done some gesturing, walking or "dancing" too, just as the rhapsode did, if even with the face and head (and why that counts as dancing for the Greeks is explained by the renowned classicist Lillian Lawler; cf. *ADMC*, pp. 74 and 116.).

112   My translation, following Fyfe; my comments in brackets, with proof shown later in the book, especially during the discussion of the definition of tragedy in Chapter 6. In a relatively happy case of inconsistency, Margoliouth uses "dance" for *rhuthmos* here, even though he had merely transliterated the same term as "rhythm" in the earlier part of the chapter (*The Poetics of Aristotle, op. cit.*, 1911, p. 132); *ADMC* p. 145, footnote 212.

Overview & Comments: Chapter 1

and no tragedian who composes the kinds of plays to be examined in the *Dramatics*—is included in the section in Chapter 1 on "pure language." That is, no tragedy is given alongside of mimes and Socratic dialogues—the examples of pure language with plot. Further confirmation that the restricted Diotiman usage of *poiēsis* continues to be primary for Aristotle comes, as we will see, throughout the book, especially in Chapters 4, 6, 24, and 26. There we will find that tragedy is without question performed, and its music and dance help Aristotle rank it higher than epic. We have well-known evidence, besides, that the three great 5th-century tragedians, Aeschylus, Sophocles, and Euripides, all were respected for their music and dance.[113] In Chapter 18, Aristotle holds the tragedian who dies at the cusp of the 4th century BCE, Agathon, responsible for creating the music.[114] In Chapter 6, the dramatic "musical" composers (*poiētai*) are suggested to be partially responsible even for the spectacle (just *less* than the set designer).

---

113   When the Athenians shockingly lost a war to Syracuse, whom by all accounts they should have defeated handily, the captured sailors were executed, except, the story goes, for some who knew Euripides' songs, the implication being that the captured sailors would teach them to the Syracusans or at least would entertain them!

114   Note additionally what Sultan says with respect to Sophocles' musical abilities, given that Sophocles was always called a "poet" before me:
   ...Plato and Aristotle seem to disagree on whether the *kithara* is a proper instrument for use in educating the youth of ancient Greece. We do have scenes on vases depicting music lessons given on the *kithara*. The instrument was played during religious festivals, and soloists (*kitharōdoi kitharistai*) competed for recognition and prizes in music competition (*agōn*) during the 5th-4th centuries BC. *It was also played to accompany the chorus' song and dance performances in Tragedy—Sophocles himself was a player of some fame in his Thamyras* [my italics]" (op. cit., online Perseus Encyclopedia).
Sultan's sources are: Maas, Martha and Jane Snyder, *Stringed Instruments of Ancient Greece* (New Haven: Yale University Press, 1989). *New Grove Dictionary of Musical Instruments,* 3 vols., ed. Stanley Sadic, London, 1984. "Music.9. Instruments," *Oxford Classical Dictionary* (second ed.) Oxford, 1978.

Likewise at the end of Chapter 15: Aristotle will not talk more about the dramatist concerning himself with the stage effects, and more precisely with mistakes regarding stage effects, because, the Northern Greek states, this topic had already been discussed in his own exoteric work. Surely, therefore, the tragedian was not concerned only with the word-smithing.

Summary of Chapter 1

Considering how dense Chapter 1 is, a summary is not only appropriate but necessary.

Aristotle starts by laying out his plan to discuss the types of (the art of) "dramatic 'musical' composition" (*poiētikēs*) and how to construct the plots well. He promises also a discussion of the powers of the parts they have (all following his own recommendation from his biological treatises how to get the best understanding of something along with Plato's recommendation in the *Phaedrus* to analyze the part recursively). Aristotle then immediately shifts to mimesis, which was so well known in Plato's Academy and Aristotle's Lyceum as being foundational to art that he does not even explain why it is crucial. Its importance is simply taken for granted.

Instead, though, of using the Platonic analytical tool of form-content, Aristotle notes the three modes of mimesis in order to explain "musical" drama more precisely: means (music, dance, and language), objects (or "subjects"), and manner. This is not to say that Aristotle will not use a form-content distinction in other places, just that he chooses to be more precise here. He postpones the latter two modes of mimesis until Chapters 2 and 3 and focusses only on the means in Chapter 1, "used separately or together."

Aristotle touches on two means "separately," that is, each by itself.

Overview & Comments: Chapter 1

They are dance and then language. However, for whatever reason, Aristotle does not analyze them in what we might think is the most logical order, starting with the simplest options before graduating to more complex combinations. Rather he first mentions the way in which two means, music and dance, can be used together, with the context being the theatrical arts he had just circumscribed: musicians dancing, at least in the sense of "stepping rightly." Because Aristotle does not explain this in detail and because he uses the term *rhuthmos*, commentators for centuries misinterpreted the statement and assumed he was only speaking of music, with the term *harmonia* meaning something like the vertical choice of pitches and *rhuthmos* meaning a (horizontal) ordering of time. With very rare exceptions, the commentators either were baffled by the oddity that language was also included as the third means of mimesis, which entailed that a temporal ordering should be applicable to it also, or they just ignored the whole problem. Yet, once we see that the musicians dance and that *rhuthmos* means dance in the sense of "ordered body movement (whether in space or in time or in both)," following Plato at *Laws* II, 665a, the rest of Chapter 1 becomes much clearer.

One final consideration is that *orchēsis* also means dance, but typically a more sophisticated kind that involves training and complex representation, even if at times in their corpus both Aristotle and Plato treat the terms synonymously. Not recognizing this has also caused generations of previous commentators to muddle the passage on dance in Chapter 1.

After discussing dance (*rhuthmos*) separately, language (*logos*) gets discussed separately, whether in prose or verse. The focus of the discussion of language is to emphasize how representation, and not considerations like verse, is crucial. We can easily deduce that Aristotle emphasizes the importance of representation because plot is absolutely crucial. Without representation (or mimesis as impersonation), plot would be impossible, and the points that Aristotle makes in the passage on "pure language" are all subservient to the emphasis on language being representational.

The reader must be careful, however, because Aristotle speaks about how *others* use terms (like *poiētēs*) or because he speaks elliptically for the sake of brevity or because he allows *poiētēs* to take on a secondary, temporary meaning to accomplish his goal. At any rate, he could not very well discuss the issues of pure representational language, when language is being analyzed in and of itself, were he to insist on using *poiētēs* as Diotima does, as music, dance *and* verse. Thus, it is perfectly appropriate for him to switch to a Gorgian-like sense of *poiētēs* as "poet" to make his points *while he discusses pure language*. Whatever ambiguity might be created in this context, though, gets resolved at the end of the chapter when Aristotle very clearly states that, e.g., tragedy and comedy use *all* three means of mimesis: *rhuthmos* (dance), *melos* (music), and *metron* (verse).

Finally, Aristotle's choice of *melos* and *metron* here as the substitute for the earlier *harmonia* (music) and *logos* (language or speech) doubly confirms that *rhuthmos* must mean not "rhythm" but "dance." Otherwise, if *rhuthmos* means only a ("horizontal") temporal ordering, which is surely what we mean by "rhythm," Aristotle is being inexplicably redundant. *Both melos* and *metron* necessarily have their own "rhythms" and only confusion results from Aristotle now adding "temporal ordering" to what would have been known already to have temporal orderings. (No one would argue that *melos* only involves potential "vertical" pitches for the Greeks.)

Now that the means of mimesis have been explained, separately and in combination, Aristotle proceeds to the objects of mimesis, which takes us to the next chapter.

Chapters 2-5

Overview: Chapter 2

For the purposes of this *Primer*, the typical translations and remarks suffice, with a few points benefitting from further comments. The chapter is clearly about the second mode of mimesis that Aristotle had promised to explain, the "objects," or what one translator calls instead the "subjects," of the representation.[115]

Comments

Sometimes commentators speak elliptically and say the objects (or subjects) of the representation are good or bad men, but as the beginning of the chapter makes perfectly clear, the objects are *actions* of good or bad men. If Aristotle were only to say that good men are represented, a painting of a good man could be meant.

While on the subject of painting: Even though Aristotle uses three painters to make a point, namely, about distinguishing individuals better, equal or worse than ourselves, he restates the point with "musical" drama as the focus. In this chapter the *mimēsis* is primarily an impersonation (or any word conveying that, as long as it is understood that "representation" or "imitation" means a person emulating another person or character). Even though other arts, like painting, are mentioned to help explain the concept and its "modes," and even though "imitation" may be the best translation in those sentences, the focus is nevertheless still on the performing arts: tragedy, comedy, dithyramb, and nome. This extends a tendency that I ignored in

---

115 Whalley argues that "subject" is more satisfactory here for the Greek "of what" (*op. cit.*, 1997, pp. 46-48); also cf. *ADMC*, p. 392. For this *Primer*, it will not matter who is right. Both translations convey Aristotle's point.

Chapter 1, but that continues through later chapters, whereby Aristotle explains topics involving mimesis both with painting and then dramatic "musical" performing arts (or vice-versa). The reason is this: Plato in the *Republic* uses *mimēsis* primarily as "impersonate" in Book 3, which most often focusses on the "musical"story-telling arts, and then as "imitate" in Book 10, which primarily focusses on painting or other static productions. Aristotle thereby explains the issues to a readership (of the Lyceum) in ways that would be exhaustive (for they all would have been familiar with this masterpiece of Plato). Still, the Greeks would not be confused, just as we are not confused by the different senses of "play" even when they are used in one and the same sentence. It is not just the word itself that gives meaning, instead it is the word with any precise context, if only a direct object.

What has also been often completely ignored or under-appreciated in Chapter 2 is that at 1448a8-11 Aristotle says:

> For these divergences can arise in dancing (*orchēsei*)
> and in playing the oboe (*aulēsei*) and kithara (*kitharsei*).
> They can also arise in prose and in verse without music.[116]

Regarding the first sentence: The "divergences" are without question divergences *of character*, given the previous sentences and the rest of the chapter. Character will be Aristotle's second most important quality in the six necessary conditions of tragedy in Chapter 6. Note now the repeated combination of dancing and playing the oboe and kithara. Given the identical combination of *rhuthmos* with the oboe- and kithara-playing of Chapter 1 just a few paragraphs before—"For on the one hand music and 'dance' (*rhuthmō*) alone are employed in oboe-playing and kithara-playing..."—which was followed by the claim that the *corps de ballet* can convey *character*, emotion, and actions

---

116   My translation, following Janko, *op. cit.*, 1987. In a feat that stupefyingly takes an unwarranted liberty with the Greek word that is in all the manuscripts, Fyfe in the Perseus Project online changes the legitimate "dancing" (*orchēsei*) to "painting" (1448a9). The Greek by Kassel on the same site is actually correct, as is confirmed by Tarán and Gutas, *op. cit.*, p. 167.

solely through dance figures, *orchēsei* and *rhuthmō* must be functioning the same way in the first two chapters, even if they have slight differences in emphasis at other times (the former suggesting more training, like our ballet, and the latter being more natural or simpler). This is another reason why *rhuthmos* must mean dance in Chapter 1.[117] Aristotle may have other reasons in Chapter 2 than the ones given in Chapter 1 for associating dance with the oboe- and kithara-playing and saying now that they can express *divergences in character*, of which more in a moment. Be that as it may, the phrase in Chapter 2 means that the dancing, oboe-playing and kithara-playing *all together* evince divergences in character or each of the artistic practices *separately* portrays the divergences. It is impossible to determine just from this chapter which option is correct, and no commentator ever discusses this ambiguity to my knowledge. However, the fact that in Chapter 1 the *corps de ballet* can convey character with only dance shows that at least dance separately can do it.[118]

---

117 Subconsciously or not, Aristotle mimics Plato, who does the exact same thing in the *Laws* II, albeit in reverse order: At 653d, the Athenian Stranger (who usually gives Plato's views) states that *choreia* (the choral or orchestral art) comprises song and dance. The Greek words are variants of *ōdē* (from which our "ode" derives) and *orchēsis*, to wit, *ōdais* and *orchēsesin*. Then, at 665a, the Stranger recalls explicitly the previous conversation, saying that *choreia* comprises *rhuthmos* as the (name of) "ordered body movement" and *harmonia* as the (name of) "ordered voice." Obviously, *rhuthmos* substitutes for *orchēsis,* and *harmonia* for *ōdē*.

118 In *ADMC* 4, I discuss this matter more with respect to *Politics* VIII 5 and Aristotle's discussion of "music" (in the Greek sense) and character. The conclusions there have been missed by all commentators because they thought Aristotle was speaking only of *mousikē* as an aural phenomenon, not as mixed music-dance, and they do not distinguish between character and (emotional) moods, which are different for Aristotle, psychologically and ethically. That is, dancers can convey character whereas music (in our strictly aural sense) by itself as I interpret the *Politics* usually only conveys moods or emotions (but *not* character *per se* in Aristotle's meaning of the term). This all suggests that in *Dramatics* 2 it is the dancers who convey character or that, at least, it is the combination of the dancing and music. In *Laws* II, especially 669e, Plato could not understand how music by itself or even music and dance in combi-

Consider another reason for Aristotle suggesting that the dancers (or the dancing musicians or the dancers with accompanying musicians) convey differences of character *per se*. For him character is different from a mere mood like sadness or an emotion like anger and involves choice and a disposition to act, with examples including courage, cowardice, and temperance, as explained in his *Nicomachean Ethics*.[119] The reason for the dancers (with music) conveying character pertains to his comment in Chapter 18 that the chorus in the musical interludes should be composed in such a way as to further the plot organically. This recommendation is in contrast to the Agathonian way of composing interludes[120] that could be used interchangeably in different tragedies. Aristotle indicates that the dramatist should treat the chorus *as if it were another actor* (1456a25). If the chorus in the musical interludes could not represent well, and thus could not advance either plot (action) or **character** (*ethos*) or *pathos*, the ability of the chorus to further the drama might be so difficult that Aristotle would not even recommend it. Naturally, if the "musical" chorus is dancing with gestures that can show *ethos*, *pathos* and actions (which for Aristotle implies intent), the plot can be advanced more effectively than by a chorus only singing or a musician only playing an instrument. Recall Athenaeus' statement that Aristotle recounted the chorus under Telestes making the transactions plain by the dancing gestures. Aristotle says nothing about music there.

Let us now focus on the Northern Greek's second sentence: "For these divergences ... can also arise in prose (*logous*) and in verse without

---

nation, without words, could be understood representationally, which shows a difference with Aristotle (cf. *ADMC* pp. 47; 120ff; and 316). Sigmund Freud is another who apparently could not understand what pure music "meant" and was notorious for disdaining it.

119   In Greek an excellence is *arête*, sometimes translated "virtue."

120   The Greek word in Chapter 18 is for "song," but presumably this is a synecdoche because the chorus always danced in conjunction with singing, unless Aristotle is somehow referring to an unusual practice of singing without dance during the choral interludes.

music (*psilometrian*)." Again, the divergences are divergences of character, and one implication is surely that verse with music is common, maybe even the default combination that is the traditional "song." Aristotle has no need to highlight that song can convey divergences in character because if verse can do it, then *a fortiori* verse with music can do it. Concerning prose and "unaccompanied" verse (possibly meaning "bare verse" without music, as Janko translates, but probably meaning instead "bare verse" with neither music *nor dance*, given Chapter 1): Aristotle says that these arts, which obviously include the (prose) mimes of Sophron and the Socratic dialogues of Chapter 1, can also convey divergences of character. What is important for us here is that the *arts of pure language with representation*—what we might call literature, novels, short stories or the like—were so undeveloped at that time that they did not even have a definite name! "Bare verse" is obviously vague. So much for the *Dramatics* being about literary theory. By this, I do not suggest that the literary abilities of the composers of the 5th and 4th centuries BCE were undeveloped and that they were therefore not superb writers. Indeed, even archaic Greek composers like Pindar and Sappho and others who composed before the great tragedians of the 5th century BCE are renowned to this day. Rather, I mean that the literary arts came from a history and culture that is sometimes called "primitivistic," and the linguistic paradigms were typically the last to develop, at least in the theater, as Aristotle confirms in Chapter 4. As J.W. Fitton avers:

> At a folk or primitive level, voice, music and body-rhythm are inextricably connected. The development of artistic culture lies in the gradual differentiation of the parts from this whole.[121]

We should not be surprised, therefore, that the Greeks of the 5th-4th centuries BCE held dance (as "ordered body movement") to be one of the most fundamental arts. Neither should we be surprised that

---

121   Fitton, *op. cit.*, p. 1973, p. 257. Sadly, Fitton did not have the nerve to translate "body-rhythm" (*rhuthmos*) as dance, despite dance being the phenomenon for him during the rest of his account.

literary paradigms came in only very late in their culture, relatively speaking, to supersede music and dance in some ways. Consider again poetic *feet*; "melody" (from *melos*, limb); orchestra (from *orchesthai*, to dance). The "musical" dramatists of the 5th century BCE knew music and dance as well as they knew language, although the lack of any surviving ancient Greek dance whatsoever and of almost all musical notation has obscured this. It is only because some texts survived do we think that the "musical" composers were as primarily language-oriented as we are, with books in our hands almost from birth.

Overview: Chapter 3

As with Chapter 2, the typical translations and commentaries mostly suffice for the purposes of this *Primer*. The chapter is clearly about the third mode of mimesis that Aristotle had promised to explain, the manner.

Comments

Three major issues for scholars in this chapter that students might also be intrigued by when reading the treatise follow.
- What is the antecedent of the beginning statement "A third difference in *these* arts..."?
- Does Aristotle discuss only two manners, (pure) narration and full enactment, or is there a third, "mixed (enactment)"?
- Is the full enactment merely a literary style, say, a matter of using direct discourse and the like, as is the traditional view, or is it acting on stage, the view I championed first in my doctoral dissertation and then in "The *Poetics* of Performance" (1999)?

For our purposes, we need not settle the first two questions, although I myself believe that Aristotle cannot be referring to just tragedy and comedy, the arts mentioned at the very end of Chapter 2. Rather, given that Homer (and thus epic) are immediately discussed, at least more of the various arts in Chapter 2 are probably meant. I also follow those who think that a "mixed" manner is at least strongly implied. One reason is that Aristotle's long-term mentor in *Republic* III (392ff), after discoursing on the "what"—the content—of mimesis, has Socrates address the "how," the form. Socrates then establishes a three-fold schema—(i) pure narration, (ii) dramatic impersonation, and (iii) a mixture of both (392d)—which is exactly the same schema Aristotle employs. As Socrates says:

> There is one kind of poetry [but of course "musical composition" in my view, given Diotima's explanation] and tale-telling which works wholly through impersonation (*mimēsis*) as you [Adeimantus] remarked, tragedy and comedy, and another which employs the recital of the poet ["composer"] himself, best exemplified, I presume, in the dithyramb, and there is again that which employs both, in epic poetry ["epic composition"] and in many other places, if you understand me (394c).[122]

Aristotle could not have been unaware of this passage. Another noteworthy point, besides the same three-fold schema, is that for Plato *mimēsis* in this entire section of *Republic* III is primarily a representation of voice *and gesture* (393c; 395d; 396a; 397a-b). He tends to concentrate on verbal or vocal impersonation—on "storytelling" for him—which sometimes subtly obscures the meaning of *mimesis* as a (total) impersonation, and modern commentators on the *Republic* too often unfortunately follow suit. Aristotle's re-use of Plato's tripartite schema implies not only that tragedy and comedy in *Dramatics* 3 are also *complete* representations in both voice and gesture but that epic is a mixture. Because epic is partly dramatic, it stays in the *Dramatics*, for some of the reasons given and for more reasons when we cover Chapters 23-26.[123] However, the purely narrated composition (as in

---

122   Trans. by Paul Shorey, Loeb Classical Library (Cambridge, MA: Harvard University Press, 1956). All other citations from the *Republic* are from this edition unless otherwise noted. My comments in brackets.

123   *ADMC*, pp. 140-2.

dithyramb) completely disappears after Chapter 3 because of Aristotle's lack of interest in "musical" art that has no proper plot.

Overview: Chapters 4-5

Aristotle now switches from explaining the three modes of mimesis (means, objects, and manner) to covering the history of drama, including additional commonalities and differences of tragedy, comedy and epic. We continue to see him applying not only his doctrine from the *History of Animals,* namely, showing commonalities and differences, but his doctrine of the causes, in this case the efficient one (and insofar as he mentions pleasure, the authentic final cause). Iambics (invective) and dithyramb are just touched upon in passing. The chapters were artificially created in the Renaissance, and it seems as if Chapters 4-5 can be treated as a unit. As always with the traditional translations, the reader should substitute "dramatic 'musical' composition" for "poetry," recalling of course that this kind of "musical" composition included language and specifically verse, so that any discussion of the literary aspects is as motivated for Aristotle using the Diotiman sense of *poiēsis* as it is for him using the Gorgian sense.

Comments

What is clear in the first section of these consolidated chapters is that Aristotle explains how the relevant art forms stem from human nature, as already discussed. What was not discussed are the two precise natural causes that Aristotle mentions (1448b4-9). Some scholars take them to be (i) mimesis and (ii) pleasure through mimesis. Others take them to be pleasure of learning and pleasure in mimesis.[124] Some, including me, take them to be what is said further down: (i) imitation

---

124 For example, Fendt, *op. cit.*, 2011, p. 60.

Overviews & Comments: Chapters 2-5

(perhaps subsuming the pleasure we get from it), and (ii) the natural disposition for *harmonia kai rhuthmos*.

What is noteworthy is that the phrase *harmonia kai rhuthmos*, like in Chapter 1, has always been translated as "harmony/melody *and rhythm*," suggesting a purely musical phenomenon. Of course, the same paradoxes that exist in Chapter 1 infect this reading, and again the better translation is "music and dance." No matter which translation we take, though, a new dilemma raises its ugly head. However, the dilemma is uglier if we take the traditional, literary view of tragedy (that involves tragedy only being written, with all the other elements like music, dance and spectacle being optional). The dilemma is bifurcated and stems from the additional phrase that Aristotle adds to the claim that *harmonia kai rhuthmos* are natural (1448b20-1). A typical translation of the additional phrase is: "the meters (*metra*) being obviously species of 'rhythms'."

Assuming *metra*, a cognate of *metron*, means "verses" here, the first horn of the dilemma is how verses can be part of rhythm, which means on the traditional view simply a temporal ordering. Or if *rhuthmos* continues to mean dance, how are the verses part of dance? The second horn of the dilemma: Assume instead that *metra* takes on its other meaning, of meters in the English sense (not as the European measure equaling 100 centimeters but as a musical meter, a temporal pattern of "beats"). Examples would be duple or triple meter, and naturally it would apply easily to dance. Hence, those meters are "species" of *rhuthmos,* body movement that is ordered. In this case, though, how did tragedy *qua poiēsis* (either as a *purely literary phenomenon* or as "dramatic 'musical' composition *that includes language*") result from *mimēsis, harmonia* and *rhuthmos*? If Aristotle were holding the literary view of tragedy, he could more easily have just said that *poiēsis* stems from mimesis *and language*. That would be perfectly sensible, but he does not say that.

One might claim (as the few scholars who recognize the dilemma sometimes do) that the language is built into the mimesis, but this is baffling because mimesis covers many practices and had just been explained in terms of visual arts, *not* in terms of language. Mimesis covers impersonation without words, such as presenting a caricature of someone in action; one impersonates that person just as well, if not more, than language. *Recall also that some language, like that by Empedocles in Chapter 1, is **not** mimetic.* Even granting that mimesis could include the facility for picking up language (say from one's parents, by "copying") or *at times* could include language, why does Aristotle omit such a crucial element, indeed, *the* crucial element for the literary theorist? To emphasize, he could have said that the origin of *poiēsis* is mimesis and language but he does not.

The few answers that are given to this bifurcated dilemma have been very unsatisfactory, at least in my view.[125] I summarize now my own three possible solutions, all of which involve *harmonia kai rhuthmos* being "music and dance [in the sense of ordered body movement"] and their advantages and disadvantages. We see upon reflection that a fourth solution is possible.[126]

First, taking *metra* as "verses" to be a part of "dance" keeps the meaning of all terms—*harmonia kai rhuthmos* and *metron*—exactly as they were at the end of *Dramatics 1*, as "tune/music and dance and verse." The verse stems from dance insofar as dance can include sign language, pantomime and natural gestures (as happens with children and all early cultures that had minimal language). The disadvantage

---

125   *ADMC*, pp. 182-9 for three proffered solutions of the last 40 years and their fatal difficulties.

126   *ADMC*, pp. 180-203 (although *Option 1* on p. 181 mistakenly has "Delight in" before "representation;" it should read "Option 1: Representation and delight in learning."). Again, though, nothing hinges for this book on resolving what Aristotle means by the "two natural causes for dramatic 'musical' composition."

of this solution is that verse, either as a written phenomenon or as speech, seems to come from what is often considered a visual phenomenon, dance, even if sign language and gestures themselves can communicate and even if many forms of dance (like tap dance or clogging) generate sounds along with the visuals. Even considering that language means speech here and that aural words are indubitably a result of the mouth moving (as Aristotle explains in Chapter 20 when speaking of the lips touching, etc.), there seems to be a significant difference between the mere sounds of tap dancing and the sounds that have *meaning*, which appears to be distinctive to language. However, it is an interesting question for another time why rapid taps do not convey *some* meaning, which leads to the question what meaning "meaning" has. Whether a theory of gesture or of sign language or of sounds coming from movement, including the ones that animals make, could ground the needed explanation is hard to say, but I leave that issue aside for the future; it is enough here to sketch the possible solutions. Another one is that Aristotle speaks elliptically and the sign language or a "'dance' of the lips and tongue" *leads* to vocal language which itself leads to verse.

The second solution takes *metra* to be meters in the English (musical) sense rather than to be verses, and in this case the language comes into the history during the improvisations that Aristotle indicates come later. This is all in accord with Plato's *Philebus* 17b-d and with Aristotle's theory in *On Interpretation* 2 and 4 that language is not natural but artificially created.[127] The disadvantage of this solution is that *metron* was clearly the substitute for *logos* in Chapter 1 and had to mean "verse" there, but again, we may well be able to absolve Aristotle of an inconsistency by arguing that he simply switches the sense of the term in this new context.

---

127   Cf. *ADMC*, p. 198 for a discussion of the passage from the *Philebus* passage and p. 182 for the passages from *On Interpretation*.

The third solution is to embed the verse *qua* speech in the *harmonia*, as Plato does on one reading of *Laws* II, 665a. There *harmonia* could be translated "song" as well as, or better than, "music" because Socrates describes *harmonia* as the children putting order into their *vocal* cries, which could suggest not only ordering the pitches (which he emphasizes is the blending of the high and low) but any vocal words as part of "song." Now, in *Dramatics* 4, treat *metron* again as mere meter. This, although very sensible, causes both *harmonia* and *metron* to change their meanings from *Dramatics* 1, where they had to mean only music and verse, respectively.

On any solution but the first, however, some word has to change meaning in Chapter 4. Yet one of these solutions is more preferable, it seems to me, than taking the common traditional reading, for which no compelling resolution to these related issues has ever been offered.

A fourth option now becomes clear. The phrase in which Aristotle says meter is part of *rhuthmos* was interpolated by an editor for the manuscript that became the archetype for all other copies. That editor assumed that the virtually identical phrase from *Rhetoric* III 8 (which was reproduced earlier) was applicable here, not realizing that *poiēsis* and (thus by ramification) *harmonia kai rhuthmos* were being used in a Diotiman, rather than a Gorgian, sense. I repeat part of the statement from the *Rhetoric*: "... it is the numerical limitation of the form of a composition that constitutes **rhythm, of which metres are definite sections** ..." (1408b28ff). If this fourth option is correct, we need not worry about the first fork of the dilemma, namely, *metra* being part of *rhuthmos, whatever rhuthmos means*. For the second fork of the dilemma, namely, how language in drama results, we need only select one of the three solutions just summarized that best explains how the natural causes of music and dance, along with the instinct for *mimēsis* (representation, expression or imitation), results in the Diotiman *poiēsis* (and ultimately in tragedy) as *music, dance, and* **verse**. How language becomes eventually the *predominant* means, but not the only means, of mimesis for tragedy is explained well enough by Aristotle later in Chapter 4 (and it is Aeschylus who makes it primary).

Given all of my arguments above and how also for Plato many times in *Laws* II (with an already cited passage being 665a) we dance and make music *naturally*, I continue to assert that Aristotle really means in Chapter 4 that "we are given [by nature] to mimesis, music (*harmonia*) and dance [*qua* the order of body movement] (*rhuthmos*)..." To emphasize one last time, Aristotle does *not* say that by nature we are given to language, which is a very noteworthy omission in a treatise traditionally interpreted as being devoted to "poetry" in the Gorgian sense, because music, dance and (the delight in) mimesis are here the *seeds* or origins of *poiēsis*, as even a literary proponent like Janko has well recognized, citing yet again a biological analogy that Aristotle uses.[128] Those biological words, explanations and metaphors continue to be important, as many other scholars have recognized long before me.[129]

It is noteworthy that Aristotle does not assert that by nature we are disposed to *orchēsis*. However, as stressed, that form of dance often has the implication of a complex, gestural dance that can be much more sophisticated than simple, natural dance. Also, *orchēsis* results in large part *from training* (recall that the director Telestes had to teach the dancing chorus to gesture in the correct ways). Hence, Aristotle continues in *Dramatics* 4 to employ Diotima's definition of *poiēsis*, fundamentally being music, dance, and verse. The context, as usual, is crucial in determining what the words mean.

---

128   "Seeds" might be thought to be zoological and not biological *per se*, but can refer to semen.

129   I already named Butcher, and David Gallop is an illuminating third, especially in his "Animals in the *Poetics*," *Oxford Studies in Ancient Philosophy*, Vol. VIII (1990) 145-171.

Without more texts, this is all that I can or need say on the matters related to the origin of *poiēsis*. The reader can pick whichever of the four solutions given above seems most appropriate (although the fourth, hypothesizing an interpolation, must obviously be chosen only as a last resort). The only option, however, that I insist is absolutely untenable is rendering *harmonia* as "harmony" and *rhuthmos* as "rhythm."

The rest of the basics of Chapter 4 can be easily comprehended, I believe, except for one puzzle that was introduced before and that no one to my knowledge has explained satisfactorily. I summarize and encourage the reader to re-examine the points, if only because much, arguably unrequited attention has been paid to this topic over generations by classicists. Dramatic "musical" composition is said at first to stem from Homer and epic (indeed, Plato calls Homer the first tragedian in the *Republic* at 598d and 605c-d). Aristotle says then (at 1449b10-11) that tragedy stems from dithyramb. Then he makes the satyr play the seeming origin. Are these all different accounts, perhaps from different periods in Aristotle's life? If not, does Aristotle really suggest that, e.g., the stately epic in hexameter influenced the dithyramb, which was a fairly riotous song-and-dance, with participants often at least slightly inebriated, all of which would be odd? The oddity begs for an explanation, one perhaps being that artistic novelty is sometimes odd. Another possible explanation is that the first account was from when Aristotle was younger and greatly still influenced by Plato. The second account may have resulted when Aristotle was older, and, when from empirical research, he had learned the true origins of tragedy (and comedy) as fully performed theatrical arts with choruses (but still influenced in part by epic).

Also, recall that Themistius cited Aristotle writing of Thespis separating himself from the chorus and becoming the first actor. That lost passage most naturally would have filled the gap right before Aeschylus is reported as introducing a *second* actor, at 1449a15. Is there other lost text, some of which dealt with satyr plays and them being dropped from the "fourth position" after the trilogy of tragedies in the competitions around 340 BCE? Was there a lost passage on Peisistratos and his starting the competitions? Finally, how do the histories mesh with the "first cause," of biology being the source of mimesis, music and dance? Perhaps one day a classicist will be able to reconcile clearly and for generations to come the Aristotelian accounts.[130]

---

130   Dana Lacourse Munteanu refers to:
...what is sometimes perceived as a contradiction, as well as the scholarly debate surrounding it, between the idea that tragedy derives from dithyramb a few lines earlier in the *Poetics* 4 and ...[the] statement that links the origin of tragedy to satyr drama. [However,] The two statements (*Po.* 4.1449a10 and *Po.* 4.1449a19–24) need not to be seen as contradictory: tragedy derives from dithyramb (which provides the chorus/actor format) and develops from something like satyr-drama to a more dignified form. At any rate, it is clear, as Janko 1987, 79, for example, points out, that Aristotle places the origin of all tragedy, dithyramb, and satyr play together in Dionysiac ritual ("Aristotle's Reception of Aeschylus: Reserved Without Malice," which is Chapter 3 of *Brill's Companion to the Reception of Aeschylus*, ed. Rebecca Kennedy, Leiden: Brill, 2017, p. 90).

Although I do not doubt Munteanu and Janko insofar as the three forms of *Diotiman poiēsis* may have come at least in part from Dionysiac ritual, this still leaves open the relation between tragedy and the other types of performance and between tragedy and epic. I know of no evidence that, e.g., dithyramb had a chorus/actor format. Also, without question the first cause for Aristotle is our biology and disposition for mimesis, song and dance. The first "improvisations" that Aristotle mentions then become the chronological origin of all drama and of epic, although Janko could argue that these "improvisations" were, or gave birth to, Dionysiac ritual. Homer is indicated by Plato explicitly and in effect by Aristotle (4.1448b35-a4) to be the first tragedian. The dithyramb and satyr play are indicated later in *Dramatics* 4 to be the origin of tragedy, after an interruption in the flow of the thought, in which Aristotle seems to start from the beginning to give the history. However, as noted, there is a missing passage pertaining to Thespis, the first "actor" who separates himself from the chorus. Therefore, Aristotle surely gave more details on the development of tragedy as a genre.

I myself have no definite answer to this perplexing set of questions, but cannot help but wonder whether, as alluded to, the first part of Chapter 4, with Homer being the first "tragedian," is Aristotle's youthful view when he

A Primer on Aristotle's Dramatics

To continue to new matters: At the end of Chapter 5, Aristotle indicates that epic's action has no fixed limit, whereas tragedy's limit tries to stay approximately within a "revolution of the sun." Some have taken this to mean that tragedy is performed within a day, whereas others have taken it to mean that the (fictional) action in the play is done within a (fictional) day, even if other, much earlier (fictional) actions are referred to in any (fictional) narrative in the play. The Renaissance theorist Lodovico Castelvetro derived his famous unities of time and place mostly from this passage. Arguments can be given for both sides of this debate, but for the purposes of this book, the limit, or magnitude, of the action will only acquire importance because in the next chapter the introduction of magnitude helps us see that Aristotle defines tragedy according to what is called "biological division."

---

was under the sway of Plato. The latter part of Chapter 4 is Aristotle's more mature view, after the Northern Greek discovered through research and experience the true birth of tragedy. It started with "improvisations," then, if different, Dionysiac choral song-dance, whether as dithyramb or satyr performance or a combination of both, unless the dithyramb and satyr play were still later forms. Then at least one of them was influenced concerning plot and noble personages by epic. Then tragedy evolved in the way Themistius mentions, with Thespis becoming the first actor, although perhaps he was the one who introduced the epic-type plot (but much shorter). Then, as Aristotle discusses later in Chapter 4, Aeschylus and Sophocles make further innovations. At any rate, given that tragedy has always been considered a merely literary art, remarkably no scholar discusses (to my knowledge) why tragedy did not originate from another *merely* literary form (and, again, epic was song with physical expressions by the singer-rhapsode, not pure poetry).

Chapter 6

Overview

Like Chapter 1, this chapter is so dense and so misconstrued that the reader is advised to read this *Overview*, then a typical translation (or the ancient Greek), then the *Comments*, and finally the translation or Greek again.

Dramatics 6 presents one of the most famous passages in the history of aesthetics, drama and literature, if not the most famous: Aristotle's definition of tragedy. The definition, which in Aristotelian terminology is made up of essential conditions that are necessary for something to exist or to be that kind of thing, is followed by an explanation of the various parts (recall the promise in Chapter 1 to discuss the "parts"). Those parts are *necessary*, Aristotle says a few times, and are what I call the six "merely" necessary conditions. Essential terms are also necessary but crucial enough to be in the definition, whereas the merely necessary conditions are entailed by the essential ones. I need give only one example here explaining further the difference.[131] "Having 180 degrees" is a necessary condition of the sum of the angles in a triangle because all triangles have 180 degrees. However, 180 degrees is not an essential condition; it is derived from the triangle being, by definition, a 3-sided geometrical figure. Thus, "3-sided" and "geometrical figure" are the essential conditions. A straight line also has 180 degrees, and hence by itself the number of degrees does not necessarily dictate that something is a triangle.

In the middle and end of the chapter, after first deriving the six (merely) necessary conditions from the essential ones, Aristotle starts afresh and *ranks* the six necessary conditions that he says all tragedies have: plot, character, reasoning (or thought), language, music-dance,

---

[131] *ADMC*, pp. 138ff.

and spectacle. If one counts the masks and costumes that Aeschylus famously created as part of the spectacle, these conditions capture perfectly what tragedy comprised not only for at least 100 years before Aristotle's birth but for at least 170 years after his death.[132] This "'musical' performance view" of tragedy is aptly fitting for one of the most lauded empiricists of all time.

Comments

As the chapter opens, Aristotle promises to discuss epic (the type of art done with hexameter verse) and comedy later, but says he now wishes to examine tragedy. This again reveals that no other art form, much less a whole taxonomy of all the literary arts, is supposed to be examined in the treatise. It also helps settle any dispute about whether Aristotle continued with a discussion of comedy in what would have been Chapter 27.[133]

---

132   For how long dance continued in the chorus, see *ADMC*, p. 69.

133   In spite of this promise by Aristotle, Tarán argues that Manuscript B's *peri iambōn*, ("regarding lampoons"), the words which come after the end of Chapter 26, were an interpolation by a "competent scribe" and not the words that Aristotle would have written as he begins the next section on comedy. In my opinion, Robert Mayhew convincingly rebuts Tarán in *"Peri iambōn:* A Note on Riccardianus 46 and the Lost Second Book of Aristotle's *Poetics"* (*Hermes*, 144, 2016/3, 374-9). What Mayhew does not say, however, is that Tarán rejects words from the same manuscript to which Tarán appeals in the debate about catharsis, hardly a consistent approach. That is, concerning the four branches of manuscripts, the very mangled Manuscript B is one of the outliers in terms of the word next to *katharsis* in the definition. It has *pathēmatōn* (sufferings/emotions) rather than the *mathēmatōn* (learnings/habits) of the much more complete and much less corrupted Manuscript A and all the many copies stemming from it. If a "competent scribe" could have added the words at the end of B, what was to stop the same or other scribes, dozens of whom kept *mathēmatōn*, from adding the catharsis-clause? Tarán cannot have his cake and eat it, too.

The immediate reply, I imagine, by followers of Tarán is that we should not consider the larger number of "competent scribes" who accepted

Overview & Comments: Chapter 6

Then Aristotle gives his definition of tragedy, which has been the source of much confusion for centuries. One reason is that, in Anglo-American circles, only a handful of published commentators have recognized that the definition is based on Aristotle's notion of "biological division." This type of definition involves introducing the elements beforehand (in any order) and then collecting the crucial ones in the *definiens* (what we call normally the definition and which in the case of tragedy, the so-called *definiendum*, arises in Chapter 6). To the contrary, ironically like in biology today, Platonic *diaeresis* or "division" starts with the highest and broadest category, say, kingdom, and sub-divides continually, marking off the appropriate side in order to collect the attributes, *which must be kept in the same order in the final definiens as the "divisions."* Thus, the *definiens* of (the *definiendum*) dog is "a living thing, mammal, four-legged, canine"—in that order. Modern biology changes, then, the procedure that one of the greatest biologists of all times uses to define tragedy, and follows instead Platonic *diaeresis*, because Aristotle does *not* insist on keeping the order of the elements in the *definiens* the same as in the preliminary divisions, *as long as they all appear.* The terms catharsis, pity, and fear, though, are completely missing in the first five chapters,

---

Manuscript A to be more important. That is, the "outliers" include the two additional Latin & Syriac/Arabic manuscripts and even though they are much less in number than Manuscript A and its copies, it will be argued that they have more weight when combined. This is a fair argument. Nevertheless, other scholars have, like Tarán, downplayed the philosophical contradictions and favored the paleography, perhaps because it is easier at one stage, after the difficult paleography is finish, just to look at what is written than to have to think deeply about the theoretical ramifications of the words. I take, therefore, the issue of the "competent scribe" back to the time when the manuscript rolls were being corrected and transmitted by the early Peripatetics after Theophrastus to show that one of the most extensive accounts we have, by Eduard Zeller, supports my view on catharsis rather than Tarán's own view. Those scribes were surely even more "competent" than ones from at least 700 years later. However, all of this requires more than a few pages of explanation and so I include a second Appendix at the end of this book.

which means they are completely out of place in the *definiens*.[134]

In addition, the word *katharsis* itself in the definition has never been translated to the satisfaction of ancient Greek specialists and is often simply left as "catharsis." As mentioned, in ancient Greek it can mean purgation, purification or clarification (or perhaps even a mixture of any of these) but each of these fits very awkwardly with Aristotle's commonly accepted psychology, ethics, and aesthetics. This topic is an absolutely crucial issue to resolve, and I discuss it shortly. However, I should remark first that Aristotle briefly explains what he means by one essential condition in the definition, "embellished language," stating immediately after the *definiens* (or as an extended part of it) that the phrase means speech with *rhuthmos kai harmonia kai melos*. It is as if he realizes he did not use the exact term "embellished" in the first five chapters, which his principles of "biological division" require, and he immediately corrects the lapse.

Many translate this phrase as (i) (language with) "rhythm, harmony/tune, and melody," or (ii) (language with) "rhythm, tune, that is, song." The problem with either of these translations is that, as we saw in detail in Chapter 1, musical harmony as distinct from tune is thereby suggested to exist in ancient Greece for Aristotle, when it did not. Even leaving aside that issue, the long recognized, other problem is that "rhythm" or "melody" or "song" is utterly redundant. Some scholars as a result have wanted to drop *kai melos*, as if the words do not properly exist in the Greek manuscripts, when they occur in all branches (and Tarán's new paleography confirms them).

All of these problems are easily resolved with the correct understanding of *rhuthmos* as dance, following Chapter 1. Aristotle simply says here that "embellished language" is language which has "dance and music, that is, "dance-music" [or choral composition]." This, as noted,

---

134   Cf. Chapter 5 of *ADMC*, and especially pp. 393ff of Chapter 6.

is what *melos* can mean according to some ancient music specialists. We will see also this term a few times in Chapter 12, when Aristotle discusses the chorus, which all classicists know sang *and danced*. With very compelling reason, readers might get the impression from many commentaries on the *Dramatics* that the philosophers and literary theorists, with some commendable exceptions, had and have no idea of the importance of the chorus in (musical) drama. At the best, those theorists grant some importance to music in the chorus but completely omit the importance of dance during the 5th and 4th centuries BCE, causing historians of drama to rail at Aristotle for not appreciating the full performance. The literary theorists, projecting their own interests, too often thought and still think that language was all Aristotle cared about in this arena, and the historians of drama should rail instead at the literary theorists' distortion of Aristotle.

Before returning to the problem of catharsis, let us finish with the review of the rest of Chapter 6. For the *most* part it is understandable on typical translations, but will be even more understandable with a couple of corrections. First, the term *lexis* is used in the explanation after the definition to explain the language (*logos*) in the definition itself, and *lexis* means speech or language, like *logos*. Some translators render *lexis* too narrowly as "diction," in part because they (wrongly) think that plot (*muthos*) necessarily means or entails language. *Muthos can* indeed mean myth or story. Yet Aristotle specifically says in Chapter 6 that *muthos* is the "arrangement of incidents," not the "arrangement of incidents *in words*," and the difference is absolutely crucial. Plot can be given by dancers all by themselves, with no words (as the remarks in Chapter 1, 2 and 4 necessarily imply), like our story ballets (and like silent film, although of course Aristotle did not knowingly anticipate cinema). Moreover, were *muthos* to mean or entail necessarily language, Aristotle adding *lexis* as a fourth condition for language would be unnecessary and redundant. In his theory of definition, redundancy is not permitted. Thus, readers must be careful when they read "diction" (or "style") in traditional translations. (The problem of "style" is that at least some of the necessary conditions surely had their own, relevant styles, and, at any rate, style is merely an aspect of one or more of the elements, and therefore would not be on the right level, in comparison with the other elements. It would be like Aristotle saying "grammar" rather than language.) The two renditions, diction or style, typically obscure the real meaning of *lexis* and of Aristotle's overall intentions in this chapter.

Finally, concerning the nature of tragedy as a necessarily performed art rather than a merely literary one: At the end of Chapter 6, Aristotle says that the spectacle is *least* artless and *least* governed by the "dramatic musical composition" (*poiētikēs*) (which, again, has four conditions: music, language, dance and plot). He does *not* say that the spectacle is *unnecessary for tragedy*, a very important, if subtle, distinction. He adds that the *dunamis* of *tragedy* exists without an *agōnos* and *hypokritōn*, always or almost always translated here as "performance" and "actors," and he finishes by saying that the completion of the scenery is *more* under the authority of the scenery-maker (*skeupoios*) than the dramatist. All of this has suggested to the previous commentators since Avicenna that tragedy could be merely written. Yet Aristotle is only giving reasons, or, better yet, a rhetorical argument, for why spectacle is the *least* necessary of the six *necessary* elements and his implication here is surely that spectacle is still germane *to some extent*. As James Hutton wisely says (despite his typical use of "poet" rather than the better term "dramatist" or "composer" and despite him stripping *melopoiia* of dance):

> Aristotle says little about Spectacle and Melody (music) because this treatise is about the poet's work, the poem, and [because] spectacle and music were largely the work of the stage personnel and the musicians. But he expresses himself with care ... spectacle is the part least essential to the art of the poet, but it is not inessential; the "machine" is used at the end of Euripides' plays because the

poet planned it so.¹³⁵

In Hutton's passage, "this treatise is about the poet's work, the poem" cannot be true because not one poem is found in the whole treatise. Of course, the dramatist wrote a script in verse but that is the *script*, as a necessary *part* of a *performed* play. The script is not intended (leaving aside Chaeremon and his ilk) to be an independent art *in this context* and Sophocles would have been justifiably driven from Athens with welts on his back had he dared asked for his fee after merely writing and handing over the words to be used in a tragedy that was accepted for the competitions.

In addition, since the *poiētēs qua* "dramatic 'musical' composer" cares primarily about music, dance, language and plot, it stands to reason that Aristotle leaves the spectacle *mostly* to others. Even the music and dance he leaves mostly to others, although the passage where he says this is presumably lost (or he stated it in lecture). We know this because in *Politics* VIII 7 he also explicitly leaves to others the technical details of *mousikē* as he defines it there, as *melopoiias kai rhuthmōn*, the same terms used throughout *Dramatics* 6, which I have demonstrated also make much better sense in the *Politics* if translated as "(the making of) music and dance."¹³⁶ Aristotle shows in VIII 7 that he is simply not comfortable discussing the technical details of both music and dance, and presumably he felt the same way while writing the *Dramatics*. He does, however, discuss music at a *very general, and perfectly suitable, level* in a number of places in the *Dramatics*, as we see in Chapters 12, 18, and 26. Given this and given some upcoming reasons, he covers himself throughout his treatise, or explicitly delegates to others, not only his four necessary and sufficient conditions for something to be *poiēsis* but the two additional

---

135 Hutton, *Aristotle's Poetics*, p. 90. To be perfectly precise, Hutton should be saying "necessary" rather than "essential" because spectacle as such is not in the definition *per se*. Rather it is one of the derived necessary conditions.

136 Cf. Chapter 4 of *ADMC*.

necessary parts for something to be tragedy: spectacle and *dianoia* ("thought" or "reasoning").

Aristotle leaves "reasoning," the third most important necessary condition (even above language) to his *Rhetoric*, as he explicitly says in Chapter 19, which we will examine more thoroughly there. Hence, we should not expect him to treat *in great detail* all of the six necessary (and sufficient) conditions for something to be tragedy. That would be too much for any one person, even nowadays, not just Aristotle. Nevertheless, at the end of Chapter 15 we see him noting that he discussed stage effects in another work, so clearly the staging was important for him as a part with which the dramatists concerned themselves.

Finally, *agōn/agōnos* is really more than just a performance. It is a contest or competition, and the *hypokritōn* (the basis of our "hypocrite") were not just actors but in this setting the very good, if not professional, actors of the competitions, who were awarded special privileges.[137] Thus, the import of Aristotle's claim about the *dunamis* of tragedy is *not* that performance is *unnecessary* but that the effect of tragedy can be found in dramatic performances that have none of the grand trappings of the annual competitions with the quasi-professional actors. This is a very sensible statement indeed and one not suggesting that tragedy as examined in Chapter 6 can be only a form of pure (representational) language, a position that, in any event, would stunningly contradict the explicit necessary conditions of music, dance, and spectacle earlier in Chapter 6.

Given Aristotle's strictures of definition, it is impossible that the rhetorical remark about spectacle could outweigh the very explicit passages in Chapter 6 in which spectacle is said twice to be a *necessary* part of *all* tragedies. For commentators not to have recognized this last point for so many generations is either an indication of how much

---

[137] Cf. *ADMC*, p. 162. See also the *Corrective Glossary* below.

they were blinded by their own concern for language or how language exercised hegemony over the other "means of mimesis" for all previous Western cultures after Aristotle's or how they ignored Aristotle's own theory of definition in this context.[138] For Aristotle to say that language, the fourth-ranked necessary element of tragedy, is more important than music-dance and spectacle, which were the fifth and sixth most important elements, is vastly different from him saying that language is the only necessary element. Moreover, and to re-iterate, to claim that spectacle is least necessary is also vastly different from him saying that it is (wholly) unnecessary.

---

138   Cf. *ADMC*, pp. 148-64 and the history in the Appendix, for how previous scholars followed the previous ones for hundreds of years, not even questioning how a remark about spectacle being the least necessary element could be interpreted to mean that spectacle was optional. Shockingly, not one scholar considers how the remark could overthrow essential conditions in a definition along with the derived necessary ones.

Catharsis

We now return to the problem of catharsis. The earliest, Arabic commentators were so baffled by the inclusion of the term in the definition of tragedy that they either dropped it in their translation and commentary (Avicenna) or translated it impossibly as "moderation" (Averroes). Moderation as a goal in ethics and psychology is perfectly in line with what Aristotle *might* have meant, given his ethical views that often lead to moderation. However, he then would have written the correct word for moderation (*meson* or *metrion*) instead. *Katharsis* cannot possibly mean "moderation" or its equivalent.

Starting in the 15th century, the Italian commentators working directly from the re-discovered Greek manuscripts rendered *katharsis* as purgation and tried to explain how tragedy purged us of pity and fear or of other similar emotions. However, fatal problems concerning the rest of Aristotle's theories exist with this translation, as has been seen for centuries. To repeat, pity and fear in certain circumstances are perfectly appropriate emotions for Aristotle and someone not having them is either a brute or utterly rash. Thus, purging the emotions would not necessarily be good. Likewise, as touched on, the other two possible translations, purification and clarification, generate their own absurdities. *Pure* pity would be a strange goal and would exclude any fear.[139] Clarifying what pity and fear are implies that dramatists are educators, contradicting the goals that Aristotle gives for drama in many other places in the *Dramatics* and in the *Politics*. Scholars have for a generation or two preferred one translation (usually purgation and purification). Then subsequent generations of scholars have over-

---

[139] For example, in one of the most recent and sophisticated attempts to address this issue (along with being one of the most enjoyable, despite the conclusions), Fendt writes: "Tragedy's purpose...is purification (*op. cit.*, 2011, p. 105)." However, the result of his explanation is not "pure pity," which it should be were pity being purified, but purgation or transformation. In his own words, the purification is "dissolving to joy" (p. 101).

Overview & Comments: Chapter 6

thrown that new translation and tried to re-apply one of the other two, or have tried to devise a new or modern meaning, an approach always involving the fatal problem that the Greeks did not use the term in that manner. Then the profession repeats the effort. The cycle has been repeated for hundreds of years, with some of the finest classicists in the world perpetually caught in the Sisyphean struggle to authenticate the correct meaning. (In mythology, Sisyphus was punished for his deceptions by being forced to roll a large rock up a hill, only to have it tumble down, so that he had to push it up again, eternally.)

In 1954 (and earlier), M.D. Petruševski, a Macedonian classicist from Skopje, argued that the problem of *katharsis* in Chapter 6 is artificial. We do not have to solve it because Aristotle could not have written the word himself in the definition! (Aristotle's father, a Northern Greek from Stagira, which is about 100 miles southeast of the border of modern day Macedonia/FYROM/The Republic of North Macedonia, worked as a physician for the Macedonian court, and, as mentioned, Aristotle himself tutored Alexander the Great, which makes Petruševski's contribution ironically apt.) Petruševski was inspired by two other scholars: Alfred Gudeman, a German-American specialist of Aristotle, and Anton Smerdel, a Croatian classicist. In part because of the hundreds of years of previous effort, both Gudeman and Smerdel denied that we would ever find the solution to the problem of the meaning of catharsis in Chapter 6. However, they did not take the final step that Petruševski did in cutting the Gordian Knot (or at least half of the Knot, because Petruševski thought we should keep pity and fear in the definition, of which more later).

A few other scholars accepted Petruševski's view, but it quit receiving attention by the 1980's. For some of the reasons that the Petruševskians gave, and for new ones, I started resuscitating the view in the mid-1990's, and argued in "Purging the *Poetics*" (2003), and still argue, that not only is catharsis illegitimate in the definition but so is pity and fear. In other words, the whole catharsis-clause was mistakenly interpolated by a later editor. Numerous specialists have agreed with me in print, some regarding *katharsis* and others regarding the whole clause,[140] even though, unsurprisingly, some scholars try to protect the long-lasting status quo of which they are a part.[141] I give just the basic summary here because the full set of arguments and evidence to overturn rigorously the 1000-year old tradition takes two full chapters in *ADMC* (5 and 6).

My five major claims in *ADMC* are:

1) None of the three legitimate meanings of *katharsis* from ancient Greece—purgation, purification, or clarification—mesh with the rest of Aristotle's theory, as has been realized for hundreds of years, making the phrase "accomplishing through pity and fear the *katharsis* of such emotions" incomprehensible on Aristotle grounds. To reiterate, pity and fear are good emotions at time and should *not* be purged (nor did the early commentators think they should be). Purifying pity and fear makes no sense either because pure pity (in contrast

---

140   In chronological order, three of the works are: Cláudio William Veloso, "Aristotle's *Poetics* without *Katharsis*, Fear, or Pity," *Oxford Studies in Ancient Philosophy* Vol. 33, 2007 (Oxford: Oxford University Press), 255-84. Marwan Rashed, "*Katharsis versus mimèsis*: simulation des émotions et définition aristotélicienne de la tragédie," *Littérature*, Vol. 182, No. 2, 2016, 60-77. Cláudio William Veloso, *Pourquoi, op. cit.*, 2018. For the last see the review in French at: https://www.nonfiction.fr/articlecomment-9562-la-poetique-daristote-sans-la-catharsis.htm

Other scholars give assent in reviews or their own publications without additional arguments, as seen throughout *ADMC*.

141   Although two specialists offered either remarks in passing or a brief reply, the only full, truly professional response to "Purging the *Poetics*" has been by Stephen Halliwell, *Between Ecstasy and Truth: Interpretations of Greek Poetics from Homer to Longinus* (Oxford: Oxford University Press, 2011), pp. 261-3. Cf., however, *ADMC* Chapter 6, pp. 393-440, where his four sets of arguments are systematically and completely rebutted.

to a moderated pity) would be an odd goal to have and would exclude any fear; likewise pure fear excludes any pity. Clarifying pity and fear is very implausible because dramatists for Aristotle were not in the profession of explaining concepts; that is, they were not primarily educators, and, as alluded to, the goal goes against the *Dramatics* and the *Politics* VIII 5-7. Also *katharsis* is *never* found in his ethical treatises or in the *Rhetoric*, when the two emotions are examined in depth in both places. Finally, giving *katharsis* a novel meaning takes it away from what the Greeks understood and what Aristotle expected them to understand about it from his comments in *Politics* VIII 7.

2) Neither *katharsis*, pity nor fear are mentioned in *Dramatics* 1-5 even though Aristotle proceeds with biological division, with every element except *katharsis*, pity and fear introduced in some manner before Chapter 6. However, it is crucial in this type of definition that antecedent *differentiae* are introduced before being collected.

3) Even ignoring the issue of biological division, and pretending for the sake of argument that Aristotle could have added catharsis, pity and fear at the last moment, there is no subsequent discussion of any of the concepts in Chapters 6-7 when *all* of the other essential conditions get developed into six necessary conditions. Some scholars like Halliwell and I follow the neo-Platonists, who recognized that catharsis was in the Northern Greek's youthful dialogue *On Poets* (better entitled *On Composers* or *On "Musical" Composers*, given the Diotiman meaning of *poiētēs*). However, this recognition only magnifies the problem if one claims catharsis entered at the last moment. It is preposterous that Aristotle could have forgotten about his early work as he wrote the five initial chapters, just as it is preposterous that Jacob Bernays (1821-

1881) speaks sensibly when he claims that an excerptor when through the *Dramatics* and excised *on purpose* the explanation of catharsis in *peri poiētikēs* that is promised in *Politics* VIII 7! (Bernays was a renowned philologist, commentator on the *Dramatics*, and uncle of the wife of Sigmund Freud, who, as is well known, himself initially used catharsis in his own theory of psychological therapy.)

4) Nor is there even a mention of *katharsis* in the rest of the treatise (apart from the second and final, irrelevant use in Chapter 17), including, shockingly, those passages in which the goal of tragedy is discussed or at least mentioned. In contrast, all of the other elements in the definition are treated at length or explicitly noted by Aristotle to be covered in other treatises.

5) Pity and fear are legitimate in the middle chapters of the *Dramatics* but they must be applicable to only one, or some mixture, of the sub-types of tragedy mentioned in Chapter 18, but not to all: tragedy of suffering, tragedy of character, complex tragedy, and simple or spectacular tragedy. The reason is that many of the types of tragedy that Aristotle discusses have no pity and fear, or at least no pity, *on his own accounts from Chapters 2-18*. In fact, he even rules out pity and fear for paradigmatic tragedies like Sophocles' *Antigone* or Euripides' *Trojan Women*, as we will see in Chapter 13, stating precisely that the plot of a *virtuous person going from good to bad fortune has no pity and fear* because such a plot is *miaron* (shocking or disgusting)! Thus, the two emotions cannot be required for all tragedy and hence cannot legitimately be in the *definiens*. Given his theory of definition, Aristotle could not have been so clueless as to write pity and fear.

Overview & Comments: Chapter 6

In addition, as alluded to earlier, I discuss in *ADMC* how (a proper) pleasure or any of its sub-kinds like intellectual delight, not catharsis, is shown throughout the treatise to be the goal of tragedy, which follows, empirically, the typical Greek's view of tragedy, as given by the character Callicles in Plato's dialogue entitled (ironically) *Gorgias* (501e-502c). Readers of the *Dramatics* can see the emphasis on pleasure easily for themselves even on traditional translations. If any philosopher in history is empirical, it is Aristotle, and the Greeks were no different from us. We go to the theater and to "musical" performances not primarily for catharsis or education but for enjoyment (although the enjoyment can be mixed in many possible ways at times with other psychological shadings on the part of the creator).

Moreover, I describe in *ADMC* how catharsis was almost surely explained by the Northern Greek in the lost section on comedy, given references in the *Rhetoric* and *Politics*. I also demonstrate why catharsis would have been therefore more applicable to *that* art form than to tragedy, including perhaps even the relevant *sub-type* of tragedy for which pity and fear are proper. However, these last discussions comprise another two full chapters (7 & 8) of *ADMC*, and would swell this *Primer* unnecessarily. Interested parties can read the account there.[142]

---

142 After publishing the first edition of *ADMC* and because of Alexander Mourelatos, I became aware of the view of W.D. Ross (1877-1971), one of the most prestigious translators and commentators of Aristotle's works in the last 150 years. Ross, who was well known to me through Oxford University Press for his work on the metaphysics and other Aristotelian treatises, asserts that catharsis was discussed in the lost second book on comedy, in a long unavailable little paperback that, to my surprise and delight, Mourelatos extracted from his extensive library. Ross writes:

> Tragedy and epic are the only forms of poetry of which much is said in the *Poetics*. There is a chapter on the history of comedy, and its nature seems to have been discussed in the missing second book. The chief other matter contained in that book was the full account of *katharsis* which we should give so much to have; comedy was probably described as effecting a purgation of

In short, Aristotle originally had "proper pleasure" as the final cause of tragedy in the definition or did not provide a single final cause (because multiple final causes are perhaps as possible for tragedy as the causes of eating, speaking and kissing are for the mouth). The phrase with catharsis, pity and fear was interpolated wrongly by a later editor to fill a physical or conceptual gap in the original manuscript.[143] This interpolation has caused thousands of scholars over many generations to venture forth on a fool's errand, in order to understand how catharsis, pity and fear can be the goal of all tragedies in spite of the inconsistencies shown with the rest of Aristotle's uncontested theory. We might praise the scholars for trying to protect all the words in the manuscripts (and at a massive cost), but it would be extremely unreasonable to continue this task *ad infinitum*. Indeed, prudence dictates that we mark the clause as spurious and get onto more fruitful tasks related to the treatise, including protecting the rest of Aristotle's theory in the full twenty-six chapters and the real goal(s) of tragedy for him pertaining to pleasure (of the proper sort, be it enjoyment or intellectual delight).

I finish the discussion of catharsis with more details on why the defense of the catharsis-clause by Tarán and Gutas is entirely unconvincing to an objective, critical philosopher. They say: "the context and the agreement of B and S[igma] *leave no doubt as to what Aristotle wrote*" (p. 247; my italics). "Sigma" is the name that Tarán and Gutas give to the lost manuscript that they deduce was the source of the Syriac translation, which itself became the source of the two final branches of manuscripts, other than A and B. That is, they base their conclusion about the authenticity of *katharsis*, pity and fear wholly

---

the tendency to laughter, as tragedy does of pity and fear (W.D. Ross, *Aristotle: A complete exposition of his works & thought*, New York: Meridian Books, Inc., 1959, p. 280). See also Appendix 1 here.

143   Cf. *ADMC*, pp. 439-40. For newer, complementary arguments, see also Appendix 2 here.

Overview & Comments: Chapter 6

on the words appearing in the manuscripts and with no philosophical justification for their existence.

In reply and to emphasize what was noted in the Introduction, given that Tarán and Gutas themselves demonstrate that the archetype was created 700-900 years after Aristotle's death, the evidence only shows what the archetype had, not necessarily what Aristotle wrote. Second, even Tarán prioritizes a conjecture, *analabontes* ("to take up/ to take up for the purpose of examining"), in the passage immediately before the definition of tragedy (1450b22), because of the *sense* of the argument over the clear-cut instance of the word *that exists in all three Greek and Arabic witnesses* and that is ambiguous in the Latin one, namely, *apolabontes* ("to get back/regain/consider separately"). Rightly or wrongly, Tarán claims that the clear-cut paleographical instance of *apolabontes* "does not yield the right meaning." Thus, at least at times, even superb paleologists correctly prioritize the meaning of the words rather than what the manuscripts show. Were they to apply the same principle to the phrase with catharsis, they should not be so confident in claiming that "the context and the agreement of B and S[igma] *leave no doubt as to what Aristotle wrote.*"[144]

---

[144] There are excusable mistakes and inexcusable ones. Tarán's and Gutas's complete omission of, e.g., Freire (1969), Brunius (1973), my work (2003) and Veloso's (2007) is excusable. They are not philosophers and can only read so many journals and philosophical replies. I assume, to be courteous, that they simply missed not only the four works, including the two articles in *Oxford Studies in Ancient Philosophy*, the first of which was published nine years before their own work, but any subsequent discussion in various places. (Veloso gives a different, less charitable but perhaps more realistic take on this matter, *op. cit.*, 2018, p. 377.) However, what in my view is inexcusable and, sadly, what tarnishes their reputation in this context, is their omission of Petruševski's argument that Aristotle could not have written *katharsis* in Chapter 6 (despite Petruševski knowing full well that the word occurred in all the manuscripts). Tarán and Gutas cite Petruševski (p. 154) and should therefore have known of his "doubt." It is unconscionable that they did not acknowledge him *if only to reject his view with argument*. Finally, see Appendix 2 below for where Gutas also does not take into account a statement

Moreover, *apolabontes* arguably *does* yield the right meaning. *Pace* Bernays and others like Tarán who follow him, *apolabontes* is legitimate in Chapter 6, because Aristotle is proceeding with biological division and *collecting* the *differentiae* that he had merely introduced in Chapters 1-5. The word captures Aristotle taking up or retrieving (for separate consideration) what he had introduced in Chapters 1-5, a perfectly proper sense of the word in this context.[145] Tarán and others who seemingly do not want to accept that Aristotle uses biological division to define tragedy or who want to skirt the whole issue, push for the alternative reading. One reason is that this alternative reading, that is, the conjecture, severs the link between the introductory divisions in Chapters 1-5 (which have none of the crucial words in the catharsis-clause) and the *definiens per se*. Tarán thus helps protect the alleged legitimacy of the catharsis-clause. However, Aristotle uses *apolabontes* in a similar context in Chapter 23, 1459a35, which Tarán skips over in his commentary but which helps confirm its authenticity in Chapter 6.[146]

In short, catharsis, pity and fear are illegitimate in Chapter 6. *Assuming* that Aristotle wrote a *single* goal for tragedy, it must have been something like a (proper) pleasure, given Chapter 23, where he says in the definition of epic that epic, *like tragedy*, should give its proper pleasure.

---

by al-Fārābī (c. 870-950), who, I show, is the first scholar in recorded history to definitely refer to tragedy in our *Dramatics*. Yet he has, not catharsis, but pleasure (correctly) for the goal! Tarán and Gutas cite the passage (p. 94) but then completely ignore it in claiming that there is "no doubt" that Aristotle wrote *katharsis*. If one simply ignores all the evidence to the contrary, in the same manner that fervent believers in the Bible or Koran ignore science, then it is easy to have "no doubt."

145   Cf. Liddell and Scott, *op. cit.*
146   Cf. Veloso, *op. cit.*, 2018, pp. 335 and 338, who drew this to my attention and who provides a much more extensive account of the whole issue.

Chapters 7-12

Overview: Chapters 7-11

Having stated in Chapter 6 that plot is both the soul of tragedy and its most important necessary condition, Aristotle begins examining it as "the structure of actions" in Chapters 7-11. He discusses the length and unity a play should have, the difference between simple and complex plots, and the importance of recognition and reversal for the best plots, among other topics. No fundamental misconceptions exist even on traditional interpretations, above and beyond the ones already discussed (although there are differences of opinion on some significant but not fundamental passages). Hence, I allow not only Aristotle to speak for himself but the previous scholars to translate and comment for him, except for a few passing remarks.

Comments

It should be noted that pity and fear seem to be introduced legitimately for the first time, in Chapter 9, 1452b3-4 (sometimes given in the form 9.1452b3-4 by commentators). Given the lack of any relevant, authentic discussions in the previous chapters, this shows on my view that Aristotle in lecture, or in lost passages, began narrowing the scope of tragedy to the sub-type that has pity and fear. Optionally, the sub-type might be a mixture of some of the four sub-types of Chapter 18 that we will examine. Alternatively, this chapter was interpolated from another text of Aristotle's.[147]

---

[147] Halliwell argues that pity is legitimate in Chapter 6 and thus that this occurrence in Chapter 9 refers back to it. I reply to his argument in ADMC, Chapter 6, pp. 410-1. Veloso and Rashed reject Halliwell's argument for still other reasons; cf., for example, Veloso, *op. cit.*, 2018, pp. 16-8 and 354-64.

Why Aristotle focused, at least in some of these middle chapters, on this sub-type of tragedy rather than on others is unclear, yet was probably explained in lecture or in a lost text. One possible answer is that pity and fear in some tragedy go back to the early days of drama. Another answer is that Aristotle wants to explore the paradox of how and why people get pleasure from attending an event that has great suffering. At any rate, as we read in Chapter 13, one of the two causes of pity is significant suffering; the second cause is that the suffering is undeserved. It is fairly obvious why tragedies that end happily give pleasure, and this phenomenon hardly needs discussion in the context of the extant *Dramatics*. Moreover, we will also see that we do not need pity and fear to get the pleasure from the best tragedies of Chapter 14, the ones that end happily, or some of those explained in Chapter 18. Indeed, the two emotions are painful on Aristotle's general view, and they impede the best pleasure if we are talking about tragedy *qua* serious drama in general. The fullest details of this matter are covered in my *Aristotle's Favorite Tragedy: Oedipus or Cresphontes?*, but I summarize the issue when we examine Chapter 14.

What is especially noteworthy now is that pity and fear are discussed from Chapter 9 to the middle of Chapter 14. Before and after those chapters, Aristotle seems to care not a jot about the two emotions, with the exception of Chapter 19, when pity and fear are merely two of the emotions in a list that speakers and dramatists can be concerned with (1456b1-5). Even the discussion in Chapters 23-26 of epic, which like tragedy has sufferings, reversals and recognitions, involves not a single mention of pity and fear. All of this is extremely odd on previous interpretations that correctly understood epic to be, in effect, a subset or source of tragedy. However, on my reading, this is perfectly sensible, because the two emotions only apply to a certain subset, or a mixture of some subsets, of serious drama and not to the species as a whole. In support of all of this, Aristotle mentions for the first of at least three times throughout the treatise (at 7.1451a11-15) that plays can go from misfortune *to fortune* or, what amounts to the same, that the plots in some cases can end happily. To emphasize, when one reads "tragedy" in the translations of the *Dramatics*, one should take it to mean "serious drama," not necessarily "tragic drama."

One final discussion is helpful, given how many commentators focus on only the first of Aristotle's two examples of reversal (*peripeteia*), when he introduces the concept at the very beginning of Chapter 11. As he states, it is a change in the actions to their opposite in accordance with probability and necessity (which to me means in accordance not merely with wild imagination or mere fictional possibility that would be unbelievable but with natural law or natural phenomena). I rely on Janko's translation and illuminating notes regarding this issue:

> ...in the *Lynceus*, Lynceus is being led to his death, and Danaus follows to kill him, but it comes about as a result of the preceding actions that Danaus is killed and Lynceus is rescued (1452a27-9).

As Janko explains:

> Aristotle's second example is from the lost *Lynceus* by his friend, the distinguished rhetorician and successful tragedian Theodectes (ca. 400-334), to whom he dedicated an earlier treatise on rhetoric. It is intended to illustrate the fact that *a reversal can lead from ill-fortune to good as well as the reverse; for Aristotle, an unhappy ending is not essential to tragedy* (see 54a-9). The *Lynceus* was about the daughters of King Danaus of Argos, who ordered them to murder their new husbands. Only Hypermestra dared disobey, and spared her husband Lynceus. She gave birth to a boy, Abas; upon finding out Danaus demanded Lynceus' death, but as a result of an unknown sequence of events was put to death himself. Aristotle discusses this play again at 55b29-32 [in Chapter 18; my italics].[148]

As Janko recognizes, tragedy need not have an unhappy ending for Aristotle. Unfortunately, Janko does not leverage enough this insight in

---

148   Janko, *op. cit.*, 1987, p. 95.

the rest of his work, especially concerning the translation of *tragōidia* (of which more in Chapter 14, when we see again that "serious drama" rather than "tragedy" is often the better translation). Otherwise, Janko provides us with one of the most underappreciated discussions, and one of the most underappreciated dramas, in the whole treatise.[149]

Overview: Chapter 12

At the beginning of this chapter, Aristotle refers in passing to the "parts" of tragedy for which he had promised a discussion in Chapter 1, and which he had then covered in Chapter 6, namely, the essential and necessary parts (plot, character, etc.). These are the "formal" or "qualitative" parts (in the definition of tragedy); one might also call

---

[149] The reader should keep the *Lynceus* in mind when we get to the double-structured plot of Chapter 13, ending well for the good characters and badly for the wicked ones.

Another, excellent treatment of reversal is given by Clinton Corcoran in "The Problem of Dramatic Expectation in Aristotle's *Poetics*," in *Greek, Roman and Byzantine Studies* 38(3): 285-294, September 1997. Corcoran discusses how wonder (a kind of intellectual delight) is the effect of the reversal in the plot. In a dutiful and laudatory attempt to explain how catharsis fits into the story, which too many scholars shy away from while examining pity and fear, especially in Chapters 13 and 14, he presents his take on the relevance of catharsis in one paragraph (pp. 292-3). However, this paragraph could be sliced away, like a bunion on the toe of a ballet dancer, and the whole "organism" would be left perfectly healthy and extremely illuminating. Indeed, it would be healthier! Alternatively, Corcoran's paragraph could be scoped more narrowly to apply to a relevant sub-type of tragedy that indeed has pity and fear for Aristotle (with some additional explanation to fill the logical gaps that now exist, as this *Primer* and *ADMC* show). In my view, Corcoran's approach will be the line of analysis that scholars follow when catharsis is recognized to be inauthentic in Chapter 6; when wonder and the other intellectual pleasures, as part of the proper pleasure of tragedy, are recognized to be the real goal(s) for Aristotle; and when pity and fear (and *perhaps* catharsis) are recognized to be applicable to a sub-type (or two) of tragedy but *only* to those sub-types.

Overviews & Comments: Chapters 7-12

them the logical parts. One cannot easily separate the character from the plot or language, in a complex, dynamic and "temporal art" like tragedy, which involves one slice of the multi-faceted performance disappearing as another slice comes into being. In this regard, tragedy is like music and unlike a painting or sculpture, which exists complete at any given moment. Now, in Chapter 12, Aristotle wishes to discuss the *quantitative parts*, which we can very easily mark off: the prologue, episode, and so forth. Thus, there is another structure but it is different from the structure of actions making up the plot that itself cuts across the quantitative parts. As we will see more in Chapter 18, Aristotle complains that Agathon composes musical interludes that are not organic to one play, which probably means that the plot for Agathon is *not* continuing through the choral sections. The plot gets broken and re-started once the interlude is finished, which is not ideal from Aristotle's perspective. The situation is similar to audience members today clapping and yelling vociferously during a story ballet after a difficult dance sequence (or after what they consider to be difficult, because often they clap at the movements that the dancers themselves know are relatively easy), instead of waiting until the curtain and then expressing their appreciation. The interruption destroys sometimes the continuity of the emotional response and even drowns out the music that other audience members paid to hear.

Comments

Speaking of interruptions: As some scholars remark, this chapter seems out of place because it interrupts the discussion of plot. Actually, as we will see, so do Chapters 13 and 14, and especially Chapter 15, which is on character. From Chapter 12 onwards, the treatise especially seems to be an agglomeration of Aristotelian texts. The introduction of pity and fear out of the blue in Chapter 9 already has suggested that chapters from different texts were combined with the original *Dramatics*. At the least, the ordering after Chapter 11 shows that the missing passages and transitions are major indeed. None of this, by the way, helps proponents of catharsis, who might claim that the explanation of catharsis was lost (or, in the case of Bernays, who absurdly claimed that an excerptor went through and purposefully excised the explanation). The reason is that catharsis continues to be omitted by Aristotle even in the mentions, or discussions, of the goal of serious drama throughout the rest of the book. Therefore, to emphasize, in my view we should look at the whole *Dramatics* as a collection of essays rather than the faithfully transmitted copy of the original, single book. At best, some of the chapters from the original were re-ordered incorrectly, with or without other texts of Aristotle; at minimum, substantial transitional text is missing. This issue gets discussed much more in Appendix 2.

That Chapter 12 is perfectly legitimate results from Aristotle's placing it in the followup context of the "formal parts" and discussing the quantitative parts. He also uses *melos* a number of times, which was in the (extended) *definiens* of tragedy. Again, *melos* can mean "music" or, better yet, in this context "music-dance." When one reads "song," as many translators render the word, it is often better to read "song-dance," because that is what the chorus did,—they sang *and* danced, and ignoring the dance for the chorus at that time in ancient Greek life would be like ignoring that horses have legs while examining, evaluating or describing the animals.[150]

---

[150] For the importance of dance in ancient drama, see the two books of perhaps the most important Anglo-American classicist working in that area in the 20th century, Lillian Lawler, *The Dance in Ancient Greece* (Middletown, CT: Wesleyan University Press, 1964) and *The Dance of the Ancient Greek Theatre* (Iowa City: University of Iowa Press, 1964). For a more recent treatment of one topic and a much more up-to-date bibliography of valuable research, see Eric Csapo, "Imagining the shape of choral dance and inventing the cultic in Euripides' later tragedies," in *Choreutika: Performing and Theorising Dance in Ancient Greece*, ed. by Laura Gianvittorio, 119-56 (Pisa/Rome: Fabrizio Serra Editore, 2017). For music in ancient Greece and in the theater, one place to start is Thomas J. Mathiesen, *op. cit.*, 1999.

Chapters 13-14

Overview: Chapters 13-14

Chapters 13 and 14 revert to plot, with Aristotle exploring the best types. However, as just noted, the ship-shod order of the current *Dramatics* becomes more apparent with these two chapters. Why would Aristotle return to plot, even though he had already left it for the choral aspects of Chapter 12? In addition, at the end of Chapter 14, Aristotle says "enough has been said about plot," which makes the transition to the discussion in Chapter 15 of the second most important condition of tragedy, character, very apropos. However, the Northern Greek then returns to plot yet again in Chapters 16-18, which is all triply puzzling. Should Chapter 14 have been much later in the treatise and was it the last chapter on plot of the original treatise? Appendix 2 discusses this issue more.

While discussing in Chapter 13 the best plot-types for tragedy along with the "fatal flaw" or mistake (*hamartia*) that has been historically famous for causing a hero's downfall, Aristotle allows unproblematically the relevant protagonist to be worthy of pity and fear. Clearly, at least one type of tragedy of this chapter and the beginning of Chapter 14, like *Oedipus*, is supposed to convey pity and fear, although another baffling issue is why Aristotle only mentions the *pleasure* through pity and fear, if catharsis is supposed to be the end of tragedy. "Pleasure through pity and fear" is equally mysterious as a concept but perhaps is elliptical for something very sensible, of which more later.

Also, Chapters 13 and 14 have grave inconsistencies, pertaining, for example, to what kind of tragedy is best These inconsistencies are not minor issues but involve very fundamental criteria. Perhaps the most striking discrepancy of the two chapters but one that commentators too infrequently address and one that has vexed occasional specialists for generations, is Aristotle suggesting that *Oedipus* (by Sophocles) in Chapter 13 is the best tragic play but then making its type in Chapter 14 only second-best, behind the type *that ends happily*, e.g., *Cresphontes* and *Iphigenia*.

The last must be the version *"in Tauris,"* by Euripides (rather than *Iphigenia in Aulis*), given our knowledge of other dramatic treatments of Iphigenia. In most plays with her name, she is brutally sacrificed by her father, Agamemnon, in order to accommodate the priests. As they prophesized in an oracle (perhaps for devious political ends), only with her sacrifice will the winds start blowing for the Greek ships to attack Troy.[151] In the happily-ending version by Euripides, the sacrifice is faked, with the heart of a deer shown to the army. Iphigenia is then spirited away to the country of Tauris, where ironically she becomes the priestess in charge of sacrificing foreigners who dare enter the country. Her brother Orestes tries to find her but is captured while landing on a ship. Fortunately, they discover each other's true identity right before she puts him to death and they sail away from Tauris after evading further dangers.

Let us cover the dilemmas of Chapters 13 and 14 more after noting, with respect to the overall structure of the two chapters, that the renowned French commentator André Dacier (1651-1722) did not completely follow the Renaissance division of chapters but split Chapter 14 into two, making the whole treatise twenty-seven rather than twenty-six chapters. I myself would continue Chapter 13 until halfway through Chapter 14, to 1453b21, at which point we have a natural division. After this point Aristotle has absolutely no concern for pity and fear, and in fact he seems to forget entirely at that moment the criteria that he had just used in Chapter 13 to arrive at the different ranking of

---

[151] For a noteworthy cinematic treatment of the tragic story, see the Greek film (with English subtitles), *Iphigenia*, directed by Michael Cacoyannis, 1977.

Overviews & Comments: Chapters 13-14

types of tragedies! (It will not generally matter that plot and tragedy are often used interchangeably, given that plot is the soul of tragedy, but occasionally we have to be careful because in some situations plot is only the most important of the six necessary conditions of tragedy, as we saw in Chapter 6.) Given Aristotle's *seeming* forgetfulness, it is no wonder that Chapters 13 and 14 reflect a discrepancy about the best plays, although an easy solution is available, which does not suggest that the great philosopher had such a bad memory. I provide in the *Comments* a summary of that solution, already published in significant detail in my *Aristotle's Favorite Tragedy*.[152] I should acknowledge, however, that splitting the chapters in a more natural position still does not resolve the paradox of the competing best plays, or, to mention a new issue, *why* the best type of tragedy in Chapter 14, which ends happily, is better for Aristotle than the second-best, *Oedipus*-type play. However, again, the fuller details must also be left to *ADMC* and *Aristotle's Favorite Tragedy*.

My alternative beginning of Chapter 14 (rather than what is now the middle) would start "The traditional stories, accordingly, must be kept as they are, e.g. the murder of Clytaemnestra by Orestes...[153]" This has often been taken to be a comment on, or in a way a continuation of, Aristotle's account of the absurdity of Orestes and Aegisthus exiting as friends at the end of Chapter 13. By contrast, in the well-known myth, Orestes kills Aegisthus in revenge for Aegisthus not only becoming the consort of Orestes' mother Clytaemnestra while Agamemnon (Orestes' father) was at war in Troy but for Aegisthus helping her kill Agamemnon upon his return. However, if Aristotle is merely continuing the same example from the end of Chapter 13, why does he not say "the murder of Aegisthus by Orestes"? If Orestes did not kill Aegisthus, why would he have killed Clytaemnestra? Why make the reference

---

152   *Op. cit.* A summary of most, but only most, of the issues is in *ADMC*, pp. 417-21.

153   1453b21ff. Translated by I. Bywater, in *The Complete Works of Aristotle,* ed. Barnes, *op. cit.*

indirect, alluding to Clytaemnestra? Whatever the answer, the general topic at this point seems instead to continue Aristotle's discussion back in Chapter 13 when he says at 1453a18-21 that the best tragedies focus on a few (well-known) houses. This may have been the reason an editor assembling a loose collection of papyri on the same general topic assumed the present order. However, the view in Chapter 13 and towards the middle of the current Chapter 14 appears to be from a different period of Aristotle's life, or from a different treatment of tragedy, because in Chapter 9 Aristotle emphasizes that the plots can be completely constructed without a known name, as the 5th century dramatist Agathon had already done with his *Antheus* (9.1451b20-1).

Agathon's example establishes an extreme tension with the view that only a few (well-known) houses should provide the material for the plots. Thus, one possibility is that Chapter 13 and the standard first half of Chapter 14 were very early texts by Aristotle and that at least part of Chapter 9 along with the latter half of Chapter 14, with its new criteria for ranking the four types of tragedy, later. Another possibility is, as mentioned, that all sections were from a unified whole but with substantial missing text to explain the transitions and current dilemmas. In fairness to Aristotle and to appreciate his insights most, I emphasize that it is better to read at least the chapters from 9 onward as "collected essays" that may have been written at different times and that may show his evolution of thought over forty years rather than to read the book as an organic single whole. Indeed, we already saw how important "organic wholes" are to both Plato and Aristotle, and the treatise now has arms where legs should be, and a tail where the neck belongs. Some of these middle and later chapters, but only some, may have been in the original *Dramatics*. Also, readers should not think that the chapter demarcations capture Aristotle's own divisions because it is possible, even if Chapter 14 is the only example, that one chapter may be cutting across two different original texts. Finally, it may be that we can take the chapters that are clearly in line with Chapters 1-8 as being part of the original, with the rest being interpolated from other texts of Aristotle.

Comments

Let us start at the beginning of Chapter 13 and work our way slowly through the two chapters.

Aristotle begins by trying to explain how the dramatist (typically translated as "poet" of course) should create the best, "complex" plots. He then cautions the reader (who, I add, might be an aspiring dramatist or drama critic) to avoid three kinds of plots, one being a virtuous person going from fortune to misfortune! In some ways, this caution is absolutely stunning for modern readers who actually attend to the passage carefully. This type of plot, the Northern Greek clearly says, does not have either pity or fear because it is *miaron* (shocking or disgusting). On the assumption that pity and fear are authentically necessary conditions in the definition of tragedy, this not only means that Aristotle would be ruling out this type of plot as a tragedy but that he is advising against a play like Sophocles' *Antigone*. On one (if only one) interpretation, Antigone is virtuous and in fortune at the beginning of the play but by the end has committed suicide because King Creon not only forbids her from burying her brother but punishes her. On another interpretation, Antigone is not so innocent because she goes against the laws of the city and its ruler, sowing the seeds possibly for insurrection, in which case we might use instead *The Trojan Women* by Euripides as causing the same dilemmas.[154] The Northern Greek

---

[154] I am obliged to Paul Woodruff for giving the reasons why Antigone may not be so innocent in his *Antigone: Translated with Introduction and Notes* (Indianapolis/Cambridge: Hackett Publishing Company, 2001); cf. *ADMC*, p. 418. Butcher long ago recognized some of the stunning ramifications of Aristotle's claim about the plot with a virtuous person going to misfortune not having pity or fear, but he could not resolve it properly; cf. *ADMC*, pp. 415 and 462.

Although far from conclusive, some evidence that Aristotle took the side that Antigone was innocent (or at least had mixed innocence and guilt)

then gives two other plot-types that have *neither pity nor fear*: a despicable individual going from misfortune to fortune and a thoroughly (*sphodra*) evil individual going from fortune to misfortune.

For those understanding Aristotle's ethics, the reasons the Northern Greek explicitly gives for these types of play having neither pity nor fear are compelling. People who are very good should not suffer unjustly, whether or not in tragedy. At the least, we should not highlight such injustice in a play if avoidable. To have them suffer *is shocking or repulsive and this drives out any pity (and fear),* for reasons we see below. The final two types of plot cannot engender pity and fear because, as Aristotle explains later in the chapter, pity requires that the person to be pitied suffers *without deserving it.* The evil man does not suffer and thus there is no ground for pity in that case, and the *thoroughly* evil man deserves his suffering. Again, there is no ground for pity.

Fear is the expectation of upcoming destruction or pain (*Rhetoric* II 5) and for Aristotle the person who suffers should be like ourselves. Regarding a play with an innocent Antigone, it is doubtful that the men in the audience see themselves as a (female) Antigone, although perhaps everyone can see himself as an individual having family obligations, and, in that sense, we are all like Antigone. Likewise with her royalty: Perhaps we all are lords of our own residence, or our own bedrooms, and thus share enough with her to feel fear.

Still, even if the audience is legitimately afraid because of generally humane reasons, given that Antigone or the Trojan Women or any virtuous protagonist suffers *without deserving it*, the question becomes why is *pity* inappropriate? Aristotle only says here that the

---

arises in *Rhetoric* I 13 (1373b9-13) when he seems to accept her view that the burial of Polyneices was just. Aristotle says that this is correct, insofar as she meant "just by nature," or in accordance with universal law, in contrast to what is "just in particular," as given by a certain community.

play is *miaron*. Surely, the disgust or odiousness, then, drives out any relevant pity, and this is confirmed in the *Rhetoric* and in my further discussion of the other cited *Antigone* of Chapter 14, of which more shortly (I have demonstrated that this version must be by Euripides, not, as the tradition has assumed, by Sophocles). We might feel pity for, and be helping, a good neighbor lying on the sidewalk who has been injured by a bicyclist who left the scene of the accident. Nevertheless, if a Mack truck goes out of control and comes bearing down on us, the fear will cause the pity to dissipate and we act in desperation to escape harm. To bring both a second example and disgust into the explanation: Most often the Allied soldiers coming across the innocent victims, especially children, gassed in Nazi concentration camps at the end of World War II felt horror, disbelief and anger, not pity, reflecting Aristotle's view of the matter. The odiousness of the experience overwhelmed the pity, which itself hardly ever gets mentioned by the soldiers in their accounts. As Aristotle himself states in *Rhetoric* II 8:

> The people we pity are: those whom we know, if only they are not very closely related to us—in that case *we feel about them as if we were in danger ourselves*. For this reason Amasis did not weep, they say, at the sight of his son being led to death, but did weep when he saw his friend begging: *the latter sight was pitiful, the former terrible,* **and the terrible is different from the pitiful; it tends to cast out pity, and often helps to produce the opposite of pity** (1386a17-23; tr. W. Rhys Roberts; my emphases).

The opposite of pity is described in the next chapter of the *Rhetoric*. It is indignation.

"Intermediate good" individuals like Oedipus can reasonably cause pity and fear because of his mistakes, similar to ones we probably all make. It turns out, too, as we see in Chapter 18, that a *somewhat* evil man (perhaps like Shakespeare's *Richard III*) going to misfortune can also engender a certain degree of pity and fear, but discussing this rather complicated case in an introduction to the treatise is too time-consuming.[155]

Now that we understand better when pity and fear are applicable, we can continue with Chapter 13: After the discussion of Oedipus and the types of houses to which dramatists should restrict themselves, Aristotle defends Euripides for sometimes ending his plays badly. Indeed most, if not all, of the plays of Aeschylus and Sophocles, the two other great dramatists of 5th-century Athens, end badly, too. By "tragedy" here, I mean only the trilogy (or any of the parts of the trilogy) that was done at the competitions *before the satyr play*.

Because of the lack of any text by Aristotle on the topic, I ignore the satyr play. It apparently was added by Pratinas of Phlius at the annual Dionysia around the beginning of the 5th century BCE and lasted in the competition of tragedy until 340 BCE, when Aristotle had been away for eight years from Athens, following Plato's death. In 340/339, by law, the tetralogies became mere trilogies. The satyr play was excluded and went its own way. Even if sophisticated, it often had some markedly comic elements and over time seems to have grown into, e.g., pastoral drama. When in the "fourth position," the satyr play is commonly known to have given the audience relief from the typically sad events that preceded it, in the trilogy. Thus, when Aristotle returned to Athens about 335 the experience of tragedy had drastically changed. Although we have no extant tragedy from the whole 4th century BCE, it is reasonable to assume, since five of the eighteen surviving plays of Euripides end happily, that as the plays ended more and more often with good fortune, there was no longer a need to provide

---

155   Cf. *ADMC*, pp. 413 and 425-7 for the whole discussion. Some, like Halliwell, find the example in Chapter 18 "vexing," but that is because they ignore that in Chapter 13 Aristotle only rules out the *thoroughly* (*sphodra*) wicked man whereas the protagonist in Chapter 18 has mixed virtues and vices.

relief with the satyr play.[156] (Recall how the 4th-century *Lynceus* also ended well for the good characters.) In any event, Aristotle focusses for the moment on those plays that end badly, justifying them.

Aristotle ends Chapter 13 by speaking of tragedies that *others* think best, the plays with a "double story" or "double structure," with opposite results for the good and bad personages. This seems to mean that the good do not suffer and the bad do, as in the epic that Aristotle cites, the *Odyssey*. Oddly, Aristotle does not remind us of the play *Lynceus*, of which he had spoken favorably in Chapter 11, and which also has a double ending, with the innocent Lynceus being saved and the evil, powerful Danaus dying instead, still more evidence that the chapters came from different treatises or periods of Aristotle's life.

Aristotle then explains an additional point that some translators have misconstrued, indicating that a dramatist can compose to appeal to the weakness of the audience and give a pleasure that is more (*mallon*) like comedy than like tragedy. Aristotle gives the aforementioned example of a tragedy in which Orestes and Aegisthus walk off absurdly as friends at the end. Yet, to reiterate, we know that in the traditional myth Orestes kills both Clytaemnestra and Aegisthus and is harried by the Harpies, taking sanctuary in a temple to save himself by performing purificatory rites, which Aristotle mentions in Chapter 17. (The word for "purificatory" is a cognate of *katharsis*, and, as alluded to, this is the only other time that *katharsis* is mentioned in the whole treatise other than in the definition). Yet here at the end of Chapter 13, the murderer or the co-murderer, Aegisthus, suffers no punishment; neither does Clytaemnestra, which must have been shocking to those knowing the myth, even if it humored the less educated or more starry-eyed members of the audience, those always looking for a saccharine ending in their artistic experiences.

---

156 Cf. *ADMC*, pp. 442-5 and especially Mark Griffith's excellent *Greek Satyr Play: Five Studies* (Berkeley: California Classical Studies, 2015).

Bearing in mind this shock for an upcoming discussion, the reader should first recognize that some translators render *mallon* instead as "rather," a legitimate usage of the term in other settings, suggesting that the pleasure of this play is *rather* of comedy than of tragedy and therefore that this play is a comedy. Yet surely this type of play was performed in the competitions of tragedy and not comedy, if only because, as Aristotle had just said, others think it is the best type of tragedy and it deals with noble personages and serious themes. Thus, *mallon* must mean "more" instead of "rather," and tragedy and comedy must share, as drama, *a generic goal of pleasure*.

Aristotle continues at the beginning of the heretofore standard Chapter 14 to discuss how pity and fear should be conveyed (and he notes that they are different from terror or horror). He then utters the mysterious claim already mentioned, that the *pleasure* through pity and fear is the goal of the dramatist. I leave for further and deeper reading why pleasure cannot be a synonym for catharsis here and why it would be strange for Aristotle to be speaking elliptically and to be leaving off catharsis, were it truly authentic in the definition of tragedy.[157]

Subsequently, Aristotle describes the types of plays that should be the

---

157   Cf. *ADMC*, Chapter 7, which examines all the places in the *Dramatics* that Aristotle either says pleasure is the goal of tragedy or strongly suggests it, and which also demonstrates that even some traditional literary theorists understand pleasure and catharsis cannot be used synonymously on any reasonable approach. I stress that "pleasure through pity and fear" is mysterious because pity and fear are painful emotions, according to the *Rhetoric*. Hence, unless one is a masochist, it is baffling what could be meant. Perhaps the phrase is elliptical for, e.g., "pleasure through [the plots that involve] pity and fear." The pleasure might result, then, from the music, dance, spectacle, exquisite verse, and other aspects of the play as a whole (aspects that, e.g., generate the positive cognitive reaction to reversals and recognitions). We enjoy tremendously *Romeo and Juliet* or *Swan Lake* until the very end, at which point we feel the pity. Just as with bittersweet chocolate, pain and pleasure can be mixed in tragedy (and for Plato even in comedy), but a fuller discussion of this complex issue must be left to *ADMC*, pp. 425-7.

Overviews & Comments: Chapters 13-14

focus, if the dramatist is to trigger pity: Not enemies harming enemies, *which Aristotle says involve no pity*, but family members or friends harming each other.

Then comes the new, surprising ranking of four types of plays, after Aristotle makes the remark that the traditional stories must be kept as they are. This remark is *not* the suggestion, as in Chapter 13, that the dramatist should *only* take the plots from the well-known houses. Rather, the remark means that, *if* dramatists choose to use a well-known myth (whether or not it is from one of the few houses of Chapter 13), they not distort it. Besides, unlike Chapter 13, the criteria are now whether a person (i) harms a friend or family member (or not) and (ii) knows he or she harms the family member (or not). Issues of pity and fear are completely dropped in the ranking and the rest of Chapter 14. Indeed, to re-iterate, except for a brief re-appearance in a *list* of emotions in Chapter 19, the paired emotions have no role in subsequent chapters, especially in places where we would expect Aristotle to discuss them (like in Chapter 18, where "amazement" rather than pity and fear is suggested to be the goal of the play).

Four possible combinations result, Aristotle says (1453b36-7), and then he ranks the types of tragedy. The worst play is when the protagonist has full knowledge but does not act (to kill or gravely harm). Aristotle notes the example of *Antigone*, saying it is *miaron* and has no suffering (*apathes*, which is the alpha-privative of *pathos*, like our "typical" and "atypical"). All commentators to my knowledge have assumed that this is the *Antigone* of Sophocles, but I demonstrate in *ADMC* and *Aristotle's Favorite Tragedy* that it must be the version of Euripides that ends happily.[158] Sophocles' version is full of *pathos*,

---

158 *ADMC*, p. 420. I summarize there the results from *Aristotle's Favorite Tragedy, op. cit.*, which is where (at pp. 24-7 and 32-6) I demonstrate in detail that the *Antigone* in *Dramatics* 14 must be by Euripides. Part of the demonstration is that often Aristotle does not name the dramatist if it is Euripides, but does name him otherwise. After publishing *Aristotle's Favorite*

with not only Antigone but also her betrothed Haemon, King Creon's son, and Eurydice, Creon's wife, committing suicide. To the contrary, in Euripides' version, the gods save Antigone and Haemon, they get married and everyone lives happily ever after. Only this version, then, is *apathes*.

Still, a resulting puzzle is why this version of the play is *miaron*. The answer, at least for me, is similar to what we just saw with the absurd case of Orestes and Aegisthus walking off as friends. As noted, a few sentences before the mention of Euripides' *Antigone*, Aristotle emphasizes the importance of keeping the traditional story *if* one is going to base the tragedy on a well-known myth. Euripides' version of *Antigone* is shocking (*miaron*) because it drastically changes the myth (and, like so many other Greek words, *miaron* has different shades of meaning, depending on the context). It is as bad as a dramatist nowadays modifying Shakespeare's *Romeo and Juliet* so that an angel saves Juliet right before she commits suicide in the crypt; so that she and Romeo make love among all the decaying corpses in their heated passion and because of their absence from each other; and so that the Montagues and Capulets become best of friends in a few minutes despite their long-standing hatred, duels and mutually inflicted injuries or deaths. Thus, even if the newlyweds get to live happily ever after, such modifications are illogical *and shocking*.

The third-best (and second-worst) tragedy is the type for which the agent knowingly carries out the harmful deed, and Aristotle gives the example of *Medea* right before the ranking (1453b27-9). Medea kills her own children to spite Jason for having left her. Although Aristotle does not say it, this would also be *miaron*, and, for the same reasons as in Chapter 13, any pity and fear would be thrust out. As shown

---

Tragedy, I came across a passage in *Rhetoric* I 13 in which Aristotle continues this pattern, mentioning *Antigone* and also indicating it is by Sophocles (1373b9-10). Clearly, he needed to disambiguate this version from plays of the same title coming from other tragedians.

above, the *Rhetoric* expressly says that pity cannot be felt in a situation like this. The reaction is much too painful or severe, driving out any pity.[159]

The second-best tragedy is the kind like *Oedipus*, and even though Aristotle does not mention the play by name at that point in the ranking (1454a2-4), he had just described it a few sentences before in the same manner (1453b30-1). The criteria are that the deed is done but without the agent (in this case Oedipus) knowing that the harmed person was a family member and only later discovering it. The stranger at the crossroads who mistreated or at least threatened Oedipus, and whom Oedipus killed, was *unknowingly* his own father. Thus, Aristotle explicitly says the play is *not miaron*. When one is abused or threatened, one justifiably feels anger and fights back. However, whether one should kill the other in this kind of circumstance is a question that requires an ethical analysis for Aristotle. As he says:

> both **fear** and confidence and appetite and **anger** and **pity** *and* ***in general pleasure and pain*** *may be felt both too much and too little, and in both cases not well; but to feel them at the right times, with reference to the right objects, towards the right people, with the right motive, and in the right way,* is what is both intermediate

---

[159] Again, *Rhetoric* II 8, 1386a17-24; cf. *Aristotle's Favorite Tragedy*, pp. 29-30. However, I did not cover the case in the earlier publications where someone might say that perhaps we feel pity for Jason. Yet Aristotle's statement in the *Rhetoric* is explicit: We could not feel pity for the children because of the extreme anguish. Furthermore, if pity is applicable to *any* character in the drama, the same would have held for the type of play in Chapter 13 that involves a virtuous person going from fortune to misfortune. Presumably, there would be someone else in the play who could be pitied, but Aristotle says the play has *no* pity and fear. Aristotle must be concerned, then, with the primary character(s) and, as I show in *Aristotle's Favorite Tragedy*, esp. pp. 41-6, the emotions at the end of the play. This is because, it should go without saying, a variety of emotions could be, and are, felt throughout a typical performance. Sometimes commentators write, remarkably, as if only one or two emotions are ever felt during a 2- to 3-hour play.

and best, and this is characteristic of virtue [my emphases] (*Nicomachean Ethics* II 6, 1106b13ff).

Hence, Oedipus may have made the mistake of getting too angry, although any unequivocal fault leading to his eventual self-blinding probably relates more to the subsequent actions and indolence on his part, like marrying his mother without researching their own pasts more thoroughly. Even before killing the stranger at the crossroads, he knew the oracle predicting that he would kill his father and marry his mother. Thus, if he had truly wished to ensure that he did neither, he should have only gotten betrothed to someone about his own age or younger and he should have never killed anyone (much) older than himself. Maybe this is the reason the Greeks only awarded the play the second prize when it premiered. In any event, the play eventually has a recognition, one of the criteria for being the best type of plot that all commentators have correctly recognized in the previous chapters.

The best play involves the protagonist intending to kill but desisting, because he or she (Merope in the case of her son Cresphontes in the drama of the son's name) discovers on the cusp of the planned killing that they are related and the recognition saves the day. Aristotle does not give the precise reason(s) why the happily ending play is best, although he does acknowlege the recognition, which we have seen is part of a complex plot, a requirement for the best plays in the earlier chapters. We can deduce that *Cresphontes* has the same kind of reversal as the second-best play *Oedipus*, but going in the opposite direction, from misfortune to fortune.[160] Moreover, to present but one more reason in this *Primer*, *Cresphontes* has the added delight of a *logical* happy ending (unlike the illogical ending of the Orestes-Aegisthus version noted at the end of Chapter 13).[161]

---

160 Why the best tragedies in Chapter 14 are better than the second-best type, like *Oedipus*, is almost always an unasked question. I provide the reasons stemming from the advantage of my overall interpretation of the whole treatise in *Aristotle's Favorite Tragedy*, 2018, *op. cit.*, pp. 75-81.

161 ADMC, pp. 417-8 and 449; also, *Aristotle's Favorite Tragedy*, *op.*

The upshot of all of this is that tragedy for Aristotle does not necessarily end unhappily, contrary to the suggestion of Chapter 13. Indeed, Aristotle really means what he says: The best tragedies (in his sense of the word) end happily! Before my *Aristotle's Favorite Tragedy*, no previous scholar had been able to reconcile convincingly the inconsistency of *Oedipus* in Chapter 13 ending *badly* and being the best plot-type *there*.[162] One reason is that they all (including Petruševski, even though he denied the authenticity of catharsis) accepted the legitimacy of pity and fear in the definition of tragedy. Hence, they were saddled with the impossible task of making sense of the rankings and the

---

cit., 2018, espec. pp. 75-6.

162   After publishing Edition 2 of *ADMC*, I became aware of Malcolm Heath's "Aristotle on the best kind of tragic plot: re-reading *Poetics* 13-14," in R. Polansky and W. Wians (ed.), *Reading Aristotle: Exposition and Argument* (Leiden: Brill, 2017), 334-351. Heath gives credence to the type of "tragedy" that ends happily in Chapter 14 being the best, even if he slips in this conclusion so quietly and quickly at the end of his article that a reviewer, Joachim Aufderheide (in *Byrn Mawr Classical Review*, 2018.11.53), does not even remark on its significance!

Despite some atypical and astute insights, in my view Heath resolves the discrepancy with *Oedipus* being the best type in Chapter 13 by sometimes applying very dubious reasons that are too complex to describe here. Suffice it to say that he does not even attempt to explain how the best type that includes *Cresphontes* could have both pity and fear, a requirement for him for all tragedies (following his view that the emotions are authentically in the definition), nor how the virtuous person going from fortune to misfortune can also be missing the two "required" emotions. (In the interest of full disclosure, I should add that we can get a sense of how he *might* argue because he was the one and only blind reviewer for my *ADMC* when it was originally submitted to Cambridge University Press in 2014 and rejected by Heath, who is labelled "AnonymousC/AnonC" in *ADMC*, of which more in Appendix 2. Cf. *ADMC*, pp. 413-29, for his arguments in the current context.) Nor does Heath address why catharsis does not enter into the whole issue, an omission that in Aristotle's terminology is *miaron*. He also takes the worst tragedy of Chapter 14 to be the *Antigone* of Sophocles in spite of the inherent contradiction resulting from Aristotle saying that it is *apathes* (Heath does not name the creator, but, given that everyone else historically took it to be Sophocles, it would be a grave omission to not specify that Aristotle really means Euripides).

rest of Chapters 13-14 by assuming that all the plays had to have pity and fear.[163] However, once we see that the two emotions apply only to a *subset* of tragedy, with Chapter 13 and the beginning of Chapter 14

---

[163] Even though I cited in *ADMC* a separately published portion of Fendt's *Love Song for the Life of the Mind* (*op. cit.*), I did not acquire and read the whole book because of considerations of time. While finishing this *Primer* and his book, I realized the incomplete reading was a serious omission on my part. In the sections "The Case of the *Iphigenia*" and "Resolving the Contradiction between *Poetics* 13 and 14" (pp. 97-107), he gives to my knowledge the most commendable explanation of how the happily ending play could have catharsis through pity and fear,—but it nevertheless fails in my opinion for the many, complex reasons given in *ADMC* and in this *Primer*. Still, his treatment is remarkable in its application of Aristotelian ideas and in its willingness to take up a challenge that hardly anyone even touches. Fendt, however, inadvertently gives himself one reason why catharsis is not applicable in the case of *Iphigenia* for Aristotle, quoting (on p. 100) the *Rhetoric*: "Dramatic turns of fortune and hairbreadth escapes from peril are pleasant, because we feel all such things are wonderful (*thaumastá*, Rh.1371b10-12)." This passage, which I had missed, supports my position because were catharsis (through pity and fear) applicable for Aristotle, the Northern Greek would have mentioned at least catharsis instead of focusing on what is pleasant and wonderful. What is pleasant and wonderful, on the account I give in *ADMC* and in this *Primer*, are sufficient in and of themselves to be the end of serious drama for Aristotle. They are, or are part of, the "proper" pleasure we get from "tragedy."

I hasten to add that, similar to excellent musicians being able to transpose a score to a different key even when sight-reading, specialists of the *Dramatics* will be able to transpose some of Fendt's fascinating insights in these sections to the many topics that he and I share. Because his deep and wide ranging book, with the Greek sometimes not translated, is for professional aestheticians and specialists in ancient Greek philosophy, like a string quartet is often for professional musicians, I hope he also writes one day for the general public or for undergraduate students, perhaps on how and why the pleasure of pity and fear (and maybe catharsis) apply at least to some, if only some, subtypes of "tragedy." I believe his approach in general and some of his intuitions in particular might well help resolve the open, *authentic* questions of the *Dramatics*, as much as they can be solved with the extant texts.

I also do not believe Fendt needs to handle the issues of *Iphigenia*, as he thinks he does, to continue with his purpose of comedy, the primary theme of his book. They are independent issues in my view, and none of the above touches the excellence of his subsequent chapters on comedy *per se*, of which more later.

being concerned with that subset, then an easy solution presents itself.

Aristotle *explicitly* rules out pity and fear (or at least pity) from four of the nine unique plot-types in Chapters 13-14, namely, three from Chapter 13 and one from Chapter 14, dealing with enemies, which must entail even enemy *noblemen* harming each other in the context of a serious theme. Two of the other play-types in Chapter 14, *Antigone* and *Medea*, have no pity and fear because they are *miaron*, similar to the case of the virtuous person in Chapter 13 not having pity or fear because *its* plot is *miaron*. We saw that *Medea* could not engender pity for the murdered children based on statements from the *Rhetoric*; it is simply too horrific and the horror drives out the pity. We can deduce for a second reason that the *Antigone* of Chapter 14, Euripides' version, must also have no pity. It is, as Aristotle says, *apathes*. Thus, even if the play generates the proper fear (which for Aristotle is normally at the end of a play), it still does not have pity because no one really suffers, much less suffers undeservedly, a pre-condition of pity.

We can establish likewise that the two happily-ending plot-types (the Orestes-Aegisthus type of Chapter 13 and the best plays of Chapter 14) have no relevant pity and fear. Since they have no great suffering, *a fortiori* they have no *undeserved* suffering, which, again, is a pre-condition of pity. If you object that the pity and fear can be in the middle of the play, this is shown to be irrelevant by Aristotle's claim in Chapter 13 that the type of play with a virtuous person going to misfortune, exemplified paradigmatically (we might suppose) by Sophocles' *Antigone* (or Euripides' *Trojan Women*), has no pity and fear because it is shocking. Clearly, that play-type also could have had some pity and fear *in the beginning and in the middle*. Hence, Aristotle must only be concerned with the ending emotion(s). Thus, eight of the nine plot-types of Chapters 13-14 have no (relevant) pity.[164] *Oedipus* is the

---

164 To summarize: Four of the five plots in Chapter 13 have no pity (and three have no fear either, according to Aristotle). The four new plot-types in Chapter 14 also do not have at least pity (the Oedipus-type is repeat-

only sort that has *both* pity and fear.

Because Aristotle does not consider pity to be an aspect of most "tragedies," the emotion cannot be in the definition of tragedy (and hence pity *and* fear cannot be an *essential pair* of emotions). All of this provides us with additional support for the resolution of the discrepancy of the best plot-types in Chapters 13-14. *Oedipus* is the best *sub-type* of tragedy *that has pity and fear*. *In general*, however, the best plays end happily, if they fulfill the conditions that Aristotle gives. The *Oedipus*-type, although still worth performing at times, is only second-best. No inconsistency surfaces in these rankings, just as none surfaces if I rank mango as the best type of fruit (because mangoes have perhaps more Vitamin C per ounce or are rarer or are tastier) while then adding that raspberry is the best type of fruit *that grows on bushes* and that this kind of fruit is second behind the (tree-grown) mango. Raspberry is the second-best fruit *in general* even if it is the *best sub-type* of bush-grown fruit.

Readers new (or even not new) to the *Dramatics* can now appreciate more a comment made earlier. *Tragōidia* is badly translated in this treatise as "tragedy," and really just means "serious drama" for Aristotle. Even ignoring the happily ending plays, the Northern Greeks says at least three times throughout the treatise that a *tragōidia* can go from fortune to misfortune *or vice-versa* (and I leave it as a playful challenge for the reader of the *Dramatics* to remember by the end of the treatise which chapters contain the iterations of this statement, although, as a hint, they occur after Chapter 5).

---

ed from Chapter 13). For more details, see *Aristotle's Favorite Tragedy*, pp. 24-51 and 57-60.

Chapters 15-19

Overview: Chapter 15

Aristotle now discusses character, the second most important condition in the ranking of the six necessary conditions. We can let him speak for himself with no additional explanation needed at this level to make clear the many insights he offers, except for one comment. Aristotle wrote not only published "exoteric" works for the public but "esoteric" works for the members of the Lyceum, with the latter being usually more technical.

Comments

Many scholars have argued that the *Dramatics* is an esoteric work, and whether they are right or not with respect to all the chapters, the importance of the distinction allows us further insights into whether the chapters were originally written as an organic, single whole. *Dramatics* 15 surely is esoteric, given Aristotle's remark at the end referring to "published writings." He says:

> All these rules one must keep in mind throughout, and, further, those also for such points **of stage-effect** as directly depend on the art of the dramatic musical composer (*poiētikē*), since in these too *one may often make mistakes*. Enough, however, has been said **on the subject** in one of our published writings (my emphases; tr. Janko except for the rendering of *poiētikē*).

The suggestion is that the *Dramatics*, or at least this chapter, is not a published writing. Also, clearly the *poiētēs*, the dramatic musical composer, must concern himself with stage-effects. One example of *mistaken stage-effects* will be noted later in Chapter 17 with the case of Amphiaraus (17.1455a26-9). Indeed, given that the theme of that chapter is on constructing plots (according to its first sentence), including the staging and acting, with the dramatist trying out the gestures of his personages, a very good argument can be made that Chapter 17 was part of the "published writings" that Aristotle mentions. It makes no sense that Aristotle would return to constructing plot *after* the discussion of character in Chapter 15 and after he says at the end of Chapter 14 that he is finished with plot. Hence, Chapter 17 was interpolated into the authentic *Dramatics* by a subsequent editor. Again, it is very unlike Aristotle to start on a topic, plot, move away from it completely (as with Chapter 12 and Chapter 15) and then return to it arbitrarily.

Overview: Chapters 16-18

Now come the last three chapters that are (mostly) on plot, again surprisingly appearing after the chapter on character.[165] Chapter 16 explains "discoveries" further, which Aristotle had introduced in Chapters 10-11 and which could have originally been written shortly after those chapters. Chapter 17 was just discussed briefly and appears to

---

165   Halliwell obscures this by indicating in an outline of the treatise that Chapter 16 is on "Recognition: a typology" and Chapters 17-18 on "Miscellaneous precepts and observations" (*op. cit.,* 1986, p. 30). He ignores, or utterly downplays, that in the first sentence of Chapter 19, the Northern Greek says "We have discussed the other elements [of tragedy]; it remains to discuss language and reasoning" (my translation following Janko, except my "language" rather than "diction"). Obviously, Aristotle had structured the previous chapters following the six necessary elements of tragedy; and plot, character, music-dance, and spectacle (including staging) had been discussed in various ways. This is Aristotle's "recursive" approach, following the *Phaedrus*. However, just because, e.g., music is discussed more at the end of Chapter 18 does not mean that that chapter was part of the original discussion in the *Dramatics;* rather it only means different treatments by Aristotle also covered music. Besides, it is remarkable that those like Halliwell, who think tragedy is only a literary art for Aristotle, do not themselves cite the discussion of music as evidence that Chapter 18 is interpolated or out of place.

be one of the exoteric treatments of plot and related considerations such as staging. Likewise, Chapter 18 could be an exoteric treatment, because Aristotle introduces only now, very late in the discussion of plot, the notion of complication and dénouement. The latter, he explains, is not the climax *per se*, as it sometimes is taken to be, but everything from the beginning of the protagonist's change in fortune to the end. This includes the climax but is not necessarily limited to it. Aristotle then introduces the four sub-types of tragedy, and speaks of the principles of composing tragedy in contrast to epic. Finally, he emphasizes how the chorus should be part of the organic whole of the work, being treated as an actor; in this respect, he says, follow Sophocles, not Euripides. As is well known, the chorus sang *and* danced but it was as unnecessary to mention this as it was to speak of a dog, or of being bitten by a dog, and then to add that it has eyes and ears.

What is important to highlight here is that Aristotle speaks of the musical interludes at the very end of Chapter 18 and how they should be done.[166] Whether or not the text was interpolated, this shows Aristotle to be yet again treating music and implicitly dance as important elements of tragedy.

Comments

Nothing more needs to be said here about the topic of discoveries in Chapter 16, and I believe Aristotle speaks aptly for himself, even

---

166 Aristotle uses the cognates of *aeidō*, to sing, throughout this passage and so clearly singing is primary. Yet Plato himself had used song as a synecdoche for the whole choral experience (cf. *ADMC*, pp. 45-6), and we do the same in opera. "They sang *Carmen*" conveys the most important aspect of the opera but does not mean the performers did not act, wear costumes, etc. Anyone who knows opera will simply assume that. It may be that there were purely sung parts of the interlude by Agathon's day, without the dancing, but I know of no evidence for this, and Plato's *Laws* II, especially 653-665, is powerful evidence against it, notably since the *Laws* was composed about 45-50 years after Agathon's death.

across two millennia. However, Chapter 17 deserves a few remarks. There, Aristotle says:

> In constructing his plots and using speech (*lexis*) to bring them to completion, [the dramatist] should put [the events] before his eyes... In this way, seeing them very vividly as if he were actually present at the actions [he represents], he...is least likely to miss contradictions. An indication of this is the contradiction for which Carcinus was criticized. His Amphiaraus comes up out of a shrine; *this would have been missed by anyone not seeing it as a spectator*. But [the play] failed on stage, as the spectators were upset about it. *As far as possible, [the dramatist should] also bring [his plots] to completion with gestures* (1455a22-30; my translation following Janko).

Clearly, for Aristotle the script-writing dramatist is composing for staged performance. The rest of Chapter 17 is relatively clear, with Aristotle explaining how a dramatist should outline the story in "a universal form" and then flesh it out with episodes. The Northern Greek then compares tragedy in this respect with epic, anticipating the comparison of tragedy with epic in Chapters 23-27. However, we might ask why this treatment was not combined with the later treatment, and surprisingly we will see no reference back to this discussion in the later chapters. This is more evidence that Chapter 17 came from a separate, exoteric treatise, perhaps the earlier and almost completely lost *On Poets/On "Musical" Composers*.[167]

---

167   If one uses Janko's popular and usually commendable translation (*op. cit.*, 1987), one will have a section on some fragments of the *On Poets/On "Musical" Composers*, pp. 56ff. Note, however, how Janko completely and in my view wrongly ignores the musical aspects at the bottom of p. 57, under the heading "Tragedy achieves its function through speech, not song." Under, though, that heading (also p. 57), one of Aristotle's fragments (3.11) goes "Tragedy may reasonably be thought to have...song of its own, as it represents songs to the oboe." Another fragment (3.15) goes "He manages the [choral] parts and the song with a view to the action." "He" surely refers to the composer. Thus, tragedy in *On "Musical" Composers* also was necessarily performed, with choral art.

Overviews & Comments: Chapters 15-19

For the most part, Chapter 18 is correctly understood by commentators, although two topics have been either disproportionately suppressed or misconstrued. Before delving into those two topics, however, a prefatory remark is needed. Aristotle lists four sub-types of tragedy, with only two of them—complex tragedy and spectacular (or simple) tragedy—having been introduced earlier. As noted, the text has been corrupted and arguments can be provided for both positions, "simple" or "spectacular." Part of me wishes to follow Janko and others in thinking that "spectacular" is the word, because of the examples Aristotle gives immediately, some of which are set in the underworld. Spectacle there is presumably a primary consideration, like typical Hollywood movies targeted at young teens (such as *Star Wars*).[168] However, we know almost nothing about most of the plays Aristotle lists in this chapter, and it is quite possible that a genre of "simple plots" was set also in the underworld. Moreover, in the next passage, in the middle of Chapter 18, Aristotle praises not only the complex plot makers but those who create simple plots (1456a19-20). Thus, "simple" may well have been the fourth sub-type, and we will see that this corresponds at the beginning of Chapter 24 with the four sub-types of epic. In any event, nothing hinges for the purposes of this *Primer* on an immediate resolution of this problem.

The first problem is that no mention much less discussion of the two other sub-types, tragedy of suffering or of character, had been introduced in earlier chapters. Nor do they get discussed later. It is beyond the scope of an introduction to the *Dramatics* to explore the related issues more deeply.[169] Suffice it to say here that, yet again, we have reason to believe that this chapter comes from a different work of Aristotle or that we are missing large amounts of text. In spite of that, I also believe he provides great value in the points he makes.

---

168 Cf. Janko and his informative discussion also of the various plays mentioned in this section, *op. cit.*, 1987, pp. 120-1.

169 For the full arguments, cf. *ADMC*, Chapter 6, especially pp. 422-5.

The second problem is that translators too often translate the word *lexis* (speech or language) as "diction" here. Yet diction is much too narrow, suggesting in English only the choice of words or enunciation. As Chapters 19-22 prove, *lexis* is much broader and includes all aspects of speech: grammar, mood, metaphor, etc. Let us wait, then, and examine the relevant issues there because, even though language is extremely broad, it does not follow that Aristotle in a treatise on three and only three "dramatic" forms will want to cover *all* aspects of language, merely the relevant ones at the appropriate level.

Overview: Chapter 19

As alluded to, at the very beginning of Chapter 19, the Northern Greek indicates that he has discussed the other elements (of the six in the definition) and that it remains to discuss speech (*lexis*) and thought (*dianoia*), respectively the fourth and third most important necessary conditions in Chapter 6. He starts with thought and the last half of the chapter introduces language, the fourth most important element, which *on the surface but only on the surface* will carry over to Chapter 22.

We can see now that the only necessary element of tragedy not discussed in detail in the treatise is spectacle. However, we saw Aristotle placing it last in the list of necessary conditions, and so a limited treatment is warranted. He would leave it for the most part to the experts, although we have also noticed across the treatise a few passages where he emphasizes the importance of the dramatist paying attention to the scenic presentation and stage-craft. Moreover, and to anticipate a parallel with *dianoia* that we examine in a moment, Aristotle does not cover spectacle or stage-effects in detail because he had just indicated at the end of Chapter 15 that stage-effects had been talked about enough in his published writings.

Overviews & Comments: Chapters 15-19

Comments

Aristotle barely touches upon *dianoia* (thought or reasoning) because he refers the reader here to his *Rhetoric*, which covers the same topic. He adds, though, a few points on thought, most of which are relatively understandable. One, however, perplexes traditional literary theorists.[170] Aristotle distinguishes between effects produced by incidents and those by speech and asks what the function of a speaker is if the effect is produced without speech. If tragedy is considered to be completely in language, the passage is puzzling indeed. Yet, if we recognize that the incidents are the enacted ones on stage, Aristotle's point is very prudent. As Hutton—who ironically took a literary view of the *Dramatics*—perspicaciously reminds us: "Cassandra throws her garland and her wand to the ground and crushes them, *and it is the act that expresses her thought,* not the statement that accompanies it *(Agamemnon 1264-8)* [my italics]."[171] In other words, at times reasoning, thought, intention, and many other mental states are conveyed by one's gestures and actions, or are conveyed better by actions than by any words.

Aristotle's introduction in this chapter to the remaining necessary element, *lexis,* clearly evinces how broad a term it is. It is not confined to mere vocabulary or enunciation, which, again, is what "diction" typically conveys. Rather Aristotle begins discussing the "forms" of language and types of sentences. His concern is whether a "form" is a command, wish, interrogative, or a categorical statement (which from his theory of semantics is the only type that bears truth or falsity), and so forth. However, he indicates that knowledge of all of this *is part of the actor's art and not an issue to discuss with respect to poiētikēs.* Indubitably, then, not all analyses of language for Aristotle are appro-

---

170 Cf. *ADMC*, pp. 151-2 for how two well-known scholars, D.W. Lucas, a commentator of the *Dramatics*, and James Porter, a classicist who focusses on literature and rhetoric, exhibit their perplexity.

171 Hutton, *op. cit.*, p. 103, footnote 3.

priate for the current treatise.

Aristotle could sensibly have said too that knowledge of the forms of language is part of the grammarian's skill. Nevertheless, for the reasons given above, it seems as if the treatment at the end of Chapter 19 is authentically in the original *Dramatics*, not only being consistent with Chapters 1-8 but finishing his treatment of the six necessary conditions of tragedy. This section fulfills at least part of that concern.

However, to anticipate the next chapter, whether or not one translates *poiētikēs* in the Gorgian sense or, as I recommend, the Diotiman sense, it becomes utterly puzzling why Aristotle would immediately continue in Chapter 20 to discuss the basics of grammar. If sentence-types are not relevant to the art of poetry or of dramatic "musical" composition, as we just saw, why the distinctions between a verb and noun and the other picayune grammatical points?

Chapters 20-22

Overview: Chapters 20-22

Gerald Else skipped Chapters 20-22, along with the last half of Chapter 19, in his extensive commentary. He very sensibly suggests (at least with respect to Chapters 20-21) that they are from a grammatical treatise, whether by Aristotle or by others who filled in the precise points later. I discuss Chapter 22 in a moment. Apart from my disagreement, however, with Else on the last half of Chapter 19, which strikes me as legitimate because of the need to cover *lexis* as given in Chapter 6, all of this is why typical readers interested in dramatic theory—unless they are extremely fascinated by language and how, for example, syllables are formed by the mouth—can simply skip Chapter 20 and part of 21. The middle of Chapter 21, though, has interesting thoughts on metaphor and even if interpolated will help make fuller sense of Chapter 22. Another reason why Else was right in general on this matter and why our treatise is a collection of different works of Aristotle surfaces in the *Comments* because of a different title for the content of Chapter 20.

I discuss now some of the basics of the passages on metaphor before continuing to Chapter 23. However, any reader interested in the precise points of language in Chapters 20-22 will find most, if not all, of the standard translations and commentaries sufficient for this level of introduction, and in any event, I can do no better than what others have done on the fine points of the ancient Greek.

Comments

Apart from *lexis* as language being one of the necessary conditions of tragedy and for many commentators (wrongly) the *primary or only* necessary condition, the most obvious reason that some (but not all) scholars have accepted that Chapters 20-22 are part of an original, unified treatise, is that Aristotle in the *Rhetoric* III 2 refers to a treatise *peri poiētikēs*. He indicates that he discusses in the *peri poiētikēs* regular and metaphorical types of language, along with the topic of avoiding meanness and adorning language. Our *Dramatics* begins, of course, with the two words *peri poiētikēs*, and those topics are found in parts of the chapters now under review.

However, what is too often ignored is that in the *Rhetoric* III 2 Aristotle also says that in *peri poiētikēs* he gives: definitions of the words he had just mentioned, synonyms being one; a classification of metaphors; and "mention of the fact metaphor is of great value both in poetry *and in prose*" (*Rhetoric* III 2, 1405a4-7; my italics). He suggests immediately that *prose* writers have to pay more attention to metaphor than *verse* writers (who themselves are obviously the ones relevant to drama). Then the Northern Greek spends nine more chapters on related issues, often classifying metaphor. For instance, he says at *Rhetoric* III 11, 1411a1 "of the four kinds of metaphor the most taking is the proportional kind," and he repeats what he had said earlier, that *a simile is a kind of metaphor*. **Similes** had been stressed in *Rhetoric* III 4 to be "*useful in prose as well as in verse*; **but not often since they are of the nature of poetry**" (1406b24-6; my italics). **Simile is never mentioned in our *Dramatics* but is given a chapter in the *Rhetoric*, namely III 4!**

This statement of III 4 at 1406b24-6 could well be, and probably is, the "mention" of metaphor being of great value both in poetry and in prose, from III 2. Indeed, given the classification of metaphor throughout these chapters, all of this is powerful evidence that III 4 entirely or in part was originally in *peri poiētikēs* and then interpolated into *Rhetoric* III, because there is no mention of the value of metaphor for *both* poetry *and* prose in our extant *Dramatics*. Neither do we get in the *Dramatics* a definition of synonyms, or a classification of metaphors, as promised in the *Rhetoric* III 2 in anywhere near the detail as in the *Rhetoric* III 4-11, although the middle section of *Dramatics* 21 might be an appropriate, *very* brief classification (buried between two passages on nouns). This is similar to *Dramatics* 17 being the reference of (at least part of) the "exoteric" work mentioned at the end of *Dramatics* 15.

In short, all of this confirms that Aristotle wrote other lost passages or perhaps other books *peri poiētikēs* or, better yet in my opinion, that some of the authentic passages on language in the original *Dramatics* were wrongly interpolated into the *Rhetoric* III, of which more in Appendix 2.

Even leaving aside books on rhetoric or language, Diogenes Laertius (180-240 CE) gives a list of Aristotle's treatises on the topics of drama, tragedy, and music, including, according to standard translations that take the Gorgian meaning of *poiēsis/poiētikēs*: *On Poets* (3 books), *Treatise on the Art of Poetry* (2 books) [this is the one typically thought to be our *Poetics/Dramatics*, with the second book on comedy lost], *Poetics* (1 book) [some, like Daniel de Montmollin, think that this is our treatise, or at least the main part of our treatise, perhaps with parts of other treatises interpolated], *Of Tragedies* (1 book[172]), *Dramatic Records* (1 book), *Dionysian Dramatic Victories* (1 book), *Homeric Problems* (6 books) [as indicated, some think that Chapter 25 of our work comes from this treatise], *Collection of the Art*

---

172 There is an 80-line miniature *On Tragedy* that John Browning in 1963 thought might be written by Theophrastus; others attribute it to a later Byzantine author, which is peculiar given the lack of drama after Justinian. It is very rarely discussed. One possibility is that this is the work by Aristotle. Cf. *ADMC*, p. 231, footnote 359.

of Theodectes [as we saw, he was Aristotle's friend and the dramatist who created *Lynceus*], and other books on art and music.[173]

Most of these books are lost. However, given the lack of a Gutenberg-type publishing tradition in the 4th century BCE until long after the time that Justinian closed the schools of philosophy in the 6th century CE, when copying was often done by a literate slave, we must wonder whether parts of those other treatises got combined to give us our extant *Dramatics* (and our extant *Rhetoric*). Treating all of this in detail is far beyond the scope of this work and is a topic for a new doctoral dissertation or scholarly tract, or perhaps a few of them, with one exception that I need to discuss here. In *Rhetoric* III 2 (1404b28), *peri poiēseōs* (usually translated as *Poetics* or "treatise on poetry") is said to have a discussion of nouns. Every translator and commentator to my knowledge has taken this title to refer to the same treatise as *peri poiētikēs*. What I show in Appendix 2, however, when discussing Eduard Zeller and the Alexandrian Library, is that Aristotle wrote two different, but related, manuscripts and that they were combined by a later editor.

To summarize now that upcoming discussion, *Dramatics* 20 can safely be said to be interpolated from *peri poiēseōs*. Chapter 21 may also be from that treatise, even though it has an overlapping treatment of metaphor. The *Rhetoric* indicates that metaphor is a topic for *peri poiētikēs*, all of which may have caused (at least the middle part of) Chapter 21 to be included by an ancient editor and all of which has caused commentators to take Chapter 21 as part of the original *Dramatics*. Whether Chapter 21 was truly original or interpolated,

---

[173] *Diogenes Laertius: Lives of the Eminent Philosophers*, 2 vol., tr. R.D. Hicks (Cambridge, MA: Harvard University Press) 1950, Vol. 1, Bk. V, pp. 22-7. Theodectes is one of the three fourth-century tragedians that Aristotle mentions. The other two are Carcinus and Astydamas. I owe this last point to Hutton (*op. cit.*, p. 23).

though, needs more examination. Chapter 22 appears to be legitimately part of the *peri poiētikēs* (referred to by the *Rhetoric*) given its subject matter. However, at least some of the truly original passages in the *Dramatics* on language, metaphor and simile (which Aristotle considers to be a type of metaphor that is more relevant to verse writers than to prose writers) appear to be living away from home, residing now within *Rhetoric* III 4-11.

On these hypotheses and conclusions, the references of the *Rhetoric* are almost completely, if not completely, satisfied. The only one missing is the seemingly promised definition of synonyms in the extant *Dramatics*. However, maybe when Aristotle says that in the treatise on dramatic "musical" composition will be found "these kinds of words" at 1405a4-5, he really only means regular and metaphorical expressions that he had just mentioned before synonyms, especially since he gives "synonym" its definition at this point, at 1405a1-3. Why repeat its definition ("ordinary words that have the same meaning") if it is given somewhere else or why mention that the definition is somewhere else when it has just been given?

Unless my solution is accepted, more texts must have been lost, given the absence in the *Dramatics* of some of the topics mentioned in the *Rhetoric*.

In summary, the reader new to Aristotle and wishing only an introduction to dramatic theory can skip both Chapter 20 and the beginning and end of Chapter 21 (on nouns), and get the relevant discussion of language by reading only the material on metaphor in Chapter 21 along with Chapter 22. Naturally, those very interested in language will wish to read, too, Chapter 20 and the few additional paragraphs of Chapter 21. They are also strongly advised to read *Rhetoric* III 2-11.

By the end of *Dramatics* 22, all six "parts" of the definition of tragedy have been covered, to greater or lesser extent. Following his blueprint from Chapter 1 to examine the kinds of *poiēsis,* along with his promise at the beginning of Chapter 6, Aristotle now begins in Chapter 23 to cover epic.

Chapters 23-26

Overview: Chapters 23-25

Chapters 23-24 provide not only the definition of epic but more of its differences and commonalities with tragedy. The astute reader will wonder why and how the two chapters augment or complement the initial differences and commonalities given in Chapters 1-5 and then in Chapter 18 (1456a10-9) because Aristotle does not clearly refer back to these chapters (except for one possible remark about the difference in length between epic and tragedy in Chapter 5, but that still leaves open the puzzle about Chapter 18). In any event, Aristotle then develops principles of criticism in Chapter 25, defending epic against those who would denigrate it, including, presumably, Platonists. As mentioned, some scholars think that this chapter came originally from the *Homeric Problems* of six books, so the reader should not be surprised to detect both a different texture and a greater concern with details.[174]

---

174 Immediately before publication of this *Primer*, I became aware of a forthcoming book on the *Homeric Problems*. I report how the author, Robert Mayhew, replied to my asking whether Chapter 25 came from that book:
> The first chapter in my forthcoming book on Aristotle's lost *Homeric Problems* has two parts, one on Homeric scholarship before Aristotle, and the other on *Poetics* 25. In the conclusion to that chapter (p. 23 of the proofs, and that's not likely to change), I write:
> "First, although there are not numerous examples among the fragmentary remains of the *Problems* that illustrate every kind of solution, I think there are enough such connections to conclude that *Poetics* 25 does give us a general idea of how Aristotle proceeded in that work."
> And in the second chapter ("The Titles (and Subtitles) of Aristotle's Lost Work on Homer"), I write (p. 28):
> "One last piece of evidence for the title of Aristotle's work on Homer is *Poetics* 25, which as we have seen is devoted to Homeric epic. It begins *peri de problēmatōn kai luseōn* ["regarding problems and (their) dissolutions," my (GS) transla-

Comments

It might seem odd that Aristotle spends so much time defining tragedy and that, by contrast, so little to impart a brief "quasi-definition" for epic at the beginning of Chapter 23. However, in a number of places throughout his treatise he indicates that epic is the source of tragedy and that both epic and tragedy are concerned with "good" individuals, which at least at times could mean "noble" individuals. He adds that epic is a subset of tragedy and that whoever knows tragedy therefore knows epic. Given that he had already proceeded with "biological division" for tragedy and, for instance, had articulated in the first three chapters some commonalities and the differences between it and epic (and comedy), it hardly makes sense to repeat the procedure. All he need present now is the new *definiens qua* collection of previously introduced *differentiae*. The result is very much like the definition of serious drama. Epic composers should, he says, *create plots that are dramatic*, with a beginning, middle and end, which he had said, too, about tragedy. These are two of the reasons that epic is included in a treatise on *drama*, even though epic does not have spectacle and choral dancing. Strikingly, he does not say that the goal is catharsis, but that, *like tragedy*, epic is to give a *proper pleasure*, which helps confirm my views on the topic of catharsis. In *ADMC*, I spend a third of Chapter 7 showing that (proper) pleasure is the primary goal of tragedy, given this statement in Chapter 23 and many others in the treatise, some of which readers have already noticed (with a very im-

---

tion]. This incipit arguably offers mild support to *Problēmata Homērika* as a title for Aristotle's work on Homer. Though perhaps—and this leads us to another topic (on which more shortly)— *Peri de problēmatōn kai luseōn* was the title of one of the six (or ten) books of this work."

In other words—and to answer your question—I don't know whether *Poetics* 25 "came from the *Homeric Problems*," but it may have, and in any case I think the two are clearly related.
Robert Mayhew, *Aristotle's Lost Homeric Problems* (Oxford: Oxford University Press) anticipated publication 2019.

Overviews & Comments: Chapters 23-26

portant one still to be seen at the end of Chapter 26).

A source of confusion has been that the use of "plot" here is assumed to be exactly identical to the sense of "the structure of incidents" of tragedy, as given in Chapter 6, which I have argued must mean there "the structure of incidents [as enacted, on stage]." Again, scholars have simplistically tried to make a word behave univocally no matter what the scope of the discussion. Rather, because Aristotle indicates in the very first sentence of Chapter 23 that epic is an art of exposition (in verse), "plot" cannot have the identical meaning it has for tragedy. The same would hold if we were to speak of the plot of a silent film or of a story ballet like *Swan Lake* (without words). Clearly, in those cases plot is *not* equivalent to a story *being given wholly or almost wholly in language*, but all competent English speakers know what you mean if you speak of the plot of a silent film or of a story ballet. In tragedy, according to Chapter 6, the plot could be given without even the second most important element, character, and *a fortiori*, without the fourth most important, language. To the contrary, in epic, the plot, or the structure of the incidents (or actions), *is imagined and happens primarily through the language*. However, the gestures, facial expressions, and mimicking of different characters' voices by the rhapsode help advance, too, the elements of the plot (which is one reason apparently why Homer was very dramatic without using a chorus). Again, like our word "play," Greek words like *muthos* (plot) are often very ambiguous, rich in meanings, and—dare I repeat the caution yet again?—context is key.

Except for three points, the ancient Greek or the typical translations of the rest of Chapters 23-24 should pose no problem for the classicist or introductory reader. I leave aside the matter of recognizing various plays that Aristotle lists, some of which are not even known by specialists in ancient drama. First, "the epic composer creating dramatically" in part means, as just mentioned and as the discussion and praise of Homer implies, the use of gestures, facial expressions, and changes in speech patterns, along with the story-telling.

The other two noteworthy points are at the very beginning of Chapter 24. The first relates to Aristotle saying that epic has the same kinds of tragedy: simple, complex, of character, and of suffering. However, as we saw in Chapter 18, two of the sub-kinds of tragedy are never discussed elsewhere in the treatise. Whatever the reason, and an obvious option is that we are dealing with an agglomeration of texts, Aristotle clearly in Chapter 24 continues to fulfill his plan from the very first sentence in the whole book, when he indicates that he will discuss the *types* of dramatic musical composition (and other texts must also have recognized sub-types given the absence of any discussion in the *Dramatics* of tragedy of character and of suffering). As mentioned, tragedy, comedy and epic are the major types, and here we have four sub-types of epic, which themselves suggest that "simple" rather than "spectacular" is the fourth sub-type of tragedy mentioned in Chapter 18.

The second (and mysterious) point is that, after listing the four sub-types of epic, Aristotle immediately adds that its parts are the same as tragedy except for *melopoiia* ("the making of the *melos*") and spectacle (*opsis*), two of the six necessary conditions of tragedy in Chapter 6. Then Aristotle states that the reasoning and *lexis* should be fine. Oddly, he does not explicitly add character, the final necessary condition, but he immediately speaks of it. Given, however, that he had just mentioned the sub-type of "epic of character," similar to "tragedy of character," we can assume that he knows the reader will easily recall the six necessary conditions and that epic therefore also has the four most important necessary conditions of tragedy: plot (but in words with some dramatic elements like tone of voice or facial gestures), character, reasoning, and language (*lexis*). Epic simply lacks the *melos*/*melopoiia qua* choral art and the spectacle. Whether it has instrumental music or music in the sense of the rhapsode singing or chanting the song, and whether there are different sub-types of epic with respect to singing or merely declaiming, is a fascinating, and unresolved question.

Unfortunately, *melopoiia* here has been translated for centuries as "music" or "song." When translated as "song" it suggests that the epic rhapsode only speaks the words, like poets do nowadays (because Aristotle rules out the *melopoiia* for epic). However, if you have no song, then because song is composed of *both* music and words, you have no words either, which blatantly contradicts not only what Aristotle had just said earlier but everything we know about epic.[175] Thus, "song" cannot be the correct translation. "(The making of the) music" might seem like the better translation for *melopoiia*, but this also goes against historical practice, at least according to Plato's dialog *Ion,* in which the rhapsode clearly sings. It also goes against Aristotle having included epic because it is a form of Diotiman *poiēsis qua* music, verse, and dance (with gesturing in an ordered fashion counting as dance for the Greeks and functioning like the movements that our solo singers on stage use). Historically the epic performer accompanied himself with some type of instruments, other than an *aulos* or other wind instrument because obviously he could not sing while blowing into an instrument. In Book 8, lines 250ff, of the *Odyssey* the assembled guests must wait while Demodocus gets a lyre before singing.[176]

Classicists debate whether during Aristotle's time the rhapsodes who performed the Homeric epics (i) only recited them in the sense of

---

[175] Some have used these statements about epic to claim that epic was only spoken during the 4th century BCE, but this can only be partially right at best. I have argued in *ADMC* that at Aristotle's time there may be new species of epic that were only recited, without even chanting, but that they were new and thus unusual. We have seen and see more in these chapters how for Aristotle the type of rhapsode he is concerned with (following Plato's *Ion*) normally at least chants.

[176] To my knowledge, scholars do not know if the epic performer completely sang all words, or mostly sang and partially recited, perhaps along of the line (if I may speak anachronistically) of *récitatif simple* in modern opera.

speaking or (ii) whether they continued what the earlier rhapsodes did, either accompany themselves with an instrument or sing the words or both. Indeed, Notomi has shown that the earlier performers were called "singers."[177] One answer is that some rhapsodes sung or chanted while some might only have recited (although presumably not in one and same competition against singers); others might have still accompanied themselves (and probably sang or chanted too). Yet this debate is irrelevant to what Aristotle is discussing. His crucial point is that epic does not have *melopoiia*–the making of the (choral) *melos*– as in Chapter 6. Thus, *melopoiia* here means, or is a synecdoche for the choral (music and dance) performance. Aristotle therefore leaves the whole issue of performance style for epic open in the context of Chapter 24, by simply not specifying whether the rhapsode sang or not. He allows that the rhapsode could do either, depending on the setting, all of which may be one reason music is not emphasized in Chapter 23.

In short, Aristotle is only saying that epic does not have either the "making of the (choral) music-dance" (*melopoiia*) or the spectacle that tragedy has. Just as he assumes that the reader will know that epic has character even though he does not spell it out, he assumes that all readers know that rhapsodes sang or chanted the words, at least historically or at least still much of the time in the mid-4th century BCE. Perhaps there were debates going on about whether the rhapsode *should* sing or not, and Aristotle wishes to stay removed from them, allowing the rhapsode to do either. In *ADMC*, I discuss this with respect to Plato, who disagrees with the practice of removing music from words in the theater.[178]

I finish commenting on Chapter 24 with one final remark, because the

---

177   Nagy, *op. cit.*, shows, too, that the compositions by Pindar and Sappho were also sung, and so are better called songs rather than poems; cf. *ADMC* p. 210.

178   *ADMC*, pp. 119-24.

chapter is reasonably clear and includes powerful insights, such as "A likely impossibility is always preferable to an unconvincing possibility" (1460a27) and "elaborate diction is required only in places where there is no action [on stage] and no character or thought to be revealed [by gestures or acting]" (1460b2-3; my explanations in brackets). Aristotle makes another observation worth emphasizing, if only because he will subsequently rank tragedy above epic in Chapter 26. Here, though, he intriguingly says that epic has an advantage over tragedy because one can with words (sung or merely recited) give more splendor and diversity. The epic maker or rhapsode and audience can time-travel, as it were, with epic, that is, imagine multiple incidents happening simultaneously. Aristotle indicates that, to the contrary, tragedy is done on the stage, and there you can only have one episode at a time, presumably in unidirectional temporal order, as in nature. Because epic can have multiple episodes happening simultaneously, the Northern Greek remarks that it has more wonder or amazement than tragedy. This is surely similar to novels for us.

Now, were tragedy merely literature, it would come closer to epic than to performed serious drama, with the latter's singing and dancing chorus. Tragedy *also* would involve the incidents of the plot being able to move around in time, almost magically. In that case, Aristotle would, could, and should have given an equal advantage to tragedy. That is, he would *not* have mentioned greater diversity and amazement as one advantage *of epic*. I discuss this in detail in Chapter 9 of *ADMC* but suffice it to say here that epic requires only a solo rhapsode with chanting or musical accompaniment (and gestures, if performed in the theater) whereas drama requires very expensive resources, given Aristotle's definition of tragedy.

Of course, if we use a modern definition of tragedy or of drama, the results are different. We might have a purely literary work, which can jump around in time like epic, or we might have a performance of bare-bone plays, such as by Athol Fugard, which involve only a few actors in street clothes and maybe a table and a few chairs, all of which may not qualify as true "spectacle." One of my favorite, and in my view one of the most admirable, dramas of the 20th century, Fugard's *The Road to Mecca*, does require a lot more, including hundreds of candles, but still no choral song and dance. Aristotelian tragedy is therefore closest to our serious Broadway musical "in look."

To summarize: For Aristotle, tragedy is very constrained because of the exigencies of production and of staging a believable scene, whereas epic appeals not primarily to the eyes directly but to the imagination and the ears (although the rhapsode's gestures and facial expressions also appeal to the eyes to some extent). As Aristotle explains (1460a15-8), the pursuit of Hector by Achilles would be ridiculous on stage (because presumably the other warriors could just trip Hector or stop him to force him to fight) but in epic (song) the absurdity is overlooked or never gets imagined. In short, the epic rhapsode, in merely singing or reciting, can paint any kind of picture very quickly and immediately jump to another country or time.

We say a picture, though, is worth a thousand words, which means that the visual, dynamic aspects of the actors and the spectacle in ancient drama or opera or Broadway musical theater or so-called "straight plays" (those without music) are worth millions of words. Why Aristotle does not address this issue, because the same would hold for his type of tragedy, is a fascinating topic, but one I leave for the future. Actually, he suggests the point, but only suggests it in giving the reasons that tragedy is better than epic in Chapter 26. In conclusion, if tragedy were merely literary, then epic would not have the advantage of amazement that Aristotle attributes to it now, of which more when reviewing the competition between the two art forms in Chapter 26.

Chapter 25 states that the *poiētēs* represents things either as they were or are; as people say they are; or, thirdly, as the things should be. This had never been said in quite this way before in the treatise (in Chap-

Overviews & Comments: Chapters 23-26

ter 2 the representation could be done of people worse, the same, or better than us), which is another reason that the chapter may be from another Aristotelian work, whether *Homeric Problems* or not. Aristotle then explains how to rebut criticisms about *poiēsis* but this whole topic I leave to the translation the reader has chosen to be used in tandem with this *Primer,* because the typical ones suffice.

Nevertheless, a few remarks here are still prudent. First, the chapter is important in this context even if interpolated because tragedians are sometimes discussed in it along with Homer. Obviously, then, the points Aristotle makes could at least sometimes apply to "musical" drama, which is one reason an ancient editor interpolated the whole chapter. Second, the notion of *poiētēs/poiēsis* may have been broader in this context, perhaps allowing also the Gorgian sense. Empedocles is used as an example at 1461a23-5, whereas Aristotle had emphatically said in Chapter 1 that he was not a *poiētēs* but a natural science writer (who happens to use verse) because he does not "represent." However, the inclusion of Empedocles in and of itself does not determine conclusively (although it adds weight) that the chapter is interpolated. Aristotle without question uses a single word sometimes in different ways in one and same work, however, usually signaling with a particular activity or object that the context is different. Thus, someone would have to use stylistic analysis (showing peculiarities of writing that authors favor at different points of their career) or some other method to settle the question of interpolation beyond all reasonable doubt.

Chapter 25 is valuable for one final additional point. Aestheticians– not those also called cosmetologists or beauticians who make one's skin look better, but philosophers of art or of beauty–often speak about the autonomy of art and how the practice should not serve, e.g., ethical or political ends (like propaganda).[179] The aestheticians frequently

---

179   I mention the different senses of "aesthetician" to continue highlight-

trace the origin of theories of the autonomy of art back to the German philosopher Alexander Baumgarten (1714-1762) or to the Prussian philosopher Immanuel Kant (1724-1804) or to other thinkers of the era like the Irish-Scottish Francis Hutcheson (1694-1746). However, Aristotle in this chapter emphasizes that the standard of correctness for *poiēsis* is different from that of politics *or even from other arts*. That is, *poiēsis* is autonomous, and, as we have seen to some extent, the end is not catharsis but a proper pleasure.[180]

We must be careful, though. Simply because drama is autonomous does not mean that ethics, politics, and other considerations have no relevance whatsoever. They would just be relevant secondarily from the standpoint of aesthetics or of the philosophy of art. I may be an independent, autonomous person who always makes my own decisions (as an adult) but I still have to eat and to interact with other individuals, unless I am the sole shipwrecked survivor on an island. Aristotle emphasizes that good character is very important in Chapter 15 but there is a huge difference between saying this and saying that art must serve moral purposes and be for ethical instruction. Rather, especially considering his humanistic vision of ethics, the reason, I would argue,

---

ing how words are often equivocal. Here is a more technical case than "play," and yet clearly "aesthetician" has meanings that the context determines. Consider also "Mary is a painter." Is she a fine art painter or a house painter? The surrounding discussion will normally show.

180   One might be tempted to say, and some have said, that art for art's sake is reflected in the *Dramatics*. What, though, does this phrase mean, literally? There might be a sense in which it is true because we have just seen Aristotle saying in *Dramatics* 25 that every art has its own principles just as art has different principles from politics and because Aristotle analyzes drama "from within," with respect to its parts. Still, "for art's sake" suggests that the beneficiary is *art* and not the people that create or experience it, just as when I say "for Eva's sake" the benefit is for Eva. "Art receiving the benefit" would be a difficult thesis to advance, unless it is qualified significantly, given the arguments of this book and given how inanimate objects can hardly be benefitted. In other words, we see that tragedy's "sake" for Aristotle is for pleasure for the audience or for wealth, fame or self-satisfaction for the creators.

that Aristotle states that characters must be good, except when a villain is necessary for the plot, is that by not upsetting the audience with inordinately bad characters who get unfairly rewarded, the audience can feel *more* pleasure. In the context of Aristotelian dramatic theory, *ethics is in the service of art,* not the other way around. Therefore, although we need to engage in purely formal considerations to understand the best drama (or literature or art in general) from the relevant dramatic, artistic and technical perspectives, we cannot at all times completely divorce aesthetics and art from other realms of life and from other theory.[181]

---

181   Despite Halliwell's (in my opinion, mistaken) view that the *Dramatics* is about literature and that performance for Aristotle need only be imagined, all of the above is one reason that I sympathize with the modern British scholar when he says the following, while trying to reconcile the autonomy of art in Chapter 25 with Aristotle's ethics (and notice how important pleasure is on Halliwell's account, with no mention of catharsis):

> Hence Aristotle's point that depiction of moral evil in a poem is unjustified if it contributes nothing to the achievement of the poem's goal (*ibid.*: 25.1461b19-20). *That goal is the pleasure of a certain kind of intensely emotional response.* But...Aristotle's psychology indeed takes emotions to be informed by "judgements." The experience of poetry entails, therefore, a kind of emotionally inflected understanding which cannot be dissociated from ethical value. The *Poetics*, I submit, seeks an "ethicist" mean, avoiding the extremes both of moralism (which would identify poetry's "standard of correctness" with the ethical *tout court*) and of outright poetic formalism (which would assert a pure autonomy severed from the ethical) (Halliwell, "Ancient Beginnings," *op. cit.*, 2016, p. 7; my italics).

While on the subject of the importance of pleasure for Halliwell, I should note that he draws our attention to an "assertion in an anonymous sophistic treatise, the *Dissoi Logoi,* that 'poets write in order to provide pleasure, not for the sake of truth'" (Stephen Halliwell, *Aristotle's Poetics*, Chapel Hill: The University of North Carolina Press, 1986) p. 14. One must always be careful about whether Aristotle accepts anything by a sophist (recall Gorgias' coining *poiēsis* as "language and meter"), yet the assertion is even more evidence that the Greeks in general took art to have pleasure as the goal. This is all encapsulated by the common quip that "one should not spoil a good story with the truth."

Overview: Chapter 26

Chapter 26 is a contest (*agōn*) between epic and tragedy, similar ironically to the dramatic competitions, except tragedies would compete against tragedies in those competitions, not against other art forms. The *agōn* seems motivated primarily, or in large part, because Plato had ranked epic highest, saying in the *Laws* II that the older lads prefer comedy; the educated women, young men and mass of people tragedy; and the old, best men epic.[182] In effect, Plato creates his own *agōn* with different art forms competing against each other, probably justified by comparing them generically as "works of *poiēsis*" rather than as a certain species of art such as tragedy or epic. Aristotle accepts both the challenge and the underlying generic assumptions but politely disagrees with the result. He ranks tragedy above epic for reasons that are clear, except perhaps for one usually misunderstood matter of music and another matter about movement in both epic and tragedy. I cover these issues in the *Comments*.

I only need add in this *Overview* that Manuscript B shows a few extra words at the very end of Chapter 26, indicating that Aristotle continues to another section on comedy, as he had promised at the beginning of Chapter 6. It is one of great losses of ancient times that not enough copies were made and distributed and that the one original, or any of the few copies, entirely or mostly disappeared, in part because, according to passages in the *Rhetoric* and in the *Politics,* and according to indirect evidence by some neo-Platonists, Aristotle's explanation of catharsis seemingly occurred in this lost section. (We saw the great British translator and commentator W.D. Ross remarking on this in the *Comments* of Chapter 6, but see *ADMC* Chapter 8 for the discussion of the related issues including the view of some that the *Tractatus Coisilianus* is the missing second book.) One ramification of the explanation of catharsis occurring in the treatment of comedy is that its primary relevance for Aristotle was to *this* art form, *not* to tragedy.

---

182   658d-659a. Cf. also the *Republic* III, 397d.

Another ramification is that the catharsis relevant to tragedy may well have come about when it was performed as a tetralogy, which finished with a satyr play, and the cathartic phenomenon occurred because of that often ribald play.[183] All of this permits that, in *some* (but only in some) circumstances, a *tragōidia* as one (or a mixture) of some of the sub-types given in Chapter 18 had catharsis, especially since catharsis, like pleasure, could have different sub-species. However, these topics have been barely addressed, if at all, in the literature despite all the attention paid to the *Dramatics* and to catharsis over centuries. Even were commentators able to demonstrate plausibly that the goal of *some* sub-types of serious drama for the mature Aristotle had catharsis as a goal (without the satyr play), *ADMC* and other recent publications demonstrate that those commentators will never sensibly revive the view that Aristotle authentically wrote *katharsis* as the goal for *all* serious drama.[184]

Comments

Let us proceed from the beginning of the chapter, the final one of the extant texts. Aristotle first recounts why epic is better, but, strangely, he leaves aside its advantage from Chapter 24, namely, that because it is not confined like tragedy to the one episode on stage, it can be more diverting and amazing. No one to my knowledge addresses this issue, nor have I apart from the suggestions of this book and of *ADMC*, and it must be left aside here.

The primary challenge that Aristotle addresses now is the bifurcated claim that the art which represents in all respects is vulgar and thus *not* the best. Aristotle does not give a direct object or other context for "represents" when he first lays out the claim (1461b27-9), which en-

---

183   *ADMC*, Chapter 6, pp. 442-5, and Chapter 8.
184   Veloso, *op. cit.*, 2007 and 2018, and Rashed, *op. cit.*, 2016.

tails he presumably means "represents in general." That this art must be tragedy stands to reason, however, from the explicit purpose of the chapter and from the details that follow. Furthermore, that Aristotle is reacting tactfully to his mentor without naming him is shown from Plato's remarks in the *Republic*. There Socrates, who is usually Plato's mouthpiece, claims the following, in which *mimesis* (or its verbal form *mimeisthai*) gets translated sometimes as "impersonation" (or "impersonate"), sometimes as "imitation" (or "imitate"), and sometimes as "mimicry" (or "mimic"):

> A man of the right sort, I think, when he comes in the course of his narrative to some word or act of a good man will be willing to impersonate the other in reporting it, and will feel no shame at that kind of mimicry, by preference imitating the good man when he acts steadfastly and sensibly, and less and more reluctantly when he is upset by sickness or love or drunkenness or any other mishap. But when he comes to someone unworthy of himself, he will not wish to liken himself in earnest to one who is inferior, except in the few cases where he is doing something good, but will be embarrassed both because he is unpractised in the mimicry of such characters, and also because he shrinks in distaste from molding and fitting himself to the types of baser things. His mind disdains them, unless it be for jest...
>
> *Then the narrative that he will employ will be the kind that we just now illustrated by the verses of Homer*, and his diction will be one that partakes of both, of imitation and simple narration, *but there will be a small portion of imitation in a long discourse*... the other kind of speaker, the more debased he is the less will he shrink from imitating anything and everything. He will think nothing unworthy of himself, so that he will attempt, seriously and in the presence of many, *to imitate all things*, including those we just now mentioned—claps of thunder, and the noise of wind and hail and axles and pulleys, and the notes of trumpets and flutes and pan-pipes, and the sounds of

Overviews & Comments: Chapters 23-26

all instruments, and the cries of dogs, sheep, and birds; and so his style will depend wholly on imitation **in voice and gesture**, or will contain but a little of pure narration.[185]

Aristotle continues in Chapter 26 by focusing on the movement (which would obviously include the gestures) of the mimesis, recounting how some actors are criticized for moving too much: "Mynniscus used to call Callippides a monkey, on the ground that he went to great excesses."[186] As Aristotle summarizes the charge against the fully performed tragedy, "people [surely including the Platonists] say that epic relates to decent spectators, who have no need **of gestures**."[187]

Then on behalf of tragedy Aristotle replies to these charges with three arguments. The first two arguments are related and easy to understand. The charge by "certain people" is against actors' *excessive* delivery, not against the art of tragedy *per se* or against *proper* delivery. This leads to the second reply. The delivery may be bad, but it is not delivery *itself* that it as fault (as we saw even Plato recognized to some extent); rather, it is the delivery associated with impersonating *characters not worth showing*. However, what kinds of characters should be included in tragedy and how they should be represented had already been explained in Chapter 15 and in effect covers this particular point, in defense of serious drama.

Now comes the final, difficult argument that literary theorists have appealed to, thinking that it helps demonstrate that tragedy was for Aristotle *essentially* mere language. I quote the passage in full:

> Moreover, tragedy fulfils its function even without acting, just as much as epic, and its quality can be gauged by

---

185 396c-397b; Plato. Plato in Twelve Volumes, Vols. 5 & 6, trans. by Paul Shorey (Cambridge, MA, Harvard University Press; London, William Heinemann Ltd., 1969); my italics & bolding.
186 1461b35-6; Janko transl.
187 1462a2-3; Janko transl.; my bolding and comment in brackets.

reading aloud. So, if it is in other respects superior, this disadvantage is not necessarily inherent.[188]

Three issues arise: What is the "function" of tragedy? Does "its quality can be gauged by reading aloud" mean that tragedy as a genre only has, or only need have, speech, overruling Aristotle's essential conditions of tragedy in Chapter 6 and the derived six necessary conditions that *all* tragedies have? Lastly, what is "this disadvantage": the closest antecedent, which is mere movement or gesture, or the subject of the whole passage, namely, the charge that gesture is vulgar?

In an introductory text like this *Primer*, I cannot reproduce the pages of detailed analysis to demonstrate my conclusions on these three issues.[189] A summary must suffice, after a preliminary remark.

The Northern Greek's initial statement "tragedy fulfils its function even without acting, just as much as epic" has almost always, if not always, been taken to mean that epic is pure language and that Aristotle is stripping away acting from *only* tragedy. Yet this cannot be right because a few sentences later he discusses how the rhapsode Sosistratus and the singer Mnasitheus of Opus were appropriately criticized for gesticulating too much. Again, epic is performed by a rhapsode for Aristotle. What the initial statement really means, then, is that *both* tragedy and epic fulfil their function without acting: tragedy fulfils its function even without acting, just as much as epic (fulfils *its* function without its *own* acting). That is, both of them have language and we can focus only on that element.

To evaluate now the three aforementioned issues: The easiest one to resolve is the second one, namely, whether this passage overrules the essential conditions in the definition of tragedy. Given Aristotle's theory of definition, the acting and performance are absolutely crucial.

---

188   Transl. Fyfe, *op. cit.*
189   *ADMC*, Chapter 2, pp. 164-7.

Overviews & Comments: Chapters 23-26

Thus, Aristotle cannot be intending to overrule his necessary conditions with the claim that the quality, *whatever that is*, can be given merely by reading. This claim is similar to the one at the end of Chapter 6 that we already examined, suggesting that spectacle was *least* of the six necessary conditions (but still a necessary condition) because (*gar*) the effect of tragedy can be given without the competitions and excellent actors. Aristotle must, then, be speaking rhetorically yet again.

The easiest explanation is to assume that to compare apples with apples, he focusses only on the language that both art forms have. Otherwise, he is comparing apples with oranges, because epic does not have two parts of tragedy. In this scenario, Aristotle suggests that one can get the quality *of the plot* in both art forms through the reading, presumably suggesting that the implied actions get imagined in *both* cases. Since plot is the soul of tragedy, one can ignore the other elements *for the purposes of a worthwhile comparison*. Thus, even considering merely the language, such as with a modern novel and a play-script (or screenplay for cinema), epic and tragedy can be compared. Clearly, the quality of the literary composition in either art form not only has the full range, from ridiculously bad to superb, but the ability to suggest the plot, so in this respect, as Aristotle wisely suggests, tragedy has no *inherent* disadvantage.

The function of tragedy, the first issue recounted, and the second one for us to examine, is more difficult to resolve. To begin with, no Greek exists for "function." Aristotle only says "its own," elliptically, and some translators say instead "effect" or "power" (*dunamis*). If "function" is meant, then presumably "proper pleasure" is being referred to (as was stated for *both* tragedy and epic in the definition back in Chapter 23). Aristotle, then, means that tragedy can give pleasure like epic through the language. In this regard and considered as two instances of a genus (rather than as examples of two different species), they are again tied for first place in the contest, with no winner because they both have language. If some effect (or power) that is different from pleasure is meant (perhaps, as just indicated, to convey a plot), then the effect of language as discussed in Chapter 6 is being referred to, and both art forms have it, still causing a tie. Alternatively, Aristotle means the *partial* effect (or partial power) of tragedy, given his earlier pinpointing of the partial powers that each of the different elements in the definition have. The whole statement therefore more precisely means: "...tragedy fulfils its (partial) function even without acting, just as much as epic..." However, this suggestion does not entail that tragedy is *necessarily* only words, with the other elements only optional and that its *total* function is fulfilled only with words. At any rate, again, this suggestion in no way would or could outweigh the importance of essential conditions in a definition and derived necessary ones.

Analogously, one would foolishly argue that French culture is better than the landlocked cowboy culture in the American Midwest because of the delightful seaports and vineyards in France. This reason makes for an unfair comparison. Rather, it is crucial either (i) to compare the wine-growing regions of California plus the American seaports like San Francisco and Seattle with France's wine-growing regions and seaports, or (ii) to compare the Camargue region in Southern France near Arles that has cowboys (*gardians*) with the American cowboy sub-culture. The person arguing for French culture should argue that the *gardian* culture is better than the American cowboy culture, because, say, this region gives the same function or effect as the cowboy region in America but more admirably. That is, the American cowboy's ability to round up cattle or to provide quick, tasty steaks, or what have you, is met by the *gardians* ability to do the same and arguably more (maybe the French steaks are better spiced). Yet, this comparison does not mean that French culture as a whole is confined to the Camargue region and defined as such. Similarly, just because Aristotle makes a comparison of a part of tragedy to a part of epic does not mean that the whole of tragedy is entirely linguistic. (Naturally, if

Overviews & Comments: Chapters 23-26

we compare total French and total American culture the contest gets much more interesting, but too difficult to answer here,—and there may be no definitive winner objectively in this case, even though in the full contest between tragedy and epic, tragedy obviously wins.)

The third and final issue, which pertains to the antecedent of "this disadvantage," can be easily summarized. In order to support intentionally or not their view that Aristotle considers tragedy in the *Dramatics* to be merely written, some respected literary theorists have indicated that he intends to renounce *all* gesture and movement, one of the two options (the other being to renounce vulgar movement).[190] However, given the Greek text in Chapter 26 that I did not reproduce here, to be read in translation or in the original Greek, Aristotle *rejects* giving up all movement, for otherwise he says, we would have to give up dance. He strongly suggests that he does not wish to do that, which will be doubly confirmed later in Chapter 26, and hence "this disadvantage" must refer to the charge of *vulgar* gesture: *That* kind of gesture itself is not "inherent" in tragedy (and can be renounced).

The rest of the arguments on behalf of tragedy that follow in Chapter 26 are readily comprehensible and compelling.[191] Only three final remarks are needed for our purposes in this *Primer*.

In one of the upcoming advantages for tragedy, Aristotle says that its

---

190   For example, D.W. Lucas; cf. *ADMC*, p. 164-7.

191   The arguments leave aside considerations of finance, etc. If they were brought in, along with the advantage of amazement of Chapter 24 that epic has, then epic might have another advantage added to its list because it requires less resources. Whether that comes even close, though, to bringing it near the total advantage of tragedy is an interesting question. One might say that this is not an artistic issue, but an economic one and that we are only focused here in the treatise on the artistic issues, for good or bad. Moreover, Aristotle then can compare epic with merely written tragedy, the type that Chaeremon produces, and the economic cost would therefore favor tragedy, because it is shorter and thus less labor-intensive to produce.

mousikē and spectacle give it not a little pleasure, with the implication that the pleasure is actually very considerable. Again, these are the fifth and sixth necessary elements of tragedy that epic does not have. *Mousikē* is now taking the place of *melos/melopoiia* from Chapter 6. All translators until now to my knowledge have rendered *mousikē* here as "song" or "music" but again both of these omit dance. Yet, Aristotle explains that *mousikē* is *harmonia kai rhuthmos* in *Politics* VIII 7 and I have demonstrated[192] that *mousikē* has the same meaning both there and in Chapter 26 as it does in the first six chapters of the *Dramatics*, as "music and dance," not "harmony and rhythm." As we saw much earlier, all of this follows Plato in the *Laws* II (notably 655a) and at *Alcibiades* 108c, in which *mousikē* is explained as "music and dance (*qua* ordered body movement in an orchestral setting)." It also captures what happened in Greece, a commendable policy for an empiricist like Aristotle. Thus, he treats *mousikē* as a synonym for the choral performance of tragedy and for very good reason.

Let us now proceed to the penultimate paragraph of the extant treatise. The Northern Greek states that both tragedy and epic should produce not a random pleasure *but the one mentioned*. Unfortunately, it is not clear where he had mentioned it. However, once we review the text, we see starting with Chapter 4 that pleasure (at least of a certain kind) is the goal of tragedy, and we find a number of sensible options for Aristotle's "the one mentioned." One option is the original, proper goal, namely, a (proper) pleasure, written where the catharsis-clause now sits usurping the legitimate goal that had been destroyed when the manuscript was damaged. Another plausible option is, as we saw, the (quasi-)definition of epic, where Aristotle says it has the same (proper) pleasure as tragedy, but presumably considered from a generic perspective. Other options are possible, but let these examples suffice.[193]

---

192   *ADMC*, Chapter 4. Cf. also *ADMC*, pp. 58ff.

193   They are covered in *ADMC*, Chapter 7. They have never been ex-

Overviews & Comments: Chapters 23-26

Finally, while on the topic again of catharsis: Indubitably, we have no explanation of the phenomenon in the extant text despite *Politics* VIII 7 mentioning that the explanation is given in a *peri poiētikēs*. Given some references in the *Rhetoric* to exactly the same *peri poiētikēs*, when Aristotle speaks of jests, the most logical solution is that Aristotle explained catharsis in the lost section on comedy. Some might claim that while explaining the concept there, Aristotle could have applied it significantly back to tragedy. However, the very last sentences in our treatise rule that out. As he says, returning us full circle to the very opening sentence of the whole treatise, we are done with tragedy and epic, their parts, their kinds, and how to compose well. Therefore, although catharsis might apply *peripherally* to a few, but only a few, subtypes of tragedy at most, Aristotle could have mentioned this only *in passing* in discussing comedy. This is still a far cry from catharsis being the goal of *all* tragedy or *necessarily* being the goal of the subtypes of tragedy with pity and fear discussed in Chapters 13 and 14, where we will recall Aristotle mentioned that the goal for the dramatist was *pleasure* through pity and fear, *not* catharsis through pity and fear. It would be extremely peculiar for Aristotle to claim that we are done with tragedy, as he does in the final sentence of Chapter 26, and then later in a discussion of comedy to explore in *substantial and important detail* how catharsis could apply also to tragedy.

This concludes the *Comments* and the main body of this book. For a summary of some other issues that my interpretation exposes, including the matter of catharsis in comedy and the typically unrecognized importance of that art form for Aristotle (with some rare noteworthy exceptions), see the following Appendix 1. In Appendix 2, to explain how *katharsis* entered an archetypal manuscript in *Dramatics* 6 despite the philosophical inconsistencies it causes, I examine the ancient textual evidence for how Aristotle's library was transmitted, how the

---

plored before rigorously from the advantage point that Petruševski and his followers like myself have but are easily accessible to those new to the *Dramatics*.

library was damaged, and how at least some of the books were badly edited and copied before being saved (or not) for posterity. Finally, I touch at the very end in an *Epilogue* on a new, somewhat scandalous *agōn* in certain Anglo-American and French intellectual circles. It has started because of those like Petruševski, Veloso, and myself, who have given the evidence why Aristotle could not, for instance, have written *katharsis* in *Dramatics* 6, putting an end to a whole line of scholarship, publications and cultural attitudes that have gone on for centuries. Some (but fortunately only some) of the authors impacted have complained in a not-very-scholarly fashion, perhaps feeling that it is not fair that they suffered in trying to resolve the modern day equivalent of the Gordian Knot while someone like Petruševski and his followers simply took the sword and cut it.

APPENDICES

A Primer on Aristotle's Dramatics

Appendix 1: Summary of Other Issues from *Aristotle on Dramatic Musical Composition*

Questions for Specialists to Answer

Immediate questions arise after we understand, for example, that catharsis cannot be the goal of tragedy in general for Aristotle. What *is* the goal? In its final chapters, *Aristotle on Dramatic Musical Composition* (*ADMC*) explores this question along with related ones. They are simply beyond the scope of this *Primer*, even if the final chapters in *ADMC* are at a much less sophisticated level than the previous ones. Because those chapters of *ADMC* mostly involve just reviewing the texts in which Aristotle speaks of the goals of mimesis, of serious drama, and of dramatists, the chapters are relatively accessible to the general reader. Aristotle speaks of the dramatist trying to please the audience (presumably to win a competition) but most often speaks of the kind of pleasures associated with tragedy, e.g., an intellectual delight or pleasure (that could have emotional associations also). Hardly any specialized debate on these matters has occurred because everyone for hundreds of years, until Petruševski and his followers, believed the issue was settled and believed catharsis was the goal.

What is the role of the satyr play for Aristotle? When it had the "fourth position," did it give the catharsis for the trilogies that ended tragically as opposed to those that ended happily? One of the most puzzling questions, rarely touched on, much less emphasized, by commentators, is why the satyr play is not analyzed in the treatise. Was it because it was considered more a comic art form and because Aristotle explicated it in the lost section on comedy? To emphasize, this is one of the great unanswered questions of the *Dramatics*, if not the greatest. In the last fifteen years, though, there has been a remarkable surge of interest in the satyr play. See Mark Griffith's *Greek Satyr Play: Five Studies* for a superb introduction to the whole topic and the various published scholars.[194]

Postscript on Catharsis, Pity and Fear

The difficulty with trying to ascertain Aristotle's view on catharsis is explained now, given the lack of surviving manuscripts. Anyone who enters this swamp is a brave soul,—as brave as, or braver than, Orpheus going down to Hades to try to retrieve Eurydice, who had died on their wedding day after being bitten by a snake. (Amazingly, Orpheus was allowed to retrieve Eurydice on the condition that he never look back at her before arriving above ground. Toward the end of the journey and in doubt that she was still behind him, he turned around and lost her forever.)

Given the arguments from *ADMC* and this *Primer*, if catharsis was not explained by Aristotle in a completely lost book, then the *Politics* and *Rhetoric* decidedly show that it was explained in the lost section on comedy. Does catharsis apply for Aristotle to comic drama as a general goal or only to one or more of comedy's own sub-types? In any event, presumably catharsis was primarily or only relevant to that art form.

If *primarily* relevant to comedy in his mature thought, was it also relevant to some sub-types of pure tragedy (without the satyr play), and if so how? I have already suggested that the satyr play, when it was

---

[194] Griffith, *op. cit.*, 2015. Cf. also *ADMC*, pp. 163, 206, 443, and 495. Griffith analyzes briefly the *Dramatics* in ways that did not strike me as comprehensive, e.g., ignoring that the satyr play for Aristotle could have elicited catharsis. The result of his gracious replies to my private correspondence is given in *ADMC*, p. 497. Without having any knowledge apparently of my same views on the theme, Griffith also presents very compelling thoughts regarding the ancient performing arts in an upcoming publication on how the lack of surviving music, dance, etc., has caused moderns to give very disproportionate weight to the scrolls that did survive; cf. *ADMC*, pp. 112, 179-80, 327-8, and 489.

Appendix 1: Other Issues in *ADMC*

in the "fourth position," may have given the catharsis. Alternatively, was catharsis only relevant to "tragedy" when Aristotle was younger, more under the sway of another lover of catharsis, Plato,[195] and when the Northern Greek wrote the dialogue *On "Musical" Composers (aka On Poets)*? Does some sort of catharsis apply to the sub-type, and only to the sub-type, of tragedy exemplified for Aristotle by *Oedipus*, given that the goal in Chapter 14 is *pleasure* through pity and fear? Everyone has assumed that catharsis even in this case is relevant, but it needs to be demonstrated, because Aristotle may not have thought catharsis was the *primary* goal of *any* kind of tragedy after his youthful *On "Musical" Composers*.[196] Recall that catharsis is never discussed in the *Nicomachean Ethics* or in the *Rhetoric*, and *Politics* VIII 7 suggests that it is, at best, a secondary or occasional goal, especially for pathological individuals. Enjoyment or cognitive delight in that treatise is without question the most important goal of the "musical" arts for adult citizens.

While on the subject of the *Politics*: *Musical* catharsis is introduced in VIII 6 (as something associated with music of the *aulos*) and 7, where it is said to be explained more in a treatise *peri poiētikēs*, which should be clear now does not mean for Aristotle "on the art of poetry" but "on the art of dramatic 'music' making." How many types of "musical" catharsis are there, given that analogously different kinds of pleasure exist, and how do the types of catharsis differ?

Catharsis can also come from dance, such as in the orgiastic rites (*Politics* VIII 7). Both Plato and Aristotle accept that Corybantism, a

---

[195] *ADMC*, pp. 405-6.

[196] In my view, Fendt's "The Purpose of Comedy" (*op. cit.*, 2011, espec. pp. 108-56,) is the most up-to-date and thoughtful introduction to what Aristotle *might* have said, and *did* say, on comedy and catharsis. It is indispensable reading for anyone now entering this almost wide-open topic, even if it is more Fendt at times than Aristotle (but, then, given the absence of manuscripts, anyone tackling this issue will necessarily be speculating).

delirium involving hallucinations and sleeplessness, and by implication, less extreme nervous conditions, can be relieved through movement.[197] Although not very well known, we moderns have music therapy and dance therapy at certain hospitals and other institutions (and almost everyone knows the calmness following a night of dancing to rock-and-roll, club music, tango, or ballroom styles). What about empathetic catharsis from a plot that could be done without language, as with our story-ballets? Do we, or should we, get a catharsis from the tragic ones like *Swan Lake* or *Giselle*? Or can we also get a catharsis, be it a different sort, from the comic ones like Frederick Ashton's *La Fille Mal Gardée*, Jerome Robbins' *Fancy Free*, or Jiri Kylian's *Symphony in D*?

Of course, these statements are substituting for whether, and how, the Greeks could get catharsis or not from their dance experiences, but since no dance or music work survives as a whole, we must take a best guess. This is not to suggest that they had full-length ballets before Roman times, when the so-called pantomime appeared to be full dance performances (emphasizing mimeticism), only that the dance could have been done long enough within the choral arts to convey emotions and other psychological experiences, as Aristotle in *Dramatics* 1 and 2 clearly indicates happens. Recall also from Chapter 4 that the "trivial plots" in the very early tragedies were done almost wholly with dance.

What about purely literary catharsis? In what way is this similar to, or different from, musical catharsis? If over 465 years of tradition are correct, catharsis can also come through plot and language, but there is no statement by Aristotle that catharsis comes only through these two necessary conditions of tragedy, of the six given in *Dramatics* 6. Nor does the neo-Platonist Proclus say anything more precise than catharsis was used by Aristotle in his *dialogue* to justify tragedy and comedy against Plato's attacks. In other words, the neo-Platonist

---

197   *ADMC*, pp. 327-8, 382 and 489.

Appendix 1: Other Issues in *ADMC*

never delimits the catharsis to language or to plot or to a combination of the two. If, however, plot and language in and of themselves, either separately or combined, can give a catharsis for the mature Aristotle of the *Dramatics*, then other primarily linguistic forms like epic surely can also, despite Aristotle never mentioning catharsis once in his discussion of epic. What about purely literary productions like Plato's *Symposium*? Does this have a catharsis, at least *qua* clarification?

What about spectacle or a combination of plot and spectacle, which can give terror according to Chapter 14? Could the same plot but with different spectacle at the end also not give a calming effect, dispensing with, or purging, the terror? Would this not count as a catharsis?

Now consider in addition the other logical possibilities. *Katharsis* has three meanings during Plato's and Aristotle's time: purgation, purification, and clarification. Which meaning would Aristotle accept or, given his habit of disambiguating words, would he not acknowledge all three senses? Would he restrict himself to one sense and why? Given his other habits, why would he not take the meaning given in popular and Platonic discourse for any given phenomenon and for any relevant topic?

What about mixtures of the types, for instance, a catharsis that starts to purify but then purges? Perhaps some dramatists want to teach secondarily but give pleasure and a purgation primarily. Is not clarification then also possibly relevant, so we have a complex, mixed catharsis at the end?

Maybe a catharsis begins with the music but the dance either takes it over or impedes it with a different catharsis-in-process (likewise, with language or plot if those elements can each give a catharsis). What are the possibilities with these cases of "serial" catharses that are sequential and not concomitant?

In short, how do we account for the options if there are different types of catharsis, in all the manners described above? It would be hard to answer all the questions if there were only one or two notions of catharsis, but when there are three obviously the options multiply.

If the foregoing is not complicated enough, consider also that plots come in many different kinds. Even were it shown that plot by itself can give catharsis (apart from the other, more concrete elements of drama like language and music), plots can be: tragic; serious but not tragic, e.g. *Iphigenia in Tauris*; comic; mixed comic and serious, e.g., the Aegisthus and Orestes plot given at the end of *Dramatics* 13; and mixed comic and tragic, e.g. tragicomedy like the satyr play, such as Euripides' *Cyclops* or some of Shakespeare's late plays that mix both comic and tragic elements. Would a happily-ending *tragōidia* like *Cresphontes* really trigger the same catharsis as a *tragōidia* ending horribly, like Sophocles' *Antigone*, assuming the happily-ending play (or horribly-ending play) even had a catharsis to begin with, as opposed to having the "mere" but arguably sufficient pleasures of reversal and recognition? (Any answer to these questions should assume that only some "tragedies" could have had catharsis for Aristotle, because of the arguments in *ADMC* and in this *Primer* showing that he could not have included *katharsis* in the definition of tragedy and that a "proper" pleasure was typically, or always, the goal instead, even if the catharsis led to a pleasure, as in *Politics* VIII 7.)

Chapter 18 reveals that we are far from finished with the alternatives. Now we need to go through the previous options with each of the four subtypes of tragedy *and of epic*, and determine whether they could have catharsis or not, and if so, why. Presumably any catharsis coming through tragedy of suffering would be different from a catharsis coming through a tragedy of character, especially if the latter ends well. Then, recursively, we need to examine the subtypes of the rest of the art forms, say, comedy. Then sub-types of literature. Then of music (for surely a waltz gives a different feeling than a dirge). Then

Appendix 1: Other Issues in *ADMC*

of dance.

In short, anyone trying to elucidate Aristotle's doctrine has the onus to explain why some plays have catharsis and others do not, what sense of catharsis they might have, whether the catharsis could be complex, meaning whether there might be multiple catharses, either sequentially or concomitantly, and so forth.

Finally, even if someone is successful in the previous respects, from what perspective, audience or performer, does the catharsis arise? In *Politics* VIII 7, the people engaging in the sacred rites experience the catharsis (and, again, Plato and Aristotle both agree on the advantage for nervous conditions). In dance therapy and music therapy, it is more the participant than the viewer who experiences the benefits. Gerald Else thought that the catharsis was in the structure of the play. Even if, however, Else is right in *this* regard, could not audience members also feel a catharsis empathically, and what are the possible combinations? Perhaps both the participants in a music-dance event and spectators experience a catharsis but in different degrees. Also, in *Politics* VIII 7 Aristotle recognizes that different kinds of people will want different types of performances. Would one kind get catharsis from a certain play, but the other kind not?

Now the fun really begins. Until this point I have only discussed katharsis with respect to the relevant parts of drama. Now let us introduce pity and fear, too. Consider all of the additional permutations if only pity is taken into account in the matters above (for the sake of rigor); then fear by itself; then the combination of pity and fear. Even if a play has pity does it necessarily lead to any of the kinds of catharsis alluded to above? Lessing once challenged commentators who really wanted to understand Aristotle to examine the four possibilities with catharsis, pity and fear in general, namely, whether pity with catharsis *qua* purification could accomplish pure fear, or just pure pity, and similarly with fear. However, not only has his challenge never been accepted but Lessing left aside music, dance, and spectacle and how different plot types, etc., could affect the possible answers. Whether he thought language by itself could achieve catharsis, or whether it had to be plot with language, is not discussed by him anywhere to my knowledge. Little did he realize that the issues of pity and fear just scratch the surface if one wishes to understand how the two emotions, with catharsis, could fit into Aristotle's dramatic and literary theory, because Lessing completely ignores, e.g., that some "tragedies" on Aristotle's own account have no pity.

I trust the aforementioned suffices to describe why the issue of catharsis, pity and fear as the terms relate to dramatic "musical" composition is astronomically complex. I myself will not dare attempt to resolve any of it unless and until other manuscripts are found, be they dust-covered in a nook in the extensive holdings of the Vatican or lava-covered in an unexcavated part of Herculaneum. However, perhaps there are brave and passionate descendants of Orpheus reading this book, who learned to take advice and not look back and who are willing to accept the challenge. I sincerely wish them the very best and hope that they publish their findings before I myself go to Hades.

Questions Aestheticians May Help Answer

Why is modern literary tragedy or cinematic tragedy more like epic than like staged tragedy and what are the dilemmas that result from an Aristotelian perspective once we realize this? Again, we need to make sure in discussing this that we do not equivocate on the meaning of the word "tragedy" (*tragōidia*). Is it something necessarily tragic or merely serious drama? I introduce this topic more in *ADMC* Chapter 9.

Given the clarifications of my books, the *core* Aristotelian theory of "drama" as presented in the *Dramatics* would apply nowadays *direct-*

Appendix 1: Other Issues in *ADMC*

ly only to art forms like Broadway musical theater (whether tragic in our sense or "merely" serious, like *West Side Story* and *Oklahoma!*, or comic, like *A Funny Thing Happened on the Way to the Forum* or *The Book of Mormon*). How, and why, could we extend (rigorously) the spirit of Aristotle to other art forms, like literature or ballet or cinema, given his claim in Chapter 25 that different arts have different principles? What would be the dangers? Serious drama in Chapter 6 has "music" and spectacle as necessary conditions; literature is pure language. The claim of Chapter 25 suggests, very wisely, that one cannot mechanically apply artistic principles from one art to another; one must judiciously apply them, if at all, once we drop below the most generic level of "art." This leads into deep and complex questions in the philosophy of art or of aesthetics, especially if the art forms are very different. Even if the generic goal is identical, insofar as all are species *of art*, the specific goals may differ or the manner in which composers achieve the generic goal may differ. Superb poets often are very different from superb choreographers; they can be wonderfully precise in their own ways but you need to speak German to truly appreciate Rilke whereas dance is universal (although one needs training to appreciate the subtleties of ballet).

Given the empirical humanism in Aristotle's approach, with the source of our attraction to dramatic "musical" composition in biology (which, again, can include psychology), would the basic Aristotelian principles always apply to musical theater as long as human nature stays essentially the same? What about the other arts?

Commentators have often said that tragedy is ranked over comedy, when Aristotle only ranks it over epic. Given that he praises comedy at times, one question is whether tragedy is indeed better, or whether tragedy might be better, say, morally but comedy psychologically, effecting a relief (a catharsis?) or joy that is very beneficial. Another biologist, and recent Nobel Prize recipient, Konrad Lorenz (1903-1989), in his seminal book *On Aggression*, places great importance on humor and by implication comedy and how in effect they counter natural inclinations to aggression and fighting. He states:

> I believe that humor exerts an influence on the social behavior of man which, in one respect, *is strictly analogous to that of moral responsibility*: it tends to make the world a more honest and, therewith, a better place.[198]

Aristotle as the quintessential biologist may well have similarly recognized some of the benefits that modern psychologists list for laughter, even if he did not have our techniques for experimentation and for measuring chemicals like endorphins. He certainly recognized an almost identical benefit in *Politics* VIII 7 when speaking of catharsis and the relief and pleasure that to some degree results for everyone, from orgiastic rites and from passionate "melodies" (or "music-dance"). Here is a list culled from different medical organizations, such as the Anxiety and Depression Association of America, organizations for treatment of OCD (Obsessive-Compulsive Disorder), and the Mayo Clinic: https://www.mayoclinic.org/healthy-lifestyle/stress-management/in-depth/stress-relief/art-20044456

21 Benefits of Laughter

1. Relaxes the whole body
2. Boosts the immune system
3. Triggers the release of endorphins
4. Protects the heart
5. Lowers stress hormones
6. Enhances resilience
7. Adds joy to life
8. Improves mood
9. Enhances teamwork
10. Helps defuse conflict

---

198   Konrad Lorenz, *On Aggression*, trans. by Marjorie Kerr Wilson (New York: Harcourt, Brace & Company, 1966) p. 297; originally published by Deutscher Taschenbuch, 1963; my italics.

Appendix 1: Other Issues in *ADMC*

11. Eases anxiety and fear
12. Lowers blood pressure
13. Relaxes muscles
14. Increases memory
15. Helps oxygen flow to the brain
16. Maintains healthy blood sugar
17. Promotes better sleep
18. Improves alertness
19. Increases creativity
20. Gives you more energy
21. Improves relationships

In short, the question of which art form is better, or whether they each have equally good, but different, benefits is wide open for Aristotle. To arbitrarily say that *for him* tragedy is better than comedy, without textual evidence and without specifying the respect in which the art is better, is as bad as saying that he followed Gorgias rather than Plato-Diotima without giving any evidence, especially when he was closely associated with Plato personally for 20 years of his professional life.

A Primer on Aristotle's Dramatics

Appendix 2: The Transmission of the *Dramatics* to the Later Peripatetics and Beyond

The issues of the nature of *tragōidia* and the sense of words like *poiēsis, harmonia kai rhuthmos* are either philological (meaning how the word is translated) or philosophical (meaning how well Aristotle's overall thought as a whole is made comprehensible). When Aristotle does not explain a term and when the context does not force us to accept one legitimate meaning over another, the term's sense, and the resulting apprehension of any particular doctrine, can sometimes be determined by other books of Aristotle and even of Plato, if care is taken. Although the interpretation of various words have often been disputed, no one now contests the authenticity of the "musical" terms in the *Dramatics*. If the legitimacy of the terms were questioned, as they once were (e.g., *kai melos* in Chapter 6), Tarán and Gutas's paleography has settled the issue, at least in almost all cases. The arguments of *ADMC* and of this *Primer* demonstrate that the Platonic-Diotiman senses of the terms rather than, for example, the Gorgian sense of *poiēsis*, function as the basis for Aristotle's discussions. Given, therefore, that the Platonic-Diotiman senses easily allow us to resolve many perennial dilemmas (like why Aristotle discusses *none* of the purely literary poetic forms in a treatise previously titled *Poetics*), the philological and philosophical matters pertaining to, for example, the nature of "tragedy" as performed "musical" art rather than mere literature can be considered settled, at least for our purposes.

The issue, though, of catharsis in Chapter 6 is different. The philosophical considerations overwhelmingly show that *katharsis* in the definition of tragedy hides the rest of Aristotle's correct thought, including the proper goal of pleasure. *Katharsis* also obscures that he follows his own rules of definition. However, the very painstaking and commendable paleography by Tarán and Gutas reveals that the word exists in all four branches of manuscripts. Hence, some scholars are still reluctant to athetize the catharsis-clause, perhaps because it is easier just to accept what is in front of our eyes, once the paleography and some standard philology are done, than to take the next step and achieve philosophical coherence. Scholars who read my work unsurprisingly ask "Who interpolated the catharsis-clause if it is illegitimate"? Some suggest that it would be impossible to accept the philosophical conclusions unless I can answer that question, even though there are other cases where the only word in the manuscripts is rejected because of the thought behind the word and even though *no one* knows the editor at fault in those cases.

Somehow, *katharsis* is different. Its defenders consider it too important a concept to have been mishandled (and I only speak here of its occurrence in the definition of tragedy). It is assumed that century after century of scholars could not have been so wrong in trusting in its authenticity, even if they all for the same centuries not only were unable to establish its meaning but ignored, for instance, until Smerdel and Else that Aristotle was following his own principles of definition in the definition of tragedy. This runs parallel to the issues above, with the scholars ignoring the evidence in front of our eyes in the *Symposium* that *poiēsis* meant, not plain "poetry," but verse *and* "music [in the Greek sense]" and that Aristotle was accepting this notion as the foundation for his own theory.

To augment, therefore, the philosophical and philological arguments of this *Primer* and of *ADMC*, it will behoove us to understand as much as possible how, when, by whom, and why the catharsis-clause got interpolated wrongly into the damaged manuscript during restoration. I have already spoken at times of the "why." The early *On Poets/On "Musical" Composers* was Platonic, and, like Plato, Aristotle in his youth employed catharsis in the context of art (and still does in *Politics* VIII 6 and 7). Based on that exoteric dialogue, and the reference in VIII 7 of an explanation of catharsis in *peri poiētikēs*, a subsequent editor thought catharsis was still for the mature Aristotle the

Appendix 2: The Transmission of the *Dramatics*

final cause of "tragedy." The editor accepted this despite *katharsis* being missing in the rest of the extant texts, with no explanation as promised by the *Politics*. Furthermore, the editor ignored the tensions that *katharsis* creates with, e.g., pleasure being the real goal of both tragedy and epic. Pity and fear are authentic in most, if not all, places in Chapters 9 onwards, and thus it was also assumed that the two emotions could be the intermediate goal of tragedy, in spite of Aristotle saying explicitly in Chapter 13 that a plot of a virtuous person going from fortune to misfortune has neither pity nor fear. Clearly, the editor who interpolated the whole catharsis-phrase did not realize the theoretical inconsistencies that were being generated on and below the surface. He also did not recognize how Aristotle had been using his own theory of definition *qua* biological division in defining tragedy. Yet, the wrongful interpolation was superficially plausible, as confirmed by the generations of scholars who have trusted it and performed exegetical calisthenics over centuries to fit it to the rest of Aristotle's thought. Besides, with the exception of five commentators starting with Smerdel and Else (including myself), none of them recognized the importance of biological division.

Let us address now *when, by whom*, and *how* the phrase with catharsis, pity and fear got interpolated. I should acknowledge beforehand that there is no way to prove this with absolute certainty, given the distance in time and the lack of manuscripts, but overwhelming circumstantial evidence should be as acceptable here as it is in a court of law.

There are four accounts of the transmission of the Aristotelian texts in ancient times, by the renowned Stoic Posidonius (c. 135–c. 51 BCE), who is sometimes considered the greatest polymath of his age, and by three later figures we have already touched upon. In chronological order, they are: Strabo (c. 64 BCE–24 CE), Plutarch (46 CE–c. 119), and Athenaeus (c. middle of the 2nd century CE–early 3rd century). Posidonius, Strabo, and Plutarch recount the manner in which Aristotle's library ended in Rome, whereas Athenaeus describes how books of the Lyceum, or at least of Aristotle's private collection, went directly to the great library of Alexandria. The city was named after Alexander the Great, Aristotle's pupil, and the library was founded about 295 BCE by Demetrius of Phaleron, who had been a member of the Peripatetic school and a Governor of Athens starting in 317, being appointed by the Macedonian general Cassander, who had taken control of the region after Alexander the Great died. After prudently leaving Athens when the old democracy was restored in 307, Demetrius took refuge with Ptolemy I, who with his heirs financed the library. Naturally, those who created and directed the library would have been very enthusiastic about acquiring Peripatetic texts.

I examine the two different traditions separately, starting with Posidonius, Strabo, and Plutarch.

Plutarch is thought to take his account from Strabo, although there are some minor differences in details, and some historians debate whether Plutarch reported independently of Strabo.[199] Posidonius gives, if I may reverse the chronological order, merely a very short summary of Strabo. Because Strabo gives by far the most detail, and because it therefore would be very strange for him to be making up the story, I focus on his account. He says in his *Geography*:

> From Scepsis came the Socratic philosophers Erastus and Coriscus and Neleus the son of Coriscus, this last a man who was not only a pupil of Aristotle and Theophrastus [c. 372-287] but [who] also inherited the library of Theophrastus, which included that of Aristotle. At any rate, Aristotle bequeathed his own library to Theophrastus, to whom he also left his school; and he is the first man, so far as I know, to have collected books and to have taught the kings in Egypt how to arrange a library. Theophrastus bequeathed it to Neleus; and Neleus took it to Scepsis and

---

199 Cf. Hugh Lindsay, "Strabo on Apellicon's Library," *Rheinisches Museum für Philologie*, Neue Folge, 140. Bd., H. 3/4 (1997), pp. 290-8; p. 294.

Appendix 2: The Transmission of the *Dramatics*

bequeathed it to his heirs, *ordinary people, who kept the books locked up and not even carefully stored.* But when they heard how zealously the Attalid kings to whom the city was subject were searching for books to build up the library in Pergamum, *they hid their books underground in a kind of trench. But much later, when the books had been damaged by moisture and moths, their descendants sold them to Apellicon of Teos* [birth unknown; died c. 84 BCE] for a large sum of money, both the books of Aristotle and those of Theophrastus. But Apellicon was a bibliophile rather than a philosopher; and therefore, seeking a restoration of the parts that had been eaten through, *he made new copies of the text, filling up the gaps incorrectly, and published the books full of errors.* The result was that the earlier school of *Peripatetics who came after Theophrastus had no books at all, with the exception of only a few, mostly exoteric works*, and were therefore able to philosophise about nothing in a practical way, but only to talk bombast about commonplace propositions, whereas the later school, from the time the books in question appeared [when Apellicon returned to Athens and made new copies], though better able to philosophise and Aristotelise, were forced to call most of their statements probabilities, because of the large number of errors [in the newly created copies]. Rome also contributed much to this; for, immediately after the death of Apellicon, Sulla, who had captured Athens, carried off Apellicon's library to Rome [84 BCE], where Tyrannion the grammarian, who was fond of Aristotle, got it in his hands by paying court to the librarian, *as did also certain booksellers who used bad copyists and would not collate the texts—a thing that also takes place in the case of the other books that are copied for selling, both here [at Rome] and at Alexandria* [my italics and additional comments in brackets][200]

No one questions Strabo's accounts of the Socratic philosophers and

---

200   *Strabo.* ed. H. L. Jones, *The Geography of Strabo* (Cambridge, Mass.: Harvard University Press; London: William Heinemann, Ltd., 1924).

it would be very strange that the ancient geographer is concerned with historical accuracy on that point and not on the other ones. Also, in speaking of the "zealous" Attalid kings who seemingly could have appropriated the library, with no, little, or arbitrary compensation, Strabo refers according to the translator to Eumenes II, who reigned from 197-159 BCE. If correct, this means that Aristotle's library had been bequeathed and moved multiple times, then "not carefully stored," until Neleus' heirs bequeathed the combined library to their own descendants, who themselves became concerned about Eumenes II. The combined library was then moved underground and hidden still longer by the descendants, who finally sold it. Scepsis was across the Aegean Sea and slightly inland on the coast of what is now northwest Turkey, south of the Dardanelles Strait. The town was about 150 miles to the northwest of Pergamon, which itself was about 40 miles inland and due east of the island of Lesbos, in what is now also the western part of Turkey. Thus, Scepsis was much closer to Pergamon than to Athens, even if one sailed directly and did not take the roundabout overland route that involved crossing the Dardanelles. Lesbos is where Aristotle resided during part of his 13-year hiatus from Athens after the death of Plato, before he returned and started his Lyceum. His junior colleague, Theophrastus, obviously a large part of the story of the transmission of the library, was a native of the island. Obviously, friends sometimes determined where one, or one's library, might reside at any given moment.

We have to wonder how much the papyrus rolls suffered in being moved to Scepsis around 280-250 BCE and back to Athens decades later, especially if done secretly at the later date in order to evade the agents of the Attalids. These moves would involve additional potential damage, above and beyond them being stored in two different locations for, we can calculate, about 135 years, and being damaged by the moths and moisture. The reasons for the calculation are these. The Attalid kings ruled until 133 BCE. Even if Apellicon lived to about 85 years of age and thus was born about 170 BCE, presumably he was

Appendix 2: The Transmission of the *Dramatics*

not engaging in high-powered commerce in a different dynasty, with different laws, until he was at least 25-30 years old. So his purchase of the combined libraries could only have been made about 145 BCE at the earliest, and no later than about 133, when the Attalids lost power. Let us say for simplicity's sake 140 BCE.

George Grote, a prominent British specialist of Aristotle from the mid- to late 19th century, presents a detailed history of the series of events, including the sale to Apellicon, and an arguably more attractive option. Grote indicates that the final Attalid king, Attalus, bequeathed his whole kingdom to Rome when he died in 133 BCE.[201] This is when the descendants could sell the library to Apellicon without fear of the agents of the Attalids, and, I might add, without Apellicon having to worry himself about the lack of legal protection in an Attalid regime. Hence, we can revise our estimate of the purchase from the descendants of Neleus to about 132-120 BCE, with poorly restored copies then being available in Athens for the Peripatetics from about 130–115 BCE onwards until Sulla transports the library to Rome in 84 BCE.

To return to Strabo's passage: "not carefully stored," when the library was locked by the heirs of Neleus, can simply mean the books were not kept in any good order. The phrase might also mean the paypri were not all well protected by outer scrolls. Perhaps the phrase means in addition that they were not protected against bugs but it would be odd that the heirs realized the books were valuable enough to lock away and yet took no steps to keep them from deterioration. Still, the history indicates that they took only a modicum of steps. Finally, Apellicon took the books that he is accused of badly editing back to Athens, which is where the editing probably occurred, all of which surely entailed at least a little more damage and disorder in removing the scrolls from the trench, packing, shipping, and unpacking them.

---

201   *Aristotle*, by George Grote, ed. by Alexander Bain and G. Croom Robertson, 2nd edition with additions (London: John Murray, Albemare St., 1880) p. 36.

It was only then that the later Peripatetics could buy or re-examine them, subject to the errors in the new versions. Also, "filling up the gaps incorrectly" is ambiguous. Were all gaps filled, no matter how large the damage, or just the ones for which a few letters or words could be reasonably, or *somewhat* reasonably, deduced? Strabo's account does not settle the issue, but the current state of the *Dramatics* reflects the answer. Many gaps have never been filled.

Consider now the following additional factors:
- As attested by the ancient sources, Aristotle himself wrote hundreds of rolls. Andronicus of Rhodes, allegedly the last head of the Lyceum even though he was working in Rome, is credited with establishing the (modern) Aristotelian corpus in the mid-1st century BCE. A contemporary of Grote, the equally prominent German scholar Eduard Zeller, also gives one of the most detailed accounts of the transmission of the library and of this whole episode, an account that also tries to consider the philosophical contents. According to Zeller, Andronicus notes the corpus as comprising about 1,000 books.[202]
- Theophrastus' works were also in the hidden trench at Scepsis and Theophrastus was a prolific writer, too. Thus, the "ordinary people" who had kept the combined library under lock had a massive number of rolls to contend with when transferring the library to a trench and then to Apellicon. However, probably after the sale he had complete responsibility for insuring the integrity of the library, even with respect to packing and moving it from the

---

[202] B.F.C. Costelloe and J.H. Muirhead, *Aristotle and the Earlier Peripatetics: Being a Translation from Zeller's 'Philosophy of the Greeks'*, in Two Volumes (New York: Russell & Russell, Inc., 1962). Tarán and Gutas, *op. cit.*, also give a very detailed, up-to-date account of the transmission of the *Dramatics*, especially Chapters 1-2, and thus in some ways have superseded Zeller. However, because they do not translate the Greek or Latin, which would make many of their remarks incomprehensible for an American student being introduced to Aristotle's treatise, I only note their points insofar as they impact the history I describe.

Appendix 2: The Transmission of the *Dramatics*

trench. It would have made no sense for him to restore the papyri in Scepsis and then ship the library, when the shipping could cause damage that required a second restoration in Athens.

- It is simply not believable that the "ordinary people" would have advertised and paid for a capable Peripatetic to guide them in keeping the rolls ordered in terms of content when transferring the library into the trench, considering that any publicity of the existence of the library could get the attention of the agents of Eumenes II or the other Attalids, whose ruling city was relatively close. Surely, the descendants transferred the rolls fairly hastily, even with a great concern not to damage the goods, because of their fear of the library's appropriation. Given the constraints of any trench, any ordering that existed when the library was under lock probably diminished. Moreover, we saw that the heirs of Neleus, who themselves did not sell the scrolls, were accused of not caring for the library in some sense properly even when it was under lock. This probably entailed that they cared little about any reliable *philosophical* ordering of the manuscripts, and, thus, there would have been no great concern to keep Book 2 of the *Dramatics* on comedy next to Book 1.
- Proof of the disorder of the combined library comes from Zeller himself (and from our analysis in the *Overviews* and *Comments*). He provides powerful evidence that the manuscript rolls, including specifically the ones pertaining to the *Dramatics*, eventually became very jumbled, all of which supports my arguments that the treatise is an agglomeration of Aristotelian texts and, to add a new point, that the disorder came from early on, at Scepsis, if not earlier, such as when Theophrastus had to pack and move Aristotle's library or when Neleus also had to pack and move the combined libraries. Anyone who has had to move many shelves of books knows the difficulties that can result, even when one has unlimited time to label book boxes carefully.[203] This is all inde-

---

203   According to a classicist who specializes in ancient manuscripts and

pendent of the descendants of the heirs finally being able to sell the whole collection once Attalus bequeathed the country to Rome in 133 and how the scrolls would have been packed and labelled. What would have happened, e.g., if the second book of the *Dramatics* did not fit into the same box that the first book was already in?

- Finally, I should emphasize that, according to Strabo, the practice of bad copying happens not only in Rome but in Alexandria, which had the finest and largest library in the ancient world at his time (in the first century BCE). This is relevant because some scholars think that the Syriac-Arabic branch of the *Dramatics* originally came from Alexandria, which makes sense given its proximity (compared to Rome) to Syria, the Middle East, and Persia, of which more later.

We should not downplay the mercenary considerations, seeing what happens even today. A specialist in ancient Greek philosophy recently wrote a guidebook to Plato that is translated into a number of different languages but the Chinese appropriated it without any compensation or royalties to him or to the globally-known publisher. After about 2005, at a conference in China, he found himself in the interesting position of looking at his own work, translated into Chinese (probably Mandarin), with no financial benefit to himself and all proceeds going to the pirating house.[204] Christian colleges and institutes in 2018 discovered that they had bought fake fragments of the Bible, sold very recently by unscrupulous translators who realized the money that could be made for such artifacts. For example, in October 2018, Daniel Burke reports:

> The Museum of the Bible in Washington, DC says five of

---

libraries, Matthew Nicholls, scrolls were stored or transported in "book boxes" but, at least in libraries, kept unrolled for display. Cf. his article "Greek manuscripts" for the British Library at https://www.bl.uk/greek-manuscripts/articles/ancient-libraries.

204 Private correspondence, 2017. Name protected at his request in case of future travels there.

Appendix 2: The Transmission of the *Dramatics*

its most valuable artifacts—once thought to be part of the historic Dead Sea Scrolls—are fake and will not be displayed anymore...

[and]

On the website, "*The Lying Pen of Scribes,*" scholars and scientists have identified more than 70 purported Dead Sea Scroll fragments that have surfaced on the antiquities market since 2002. *Ninety percent of those are fake*, said Arstein Justnes, a professor of biblical studies at the University of Agder in Norway, including the Museum of the Bible's [my emphases].[205]

Scholars, called "scribes" above, were obviously needed to create these fake antiquities, and those individuals surely were more interested in money than in truth or in advancing knowledge, to put it mildly.[206] To return now to Zeller and his own account of the transmission of the libraries to Rome: Repeatedly over his academic life and especially in

---

205   Daniel Burke, "Bible Museum says five of its Dead Sea Scrolls are fake," at https://www.cnn.com/2018/10/22/us/bible-museum-fake-scrolls/index.html, as given on 10/23/18.

206   Another case, much closer to home: One reason that *Aristotle on Dramatic Musical Composition* (*ADMC*) had to be self-published, even though it solves a number of fundamental and difficult problems of the *Dramatics* never resolved in over 500 years, is that an editor of Cambridge University Press, Michael Sharp, in early 2014 did not compel a blind reviewer for the admittedly rough manuscript and proposal to recuse himself, when the reviewer had a conflict of interest. The blind reviewer wrote six months later that the book should not be published, *even if all the mistakes in the manuscript were corrected.* He had accurately noted problems of grammar, editing and trivial philosophical points. While handling these and his yield-at-no-cost, more substantive criticisms, which defended that tragedy is literature and catharsis legitimate in *Dramatics* 6, I discovered shortly thereafter in an obscure Estonian journal of philosophy some of the same, idiosyncratic phrases. The author/blind reviewer is Malcolm Heath, a professor of literature and ancient Greek at the University of Leeds. He is the author of a popular Penguin paperback on the *Poetics* (1996). (One can see some of the substantive criticisms he gave because he is labelled as AnonC/AnonymousC in *ADMC*). That his blind review was made to protect his reputation and his

the work cited, he addresses why the Peripatetics after Theophrastus seemed to ignore the work of the "Master" (Aristotle). Zeller aimed to show that it was *not*, as previously thought, the result of Aristotle's library being completely unavailable to the later scholars,— and being unavailable *because* the library was jealously guarded by Theophrastus or by Neleus or by both.

To begin recounting the reasons why later Peripatetics ignored the Master, Zeller examines the various catalogues from the ancient world that assigned texts to Aristotle and properly concludes that they cannot guarantee anything relevant to the issue at hand. He writes:

> It is obvious that catalogues...offer no sufficient security either for the completeness of their reckoning *or for the authenticity of the writings they include*. Nothing but a full and accurate inquiry into the merits of each case can enable us to decide as to the claims of those texts or fragments which are handed down to us under Aristotle's name. Such an inquiry cannot here be fully carried out; but it will not be out of place to combine with a complete review of all the writings ascribed to Aristotle a concise appreciation of the points to be considered in passing

---

finances is shown by the testimonials and written support that chapters of my book, published by Cambridge and Oxford University presses, had received even before he reviewed it. Once my final editing and corrections in *ADMC* were implemented, the book necessarily swelled to its current size to become completely rigorous.

Perhaps in part because of this, not one other publisher would even view the final manuscript, much less evaluate it. However, the primary reason, as editors have told me privately, is that *ADMC* is too shocking and destroys too much work of all the scholars who for hundreds of years accepted, e.g., that catharsis is legitimate in Chapter 6. The moral of this story is twofold. At least some big publishers are unethical or unprofessional or both in not having and enforcing proper recusal policies (and Sharp, who had accepted my proposal within 24 hours of receiving it, admitted that Heath was the reviewer), surely to acquire greater profits or the same profits more easily. Also, you should not use idiosyncratic phrases in a publication that you also use in a blind review if you wish to maintain anonymity.

Appendix 2: The Transmission of the *Dramatics*

judgment on their authenticity (p. 53; my italics).

Zeller discusses the evidence for authenticating various texts and makes the distinction between Aristotle's "scientific" writings that are theoretical or that are part of the "philosophic system" and those that are personal letters, etc. He also distinguishes between two types of philosophic writing: "Exoteric" for the general public and "esoteric," that is, "acroatic," for the technically more sophisticated members of the Lyceum. He reminds us that the end of our *Dramatics* 15 (of course, *Poetics* for him) refers to one of the exoteric "published works," *ekdedomenoi logoi*, as was discussed in the *Comments* above. However, Zeller says of that exoteric work, "it is most natural to apply [the reference] to the *P[eri] poiētēn*,"[207] the so-called *On Poets*.[208] What Zeller completely ignores, is that the reference could be instead to *Dramatics* 17 in part or in whole, because Aristotle discusses exactly the points, including errors, in the art of dramatic musical composition that is the topic at end of Chapter 15. One example in Chapter 17 is how Carcinus erred in badly carrying out the stage effects concerning Amphiaraus. In this case, Zeller ignores his own admission that interpolations often happened in the final production of the texts.

Zeller also loses temporarily his critical acumen when explaining why "our *Poetics* is only a fragment" (p. 102), which in itself is true if he means the treatise is a portion of the original work. We are missing the promised section on comedy and, as Zeller notes (p. 103), the promised explanation of catharsis, among other topics referred to in extant works (such as the *Rhetoric*). However, he (like many others)

---

207 *Op. cit.*, p. 58; cf. also pp. 108-9. Zeller gives evidence that this book must have been a dialogue, confirming it was an early work of Aristotle's (p. 58).

208 To reiterate, the title should be *On "Musical" Composers*, given Aristotle's preference for the Diotiman meaning of *poiētēs* and given Janko's own translations of the extant fragments, which indubitably show the composers being concerned with music (Janko, *op. cit.*, 1987, pp. 53-7).

merely assumes that the *Poetics* is only one work even though Aristotle gives two different, if related, titles in the *Rhetoric*. Zeller mentions one, *peri poiētikēs*, which occurs in *Rhetoric* III 1 and 2. Given the topics that Aristotle notes in those chapters, namely, dramatic ability, using words in a clear but not mean manner, etc., the reference is presumably to our *Dramatics* 22. However, then Zeller mentions a different title in *Rhetoric* III 2 (at 1404b28): *peri poiēseōs*. He also indicates that this is our *Dramatics* without questioning the matter, surely because the extant treatise begins Chapter 20 with a discussion, as the *Rhetoric* says, of what a noun is. Yet, we saw in the *Comments* of Chapters 19-20 that Aristotle does not care about forms of speech, and excludes them from the current treatment, *peri poiētikēs*, which means he also would not have cared about what forms a noun has in a treatment of drama, even if it necessarily has verse. The different title is very weighty evidence that Aristotle wrote two *different* treatises, with very similar titles. The two treatises got combined by an ancient scholar who, like Zeller, did not recognize the differences or pay close enough attention to Chapter 19.[209] Presumably that ancient aggregator was one of the editors that Strabo mentions but he could have been another. The difference in title is further evidence that Chapter 20 is an interpolation into the original *Dramatics*, supporting to his credit, as we see in a moment, Zeller's recognition that often interpolations from different treatises happened in Aristotle's *ouevre*.

Regarding the absence of catharsis in our treatise, Zeller says that it "would have naturally come in the section on Tragedy, and, as we learn from sure traces, actually did occur there" (p. 103). Yet, amazingly, he cites Bernays as providing evidence for this. However, we have seen that anyone who follows Bernays in this regard has no credibility as an ancient Greek scholar. Bernays does *not* say, as Stephen Halliwell reports him saying,[210] that the explanation was lost or that it "dropped

---

209 Tarán makes the same mistake, *op. cit.*, p. 20.
210 Stephen Halliwell, *Between Ecstasy and Truth*, *op. cit.*, 2011, pp.

Appendix 2: The Transmission of the *Dramatics*

out," which makes Bernays' stance more palatable (if still unjustifiable given how certain discussions could have gotten lost or not in ancient papyrus rolls[211]). Rather, Bernays preposterously says that *an excerptor went through the treatise and purposefully cut out the explanation of catharsis and by implication any of its other significant discussions or occurrences*! Bernays, Zeller, and Halliwell, insofar as they hold that claim, are like an ancient Greek audience member who, normally commonsensical and empirical in real life, suspends all disbelief in the theater and accepts the magical intervention of the gods in some tragedies, the *deus ex machina,* as being utterly plausible and real. What is next?,—that Aristotle (as some claim about the early atomist, Leucippus) did not really exist and instead that Martians both wrote his texts and interpolated references to him in all the other papyri of ancient times to play a prank on humanity? Rather, as has been basically shown in this book, the evidence all points to the explanation of catharsis and its primary applicability for the mature Aristotle occurring in the lost section on comedy (unless there was another, completely lost text that had the explanation).

Then comes Zeller's most revealing statement:

> In other places also our text [of the *Dramatics*] shows many greater or smaller gaps, as also interpolations (as c[hapter] 12 and many smaller ones), and inversions (the most considerable that of chap. 15, which ought to come after chap. 18), *which sufficiently prove that we only possess Aristotle's work* **in a mutilated and hopelessly corrupt condition** (p. 103; my emphases).

Zeller arrives correctly at the conclusion, even if he mistakes, for example, the particular interpolations and inversions. This *Primer* and *ADMC* demonstrate that Chapter 12 is perfectly legitimate, if out of order, and not an interpolation. Chapters 17 and 18 themselves are

---

261-3; for the full discussion, cf. *ADMC,* pp. 401-2 and especially 407-8.

211   Cf. also Rashed, in the "Preface" to Veloso, *op. cit., Pourquoi,* 2018, p. 16.

indeed, we can now confidently surmise, interpolated from elsewhere, given that Chapter 18 mentions the four sub-types of "tragedy," two of which, "tragedy of suffering" and "tragedy of character," are never mentioned or discussed elsewhere. Again, though, Zeller *concludes* correctly. The *Dramatics* is mutilated and hopelessly corrupt and still has unfilled gaps. All of this helps confirm that the treatise was probably one of those that served as nutrition for the moths in Scepsis and that got badly edited by Apellicon when "restored." All of this also supports a strong possibility as to who interpolated the catharsis-clause in the definition (Apellicon) and how (working from a damaged version rather than, e.g., taking notes at a lecture) but it is only a strong possibility. There are many other options given the limited accounts we have, including that multiple editors over multiple generations could have added words, especially from the time Theophrastus inherited the original in 322 until Andronicus in the middle of the 1st century BCE reportedly creates a canon, about 250 years later.

Since the neo-Platonist Proclus in the 5th century CE had the early exoteric dialogue *On Poets/On "Musical" Composers*, or at least refers to it, the editor who interpolated the catharsis-clause presumably had the dialogue to justify the interpolation. Catharsis is leveraged in this dialogue by Aristotle to defend tragedy *and comedy* against Plato, according to Proclus, and the interpolating editor simply did not realize that Aristotle's view had matured. He had not enough time or acumen to consider the options that generations of scholars for over 465 years have considered, *with still no convincing answer as to what catharsis reasonably means and how it could mesh with Aristotle's other universally accepted doctrines*. It is impossible to say who exactly was to blame, whether Apellicon, who had money to make in Athens, or a later Peripatetic, who filled in a gap with the seeming "final cause" of tragedy as a benefit for future readers. To underscore, many options are realistically (and not merely conceptually) possible.[212]

---

212   Veloso (*op. cit.*, 2018, pp. 372-6) believes that a later Peripatetic

Appendix 2: The Transmission of the *Dramatics*

Zeller asserts (pp. 139-40) not only that Theophrastus indubitably bequeathed his library to Neleus, given Theophrastus' extant will, but that no need exists to doubt the "desperate condition" of the library in a "canal or cellar" as found by Apellicon. Zeller doubts only that *all* copies of the esoteric writings were confined to this particular library

---

could have added with good intention the clause with catharsis, pity and fear. I hypothesized (with Halliwell in partial agreement) that a later editor took the use of catharsis in the youthful and Platonic *On Poets/On "Musical" Composers* to be a doctrine to which Aristotle subscribed for his whole life (cf. *ADMC*, pp. 401-7). The combination of this youthful work with the middle chapters of the *Dramatics* and *Politics* VIII 7 convinced editors and readers of the time that the interpolated gloss was perfectly legitimate. That is, because the use of pity and fear in at least some, if not all, of the middle chapters of the *Dramatics* is legitimate, the editor felt completely justified in adding the two emotions to the goal of *all* tragedy. He simply downplayed, for the reasons given in our examination of Chapters 13-14, that pity and fear could be only relevant to a subtype of tragedy like *Oedipus*. How easy this is to miss, though, is shown by how little this problem of Chapter 13 is discussed and by the astonishment nowadays of scholars who have even published articles on some aspect of the *Dramatics* and who seem completely unaware that Aristotle ranks the happily-ending plays best in Chapter 14, with the *Oedipus*-type only second best. At the least, the scholars do not even consider how those plays could have pity. Obviously, they skimmed the passage in Chapter 14, found it irrelevant to their needs, and never returned to it.

I mention in the *Comments* of Chapters 13-14 how Heath is an exception in one but only one of these regards. Giovanni Ferrari is another but his solution that pity could happen even before suffering is about to happen, although true when the suffering actually occurs, does not jibe with Aristotle's clear-cut theory *if the suffering is averted at the last moment* (Giovanni Ferrari, "Aristotle's Literary Aesthetics," *Phronesis* 44 [3] 1999: 195). First, if no serious suffering like death or wounding of (at least a moderately good) character occurs, then the precondition for any *sustained* pity does not exist on Aristotelian grounds, and any incipient pity dissipates. Second, on Ferrari's grounds, pity could easily have happened in the beginning or middle of a play with a virtuous character going from fortune to misfortune but Aristotle does not even countenance this. Rather, the disgust (*miaros*) drives away *any* pity and fear, so the great teleologist Aristotle must be concerned with the ending emotions of the plot, not with any of the ones that occur fleetingly in the beginning or middle. For the full discussion of all of this, cf. Scott, *Aristotle's Favorite Tragedy, op. cit.*, 2018, pp. 38-51.

in Scepsis and cites his own and others' research to describe the sometimes obscure references to 12-16 of Aristotle's esoteric works by ancient philosophers (who, I should add, presumably flourished no later than about 120 BCE, because otherwise those scholars could have been using copies from Apellicon, as calculated above). Zeller concludes that there had to have been multiple copies of *at least some* of the esoteric manuscripts and adds that the lack of later Peripatetic attention to the Master's works were for other reasons, perhaps a change in intellectual climate and values.[213] However, this is all completely consistent with Strabo's history being correct, as we see more shortly, because Strabo *never* suggested that *all* the esoteric works were in Neleus' collection, only *most*. Interestingly, Zeller makes an assertion that takes us to the option Athenaeus himself describes, namely, that Ptolemy Philadelphus bought the Aristotelian-Theophrastian library from Neleus for the grand institution at Alexandria. As Zeller writes: "That the *Poetics* was also known to the Alexandrine grammarians is placed beyond doubt by recent research" (pp. 151-2).

---

213   Cf. Zeller, pp. 140ff, espec. 147-152. Finally, Zeller attempts to determine the order in which Aristotle wrote or finished books. He claims that "Judging by the internal references...the *Poetics* should be later than the *Politics* but before the *Rhetoric*" (p. 160). However, in *Dramatics* 19, Aristotle points to the *Rhetoric* for the discussion of *dianoia* (thought or reasoning). Cf. Tarán for more on the chronology, pp. 18-21, although he seems to favor that the *whole Dramatics* was written *only* during Aristotle's second Athenian stay of 13 years, after 335, whereas I believe scholars like Halliwell are probably more correct in thinking that the treatise was started earlier and then augmented throughout Aristotle's life. Grote wisely says:
> As to the treatises on Logic, Rhetoric, Ethics, Politics, Poetics, Mechanics, &c., we are left to fix for ourselves the most convenient order of study. Of no one among them can we assign the date of composition or publication. There are indeed in the Rhetorica, Politica, and Meterologica, various allusions which must have been written later than some given events of known date; but these allusions may have been later additions, and cannot be considered as conclusively proving, though they certainly raise a presumption, that the *entire* work was written subsequently to those events (*op. cit.*, p. 54; my italics).

Appendix 2: The Transmission of the *Dramatics*

There is devastating counter-evidence for this assertion, which I address shortly. In preparation, though, for evaluating that assertion and for what it means concerning the integrity of the definition of tragedy, let us first switch to Athenaeus's account, which Zeller does not consider. According to Timocrates, a figure in Athenaeus' *Deipnosophists*, in which Athenaeus himself appears:

> ...he [Laurentius] owned so many ancient Greek books that he surpassed all who have been celebrated for their large libraries, including Polycrates of Samos, Peisistratus the tyrant of Athens, Eucleides, likewise an Athenian, Nicocrates of Cyprus, the kings of Pergamum, Euripides the poet, Aristotle the philosopher, Theophrastus, and Neleus, who preserved the books of the two last named. From Neleus, he [Athenaeus] said, our King Ptolemy, surnamed Philadelphus, [308/9-246 BCE] purchased them all and transferred them with those which he had procured at Athens and at Rhodes to his beautiful capital, Alexandria.[214]

A dilemma arises. If the descendants of the heirs of Neleus sold the entire collection of books to Apellicon (at around 140-130 BCE, we deduced), how could Ptolemy Philadelphus have purchased them *all* from Neleus (anytime from about 286 BCE, right after Theophrastus' death, until Philadelphus's own death in 246)? Should we trust the history of Strabo, who lived relatively close to the time of the incidents, being born about 75 years after Apellicon allegedly purchased the whole collection, and who was also professionally acquainted with Tyrannion, one of those who reportedly edited the books that presumably including the *Dramatics*?[215] Or should we trust Athenaeus, who was born about 310 years after Apellicon's alleged purchase? Before answering, we should note again that Athenaeus says "From Neleus... our King Ptolemy...purchased them all and transferred them *with*

---

214 Athenaeus. *Deipnosophists*. Translation by Charles Burton Gulick (Cambridge: Loeb Classical Library, Harvard University Press, 1927) Book 1.3a.

215 Lindsay, *op. cit.*, pp. 295-6.

those which he had procured at Athens [my italics]." Clearly, Neleus's library was somewhere else other than in Athens. Scepsis? Even if somewhere closer to Athens, it meant Neleus had had to pack and move the combined library once Theophrastus died before he sold it, probably incurring at least a little damage.

Jonathan Barnes contributes to the debate, as reported by Carlo Natali in *Aristotle: His Life and School*.[216] Natali mentions Barnes' discussion of the editorial history of Aristotle's works until the 1st century BCE and says:

> He [Barnes] rightly thinks that Athenaeus's version of the story about the destiny of Aristotle's library is not compatible with the version of Strabo; but he [Barnes] prefers Strabo's account, notwithstanding the many impossibilities it contains, because he thinks that Strabo derives from Posidonius and that Posidonius wrote the truth... [Nevertheless] Barnes rightly contradicts the main point of Strabo's testimony, that copies of Aristotle's treatises were not available in the Hellenistic period before the time of Sulla (pp. 148-149).

The "main point" here is ambiguous: Is it "all" copies were not available or "some" copies? If "all," then this account is not quite accurate. Strabo indicates that the Peripatetics after Neleus had "a few, *mostly* exoteric, texts." Whether or not "few" means a couple, or a few handfuls, or, given the huge number of scrolls, a few dozen, this still means the Peripatetics after Neleus had *some* esoteric texts, which could account for the references that Zeller pin-pointed.

In his own publication, Barnes adds nothing conclusively new to the issues of this book and of the catharsis-clause, although I would argue that he gives much more weight to the view that the *Dramatics* could have been changed. Indeed, he gives evidence to question the authen-

---

216 Carlo Natali, *Aristotle: His Life and School*, ed. by D.S. Hutchinson (Princeton: Princeton University Press, 2013).

Appendix 2: The Transmission of the *Dramatics*

ticity of *any* extant Aristotelian phrase that sets up grave inconsistencies with other, well established Aristotelian theory:

> We possess several thousand pages of ancient commentary on Aristotle's works, many of them written by serious scholars (Alexander, Ammonius, Simplicius). *The commentators frequently refer to variant readings, and are acutely aware that different manuscripts present different texts.* So far as I know, in none of these textual discussions is there any reference to a "canonical" edition of the Aristotelian works, *or any hint that one particular manuscript tradition might be better than another.*[217]

Thus, Barnes would not accept Tarán's position that "Strabo's story is the more circumstantial and least trustworthy of all" (Tarán, *op. cit.*, p. 25). I agree with Barnes, for the following reasons. Tarán claims:

> Strabo's story...assumes as facts two things that contradict our evidence: first, that Aristotle's technical writings were unknown during most of the Hellenistic age, which is not the case...; second, that the MSS [manuscripts] of Aristotle's treatises eventually were *full of errors*, which of course cannot be true, since our MSS of Aristotle are not corrupt to *that* extent. Moreover, Strabo's story implies that the books were concealed in a trench for fifty years or more...enough time for the moths *to have eaten all or practically all* of the papyri books [according to a scholar who consulted an entomologist]."[218]

I rebut each statement in order, after a prefatory question that repeats what I asked earlier: Why would Strabo prevaricate about the overall history and yet speak about the Socratic philosophers who first came from Scepsis, which no one to my knowledge has ever disputed? Clearly there were families in the city who appreciated philosophy. If Strabo could prevaricate or simply be mistaken, then so could Athenaeus, or anyone else for that matter.

---

217   *Philosophia Togata II: Plato and Aristotle in Rome*, ed. by Jonathan Barnes and Miriam Griffin (Oxford: Clarendon Press, 1997) p. 29; my italics.
218   Tarán, *op. cit.*, p. 27; my italics but his own comment in brackets.

Concerning the first questionable point, Tarán suggests that Strabo reports that the Peripatetics had *no* technical (or "esoteric") books. However, Strabo precisely says "the earlier school of Peripatetics who came after Theophrastus had no books at all, *with the exception of only a few, **mostly** exoteric works.*" This means they had *some* esoteric works, and, if the original library had *many* hundreds, as it apparently had, then "a few" could be elliptical for a few dozen. Indeed, Tarán (pp. 28-30) gives not many more examples than Zeller does with respect to the technical books cited in Hellenistic times, about 25 total. However, some of these—e.g., citations from Cicero (106-47 BCE) and those from Epicurus (341-270 BCE)—are irrelevant because Cicero's could have come from Apellicon's restoration, which we calculated were available by 130-120 BCE. Citing Epicurus' scientific holdings even hurts Tarán's case, because Epicurus could have obtained them during Theophrastus' lifetime, and a whole branch of copies could have resulted. The issue here is what happened *with the Nelean branch and with the Dramatics itself, which there is no record of Epicurus owning*. Thus, Tarán, Strabo and Barnes are arguably in agreement on this issue, whether Tarán admits it or not.

Tarán also acknowledges in other places that *no* ancient seems to have had an interest in the *Dramatics*, which is very strange if the Hellenistic philosophers had copies. The lack of interest also undercuts his suggestion that because some of the esoteric manuscripts were of interest and copied, *all* of the manuscripts were copied,—a blatant fallacy. In brief, the more Tarán, or anyone else for that matter, insists on multiple copies being made of the *Dramatics*, the more incongruous the historical record is, in which *no one* until the Arabic commentators, not even Proclus, writes about the treatise, which I discuss soon.

Second, to return to Tarán's next comment on Strabo, "full of errors" is ambiguous and our *Dramatics* contains gaps that still have never been filled. If the gaps that could be filled were restored, reasonably or *somewhat* reasonably, and the ones that were too large were not, as

Appendix 2: The Transmission of the *Dramatics*

seems to be the case given the ellipses that remain in our *Dramatics*, then Strabo was perfectly correct. "Full of errors" just means lots of errors, not an error in every sentence or in every paragraph of every text, as Tarán implies.

Finally, the claim about the moths eating everything is both absurd *and* perfectly correct, depending on what "everything" refers to. Maybe the moths ate the *whole* second book on comedy or one of the few copies, perhaps the only copy (and the original ultimately got lost for other reasons). Maybe the moths ate most of the book on comedy but not the part on jests, which survives. Maybe the moths had a number of other rolls, including parts on tragedy, for dessert. That does not entail the absurdity, however, that they would have eaten everything in the collection, namely, hundreds of rolls. There are any number of possibilities as to how much they ate (and how much damage was created by moisture), just as there are many possibilities concerning the percentage of holes in your wool coats stored in your attic over summer because of moths. Surely the descendants of Neleus, as uneducated as they were, checked on occasion on the treasure that they had and took steps to minimize destruction. This does not mean, though, that they could have done more than what they did. Thus, nothing Tarán says undercuts Strabo. Strabo, Posidonius and Plutarch, by all objective criteria, outweigh Athenaeus.

There is, however, a resolution to the discrepancy between Athenaeus and the three others, if we assume Athenaeus was summarizing. Naturally, money could be made, and was made, from manuscript copies, and commerce frequently drove, and still drives, human action. Also the Ptolemaic kings were obsessed with adding books to the library. Making copies became seemingly a standard practice, for example, for books that were found on any ship entering Alexandria.[219] They were

---

219 As Mostafa El-Abbadi recounts:
One method to which they [the Ptolemies] reportedly resorted was to search every ship that sailed into the harbour of Alexan-

confiscated by law for the library, a copy was made, and the copy with compensation was returned to the owner. Thus, Philadelphus may have been perfectly happy with a copy, although the original, if it existed, would have been preferable.

Recall that Athenaeus suggests that Neleus's combined library was not in Athens when Philadelphus bought it. Thus, even if Neleus himself did not sell directly the original library or a copy thereof to the (agents of) Ptolemy, Athenaeus could have been reporting elliptically that *(the descendants of)* Neleus sold a copy to *(the descendants of)* Ptolemy (after 140 BCE, perhaps via Apellicon or even via a later Peripatetic making a copy of Apellicon's badly corrected version). Indeed, who believes that Ptolemy himself travelled from Alexandria to purchase the library? The king had nothing better to do in governing his kingdom than to go book-buying? Did he do his own laundry also? Surely, it was an agent, and if Athenaeus is speaking elliptically in Ptolemy's case, why not in Neleus' too?

Barnes might object and say that Strabo and Athenaeus would have reported the copies being made, which, if true, would again show Strabo offering the more plausible account. In short, the original of the *Dramatics* was taken to Scepsis, even if one version went to Alexandria, and the one from Scepsis was corrupted and then sold to Apellicon.

Whichever of the two ancient histories is more trustworthy and even if somehow the great library got some copy of the various scrolls including the *Dramatics* very early on, we can now determine that Zeller in

---

dria. If a book was found, it was taken to the library for a decision as to whether to return it or to confiscate it and replace it with a copy made on the spot (with an adequate compensation to the owner). Books acquired in that manner were designated "from the ships" ("Library of Alexandria," *Encyclopædia Britannica,* as of 9/27/18, online at:
https://www.britannica.com/topic/Library-of-Alexandria).

Appendix 2: The Transmission of the *Dramatics*

no way should have confidently asserted that "beyond doubt" a copy of the *Dramatics* was known to the Alexandrine grammarians. First, he has already stressed that a title existing on a list in general does not to establish what was contained in any given treatise and what the library had. Second, the earlier Alexandrians seemed to have had only the exoteric *On Poets/On "Musical" Composers* or some treatment that gave "Aristotelian concepts," as detailed by Francesca Schironi. She writes about the scholar Aristarchus of Samothrace (c. 217–145 BCE), who seems to have taken over as the head of the library in Alexandria after Aristophanes of Byzantium:

> If what I am going to argue is sound, Aristarchus knew what the philosopher [Aristotle] had said about the affinity between these two genres [epic and tragedy] *and therefore thought it legitimate to apply Aristotle's criteria for a good tragedy to epic poetry*. The Alexandrians knew some of the Aristotelian works, *and whether or not the Poetics was available to them, the dialogue On Poets, in which Aristotle discussed the same topics as in the Poetics, and the Homeric Problems were both known*... The *Poetics* in particular does not seem to have enjoyed great popularity in antiquity: *ancient sources are silent*, and the earliest quotation is in Porphyry [c. 234–305 CE]...
>
> As I hope to have shown, Aristarchus seems to have been aware of Aristotelian reflections on poetry. In his work on Homer, he uses Aristotelian categories and critical concepts.[220]

If the earlier Alexandrians, however, had the *Dramatics* and then tried to apply principles of good tragedy to epic, they had not read (or had not understood) from Chapter 23 onwards, when Aristotle contrasts the capabilities of each art form. Nor had they understood Chapter 25 and the very clear claim that different arts have different principles. Moreover, given that for Schironi the first reference to the *Dramatics*

---

220   Francesca Schironi. "Theory into Practice: Aristotelian Principles in Aristarchean Philology," *Classical Philology* 104 (2009), pp. 282, first paragraph, and 312; my italics.

is by Porphyry (of whom more shortly), about half a millennium after Aristotle's death, her statement "The *Poetics* ... does not seem to have enjoyed great popularity in antiquity" is either litotes, understatement for the sake of emphasis, or puts the matter so obliquely as to distort the reality. Besides, the "Aristotelian categories and critical concepts" did not include catharsis and the term never enters Schironi's examination. That is, there is absolutely no hint that the Alexandrians grasped the importance, or use by Aristotle, of catharsis. Rather, in speaking of *psuchagōgei*, the "enthrallment" that we saw Aristotle mentions in *Dramatics* 6 with respect to plot, Schironi further states:

> ...Aristarchus...never defines Homeric poetry as "useful" or remarks on the *sophia* [wisdom] of the poet. This can be seen in conjunction with the idea that Homer does not aim at *didaskalia* [instruction] but at *psuchagōgia*..." (p. 309).

Aristotle admired Homer, and, when discussing Homer and epic in Chapter 23, he states that composers should strive for its "proper pleasure." All of this is more consistent with the Alexandrians *not* having a copy of the *Dramatics* or, if they did have a copy, with it *not* having catharsis in the definition of tragedy and with a (proper) pleasure being correctly understood to be the aim of tragedy. Even if an Alexandrine copy of the *Dramatics* did have catharsis, the scholars either did not understand it or did not care to acknowledge it.

Thus, to explain Zeller's mistake, the Alexandrians had a similarly named book, not the *Dramatics,* and Zeller's mistake is identical to the one he made in thinking *peri poiētikēs* was the same exact book as *peri poiēseōs*. Tarán also reports the ancient passages showing how some post-2nd BCE scholars mixed up the *Dramatics* (*peri poiētikēs*) and *On "Musical" Composers* (*aka On Poets, peri poiētōn*).[221] Janko

---

221 Tarán, *op. cit.,* p 32. Moreover, the Arabic scholars until the 10th century had sometimes the same confusion; cf. Gutas (in Tarán and Gutas, *op. cit.*), p. 82-3. Gutas emphasizes that the titles always referred to our *Dramatics*, but he does not discuss to my knowledge whether the confusion affected

Appendix 2: The Transmission of the *Dramatics*

is another modern scholar perhaps most worthy of praise for advancing our understanding of the *Dramatics* and its further treatment in antiquity, despite him accepting like everyone else at his time (except for the followers of Petruševski concerning catharsis) that *tragōidia* is merely literary and that catharsis is legitimate in Chapter 6. Janko recounts, too, that the two treatises were mistaken for each other. He also adds, after analyzing some of the restored rolls of Philodemus [c. 110–c. 30 BCE] found in Herculaneum that had been buried by the eruption of Mount Vesuvius in 79 CE: "There is as yet no solid evidence that Philodemus, or indeed anybody until later antiquity, knew the *Poetics*."[222]

All of this seems to be additionally supported, if inadvertently, by Grote, who says, as a prefatory remark:

> What the Aristotelian Scholarchs, prior to Andronikus, chiefly possessed and studied, of the productions of their illustrious founder, were chiefly the *exoteric* or extra-philosophical and comparatively popular:—such as the **dialogues**; the legendary and historical collections; the facts respecting constitutional history of various Hellenic cities; *the variety of miscellaneous problems respecting Homer* and a number of diverse matters; the treatise on animals and on anatomy, &c. In the Alexandrine library (as we see by the Catalogue of Diogenes) there existed all

---

the scholars' interpretations of previous issues, be they from exoteric or esoteric texts, which could have made a huge difference. If catharsis were only mentioned in the early *exoteric* text, the dialogue, and the Arabic, Syriac, or Christian scholars did not distinguish the exoteric text from the later, *esoteric Dramatics*, they naturally would assume the term existed in the latter.

222   Philodemus' *On Poems and Aristotle's On Poets*, *Cronache ercolanesi*, 21 (1991), 5–64 at 64. Cf. *ADMC*, pp. 366ff, esp. ft. 526, for the fuller discussion. Below I mention more the recent developments, or shocking lack thereof, in the Herculaneum excavations. Who knows? Maybe the original version of the lost book on comedy or one of its few copies that survived to the 1st century BCE is entombed still in the unexcavated parts, one of which is thought to be the main part of the library.

these and several philosophical works also; but that library was not easily available for the use of the Scholarchs at Athens, who worked upon their own stock...[223]

Grote also explicates the very serious difficulties in the *Catalog* of Aristotle's work by Diogenes Laertius and the corpus as originated by Andronicus of Rhodes. They are shockingly different, and Grote can only resolve the oddities by appealing to Strabo's story and to Strabo's relationship with the others of the period. Grote concludes that Strabo "appears fully worthy of trust" (p. 38, *op. cit.*).

For the sake of rigor, though, let us play Devil's Advocate and leave aside the Alexandrians at the time of Aristarchus not mentioning catharsis, an omission that in and of itself seems to rule out an original *Dramatics* having catharsis in Chapter 6 being sold to Philadelphus (sometime during Neleus's life, around 280 to 246). Aristarchus died in 145 BCE and, if Strabo is correct, as appears to be the case, we calculated that Apellicon bought the library from Neleus' descendants about 130 BCE. This explains why Aristarchus did not have the "Aristotelian concept" of catharsis for his analyses. Any scroll with the term, or at least the *Dramatics*, was still in Scepsis.

Other factors favor Barnes' and Grote's confidence in Strabo, above and beyond Barnes' reliance on Posidonius and Strabo's professional acquaintanceship with Tyrannion. All of this supports the source of the archetype of the *Dramatics* ultimately coming from a badly patched original by Apellicon (or editors afterwards). It is improbable that Aristotle's private library had a copy while the original was in any library at the Lyceum that was the source of other copies. Who gives away their original and keeps a copy? More crucially, the current treatise, as Zeller well recognized, is mutilated and corrupted, *with interpolations and inversions*. That is:

- Chapter 12 is out of place, even if it belonged to the original,

---

[223] Grote, *op. cit.*, p. 39. My italics and boldfacing.

Appendix 2: The Transmission of the *Dramatics*

as I have shown it did.
- Chapters 13 and 14 could not have been written as is, as part of a single organic and continuous whole, because of the discrepancy of the best "serious dramas" and Aristotle having no concern with pity and fear in the ranking in Chapter 14.
- Chapter 15 on character, the second most important condition, is out of place, coming after a discussion of the choral aspects of Chapter 12; choral music-dance is only fifth in the list of ranked conditions in Chapter 6.
- Chapters 17 and 18 seem to be completely out of place, as Else recognized. Chapter 17 may well be the exoteric publication, or part of the publication, that Aristotle refers to at the end of Chapter 15. Chapter 18 has two sub-types of serious drama that are never discussed elsewhere, so must be interpolated (or there are *massive* sections of missing text).
- Chapter 20 is the *peri poiēseōs* (or at least part of it), on nouns and other grammar, and was interpolated after Chapter 19, which itself is legitimate but which actually says forms of language are *not* a concern of the *peri poiētikēs*.[224]

---

224 Despite his commendable 10-page examination of the inconsistencies of the *Dramatics* (op. cit., 1986, pp. 27-37) and while attempting to argue that the treatise *is* nevertheless a unified whole, Halliwell misses the problem of the last half of Chapter 19 and the evidence that Chapter 20 was interpolated from *peri poiēseōs*, along with a host of the other issues discussed in this book. This is why I can only consider that 10-page examination a whitewash, similar to his whitewash of Bernays. Granted, it is a much more sophisticated (and in many ways illuminating) whitewash than saying Bernays claimed the explanation of catharsis was lost (when, to emphasize, Bernays said someone purposefully cut out the explanation), but it is a whitewash all the same. There are so many points discussed, though, that I can only advise an interested reader to compare my points with Halliwell's, chapter by chapter. In a nutshell, his view of Aristotelian tragedy is a Gorgian, literary one; mine is a Diotiman, performance-based one. By understanding the more correct nature of drama (as something that necessarily has music and dance), the legitimate passages of the treatise cohere better, and we can better detect the inauthentic parts, especially once we see that Aristotle follows his own principles of definition in the definition of tragedy. Much else follows from this, but, again, a

Having a plausible but incorrect clause added to the definition of tragedy is perfectly in line with all of this. Furthermore, leaving aside the solution above that reconciles Athenaeus with Strabo, if Athenaeus is correct and a pristine copy of the *Dramatics* had been made or sold from Aristotle's private collection, it would not have all of the problems just listed.

To conclude the focus on the Alexandrians: As we have seen, starting with Demetrius of Phaleron the connection between the political and academic heads of the early library and the Peripatetics was very intimate. Whatever the accuracy of the history given above, which is obviously very limited, Alexandria may eventually have obtained a copy of the *Dramatics* through any number of unreported channels. Perhaps it came through Hermippus of Smyrna, who flourished in the middle and end of the 3rd century BCE and who Zeller speculates had control of Aristotle's and Theophrastus's library. However, the question then becomes whether this version of the treatise had the catharsis-clause or not, and the absolute agreement of all modern scholars, that no one until late antiquity speaks of catharsis in the *Dramatics per se* (as opposed to the exoteric *On Poets/On "Musical" Composers*), leaves us unable to prove the matter one way or the other. Nevertheless, if we can trust the limited history, then, given the philosophical doctrines, any version in Alexandria would have resulted from the corrections wrongly applied to the original found in the cellar of the descendants of Neleus, whether by Apellicon or his employees, or by any later Peripatetic, for any number of reasons. If we cannot trust the limited history, then anything goes, for *all* sides, given Barnes' report of the later commentators knowing that there was no "canon."

In addition, continuing to grant that Alexandria had a copy of the *Dramatics*, we have no way of knowing whether it was the version that helped form the archetype for the four branches of manuscripts, one

---

chapter-by-chapter comparison is necessary.

Appendix 2: The Transmission of the *Dramatics*

of which was copied into Syriac. The reasons follow. The library had two buildings, quite separated in distance. Caesar (and Cleopatra) inadvertently destroyed one when setting the shipyards on fire to get out of a trap by the Ptolemaic navy and army around 48 BCE, to the regret of Strabo.[225] The second building and its contents were completely destroyed by the Christians in 391 CE when they tried to extinguish paganism.[226] Thus, we can assert nothing about any copy that came from Alexandria, although we need to recall Strabo's caution about bad book copiers there.

Last but not least: If the Peripatetic school itself had a pristine version of the *Dramatics*, maybe the original that was used to make the copies sold to Ptolemy and to others, why the still-existing gaps, interpolations and inversions, which Zeller highlighted, even if he missed which parts were truly inversions or interpolations? *Would the book-buyer for Ptolemy or anyone else really accept a product that was missing sections of text, whether or not it came from Apellicon?* Would he not insist that the school which should know the doctrine fill in the

---

225 El-Abbadi speaks of:
...Plutarch, who, after a personal visit to Alexandria, explained that 'Caesar was forced to repel the danger by using fire, which spread from the dockyards and destroyed the Great Library'. Equally indicative is a statement by Strabo who, during a long stay in the city (*c.* 25–20 BCE), expressed in an indirect manner his regrets over the loss of that great library that had once supplied Eratosthenes and Hipparchus with the original reports of earlier discoveries, sources that were no longer there for him to consult (*op. cit.*, 2018).

226 El-Abbadi continues (*op. cit.*, 2018):
"When Christianity became the one and only religion acknowledged throughout the empire, Emperor Theodosius I in his zeal to wipe out all vestiges of paganism issued a decree in 391 sanctioning the demolition of temples in Alexandria. Empowered by the imperial decree, Theophilus, bishop of Alexandria, led an attack" on the daughter building. It was destroyed to its foundations and a church built on the ruins.

gaps, at least as much as prudent, before payment was made? *Was this perhaps why a Peripatetic himself and not Apellicon added the catharsis-clause?* Even a well-intentioned, later Peripatetic could easily have made a mistake, as the arguments in this Appendix and general accounts of manuscript corrections show, especially pertaining to the ones at the recent excavation and restoration projects at Herculaneum.[227]

When was the first copy of the *Dramatics* with *katharsis* in Chapter 6 known and where? The first reference to the *Dramatics* (as *peri poiētikēs*) was to a tiny phrase on word-play in the Antiatticist (180 CE) and to synonym in Porphyry (about 260-300 CE). Yet Janko himself believes that the first reference was to the second, lost book, *not* to our extant first book. I should add that the evidence about Porphyry comes not from Porphyry's own text, which is lost, but from a quotation in Simplicius. Yet Simplicius was one of the last Aristotelian commentators, if not the last, in the West because during his life, as we saw, Justinian closed the philosophy schools and banned drama around 528 CE. Indeed, given the Christians' desire to eradicate pa-

---

227   John Seabrook notes how scholars often made up their own text when filling in gaps of manuscripts or interpreting corrupted texts:
> Sometimes educated guesses about missing bits are wrong, causing the reader to arrive at different meanings from what was intended. One of the revelations following the Brigham Young MSI [multispectral imaging] studies was *how wrong* many of the earlier readings of the scrolls were. *Some editors were essentially making up their own texts* [my italics]. ("The Invisible Library: Can digital technology make the Herculaneum scrolls legible after two thousand years?," in *The New Yorker*, November 16, 2015. Also at:
> https://www.newyorker.com/magazine/2015/11/16/the-invisible-library

Seabrook also reports the devastating news of the recent unwillingness of the Italian and French government officials to give permission for the scrolls to be scanned further, depriving scholars of the possibility of discovering the doctrines of various ancient thinkers, at least for the foreseeable future.

Appendix 2: The Transmission of the *Dramatics*

ganism and its writings (recall the destruction of the daughter library of Alexandria about 140 years earlier), Justinian's moral police might well have destroyed any and all copies in his realm, the more important Eastern Roman Empire, also known as the Byzantine Empire. In the 4th century onwards, Rome, which was not even the capital any longer of the chaotic and secondary Western Roman Empire, was greatly weakened, being sacked, for example, twice within 40 years. It is impossible that scholarship and all or most book manuscripts survived, much less thrived, there during such times. We must look to a predominantly Muslim area (that contained the Christian Church of the East) to discover where the *Dramatics* with catharsis first gets described.

As Janko says:

> It is tantalizing to learn…that in c. 790 Timothy I, a Nestorian patriarch of Baghdad, was looking systematically for copies of the *Poetics*. He asked a colleague to enquire at St. Zenon's monastery for "the two books on the poets: For we have one of them." This is definitely a new testimony to the existence of *Poetics* Book II. Alas, the well-stocked library of this monastery at Ikalto in eastern Georgia was reputedly burned by the Persian shah 'Abbās I in 1616.[228]

However, this does not establish which book was held nor does it establish that the second book still existed at this point in time. Did Timothy I have the roll on comedy or on serious drama/epic? In a very detailed and illuminating examination, Gutas gives the reasons why the Arabic texts lead to no definite conclusion.[229] In any event, catharsis is not mentioned.

---

228 Richard Janko, *Book Reviews*, book review of Tarán and Gutas, *op. cit.*, in *Classical Philology* 108 (2013), 252–7; also found at http://www-personal.umich.edu/~rjanko/review%20Gutas%20&%20Tar%E1n.pdf,p. 4. My page number is to the version on the web.

229 Tarán and Gutas, *op. cit.*, p. 83-5.

I myself have no doubt that Aristotle wrote the second book and in fact argue that this is where the explanation of catharsis promised in *Politics* VIII 7 probably existed. Even if Timothy I, though, owned the first book, nothing follows about its pristine quality, and the location in Eastern Georgia suggests that any copy would have come originally from Alexandria via Syria, although it would not have been impossible for it to come from the much more distant Rome via Constantinople (or via Syria). Given the multitude of options, nothing can be established for sure concerning the authenticity of the definition of tragedy because of geography. In any event, even if catharsis was in Chapter 6 in the version that Timothy I owned, we have seen ample evidence that it would have been because the archetype, or the source for what Tarán and Gutas consider the archetype, had already been modified, probably between Apellicon's and Andronicus' time.

Speaking of location, given the residence in Baghdad of Timothy I, who died in 823, perhaps the key to the whole puzzle of when *katharsis* entered the *Dramatics* is shown by al-Fārābī (c. 872–950), the so-called "Second Aristotle." Al-Fārābī also spent a good portion of his life in Baghdad and may well have had access to the book that Timothy I refers to. Consider, though, how al-Fārābī himself describes the treatise and what he indicates for the goal of tragedy:

> ...This book is called *Poiētikē* in Greek, that is, the *Book of Poetry*...[230] Tragedy is a kind of poetry having a particular metre, affording *pleasure* to all who hear or recite it. In tragedy good things are mentioned... Musicians used to sing tragedies before kings, and whenever a king died, they would insert in the tragedy certain additional melodies lamenting the dead king... [my italics][231]

Pleasure instead of *katharsis* is recorded as the goal! Considering

---

230   al-Fārābī, *The Enumeration of the Sciences*, in Tarán and Gutas, as Test. 14, *op. cit.*, p. 94.
231   al-Fārābī, *Canons of the Arts of the Poets*, in Tarán and Gutas, as Test. 15, *op. cit.*, p. 94. Cf. *ADMC* pp. 527-8.

Appendix 2: The Transmission of the *Dramatics*

what we saw in Chapter 7, this reading is remarkably sound. The next discussion, by Avicenna, from about 1010-1030, is the first one having *katharsis*, which means that the word either replaced "pleasure" that al-Fārābī read or was found in a variant manuscript. We can narrow the answer, therefore, regarding when *katharsis* was added to the definition of tragedy to two options, either (1) to a corrupted manuscript from Scepsis that eventually made its way via Syriac and Arabic translations to Avicenna in Persia or (2) to a manuscript in, or from, Baghdad that was modified right after al-Fārābī, either to restore new damage or because religious sensibilities believed that *katharsis* would be more palatable than pleasure.

We should consider another factor. Absolutely no evidence exists that before the Arabic scholars there were multiple copies of Aristotle's *Dramatics* or, more importantly, multiple copies of a pristine copy of Chapter 6 (even if other chapters had been interpolated). There may have been only one copy stemming from Neleus, with corrections or additions, for centuries, just as there is only one original, fire-damaged copy of *Beowulf*, considered the "highest achievement of Old English literature and the earliest European vernacular epic," from c. 1000 CE.[232] One copy in over 1000 years!

The first clear-cut reference, then, to at least one scroll of the *Dramatics,* by someone who actally knew what was in the text after the histories of Strabo and Athenaeus, appears to be by Timothy I in 790 CE, but he says nothing about the contents, and it is debated whether it was in Greek or Syriac.[233] Al-Fārābī is the very first to say what was actually in the definition of tragedy, but he specifies pleasure and not catharsis as the goal.

---

232   The Editors of Encyclopaedia Britannica, "Beowulf: Old English Poem." At https://www.britannica.com/topic/Beowulf as of 11/5/18.

233   Tarán and Gutas, *op. cit.*, pp. 85ff.

Let us finish the brief history of the four branches of manuscripts, a history that comes almost entirely from Tarán and Gutas.[234] Manuscript A, from about the second half of the 10th century, seems unquestionably to have come to Italy in the 1400's from Constantinople. However, we have no idea whether Constantinople received it from St. Zenon's monastery or Baghdad or somewhere else. It is unclear how the Italians got Manuscript B, but Tarán and Gutas derive it, along with A and with the version that William of Moerbeke used, from a (lost) manuscript, which they call Xi. Xi itself came directly from the (lost) archetype that they call Omega. This accounts for three of the branches. The sibling of Xi is what they call Sigma, which is the "witness" that generates the last branch, namely, the Syriac translation, itself responsible for both the Arabic translations (used by Avicenna in Baghdad and Averroes in Spain) and the version that Herman the German used. Herman got access to his manuscript in Toledo and he credits the Saracens for assistance. (At the time Toledo was one of great learning centers, with peaceful interaction between Arabs, Christians and Jews.[235])

To emphasize, no precise date can be given for the creation of the archetype Omega, but, as noted, Tarán and Gutas estimate 700-900 years after Aristotle, which means 400-600 CE.

SUMMARY OF THE TRANSMISSION OF THE LIBRARY

The Peripatetics After Neleus

No Peripatetic (or anyone else for at least 1000 years after Aristotle, until Timothy I and then al-Fārābī) seems to have had any concern for the theory in the *Dramatics* and its definition of tragedy. Indeed, even

---

234   *Op. cit.*, Chapter 3 and especially the *stemma* on p. 159.
235   Cf. Rebecca Gould, "The *Poetics* from Athens to al-Andalus: Ibn Rushd's Grounds for Comparison," *Modern Philology*, 112.1 (2014): 1-24, espec. p. 1; cf. *ADMC*, p. 538-40.

Appendix 2: The Transmission of the *Dramatics*

Theophrastus does not seem to have cared about the dramatic theory in Aristotle's treatise.

The Alexandrians

The Alexandrians, especially the earlier ones who would have been very sympathetic to Peripatetic thought, in no way suggest that catharsis was the end of "poetry" and in fact seem to have no awareness of the concept insofar as it relates to Aristotle's *Dramatics*.[236] Instead, as we saw with Aristarchus, the end of epic and by extension of tragedy was *psuchagōgei* (enthrallment), which we find legitimately in *Dramatics* 6. That is, given how Aristotle says in Chapter 23 that epic imparts, like tragedy, its proper pleasure, and given that Aristotle uses the same word (*psuchagōgei*) in Chapter 6 (1450a33) in saying what the recognition and reversals of plot provide us, it would be stunning that Aristarchus ignores catharsis, were it truly functioning as, or in lieu of, the "proper pleasure" of tragedy. Obviously, if Ptolemy had purchased the library, including the *Dramatics*, by 246 BCE, or if a copy of the *Dramatics* came via another route, Aristarchus would have had decades during his adult life (about 200-143 BCE) to familiarize himself with the doctrine.

Moreover, we saw that Athenaeus says Ptolemy purchased the library *with the books from Athens*, strongly suggesting Neleus and the library were not in Athens. Even Athenaeus might allow, then, that the library was in Scepsis. In any event, the library would have been packed, moved or shipped, and unpacked three separate times over the course of approximately 38 to 75 years: Aristotle to Theophrastus, Theophrastus to Neleus, wherever he was based after Theophrastus' death in 287, and Neleus to Ptolemy. It is hard to imagine that the

---

236 For reasons I did not go into in this Appendix, the Alexandrians had already begun conceiving of tragedy as a literary genre rather than a fully performed theatrical one, which might have persuaded some of them that musical catharsis as discussed in the *Politics* was irrelevant to purely literary creation; cf. *ADMC* pp. 342-4; 526.

library was pristine when any scrolls were finally unrolled in the great library. Besides, Athenaeus had to have been speaking elliptically, because it is inconceivable that Ptolemy himself had personally travelled to buy the books and thus it is probable Athenaeus also meant, like Strabo, that it was the descendants of Neleus who sold a copy (via any intermediary like Apellicon) and not Neleus himself.

At any rate, because of the importance of Peripatetic thought for the early librarians, I granted that *somehow and through some means* a copy of the *Dramatics* got to Alexandria even after Aristarchus, who seemingly only had the dialogue On Poets/On "Musical" Composers. However, because of the two buildings of the library burning down, it is very questionable whether a pristine copy of at least the definition of tragedy survived from Alexandria into later times, although of course a copy could have been made and sent elsewhere. We saw, however, that Strabo remarked on the bad copyists that even Alexandria had. In any event, to emphasize, absolutely no evidence exists that *katharsis* occurred in any copy that the library had.

Worst of all, on the hypothesis that Athenaeus recounts the true history, one or more pristine copies spawning other (relatively) pristine copies would have had two results. First, the manuscripts we have would not have all the gaps, interpolations, and inversions that they have. Second, many scholars could, and would, have read about Aristotelian catharsis in tragedy in Hellenistic and later times. Yet there is absolutely no evidence that anyone until the Arabic scholars over a full millenium after Aristotle's demise, including the neo-Platonists and Simplicius, had a notion of catharsis in the *Dramatics*. At the most, it was catharsis in the *early exoteric dialogue* that they knew.

Posidonius, Strabo and Plutarch

Apart from their sheer numbers and from their confirming each other, it is probable that Posidonius, Strabo, and Plutarch correctly describe how Aristotle's library got transmitted. Zeller, Grote, Barnes and I

Appendix 2: The Transmission of the *Dramatics*

support their view, and Tarán's rejection of Strabo was shown to be completely flawed. I also gave an account in which Athenaeus was speaking elliptically, making him consistent with Strabo *et al*, but this still confirms the poor reconstruction of the library from Scepsis because of the mutilated and corrupt versions we have.

Andronicus and any "Canon"

Andronicus took the copy or copies that he had and, with very minimal editing at the most, organized the major works in the corpus that is *now* called the "canon" by some. Whether Andronicus is responsible for the interpolations and inversions that exist in our *Dramatics* or whether he "merely" organized the whole corpus that included as one whole treatise the already corrupt *Dramatics* is impossible to say, although the textual evidence suggests that someone previously edited the definition of tragedy. That is, Andronicus reportedly organized the texts as opposed to edited them. Thus, the editor who interpolated *katharsis* in the definition of tragedy probably was Apellicon (or his hired hand), Hermippus, or a Peripatetic scribe patching whatever gaps could be reasonably filled from the damaged original to "perfect" the philosophy or to get payment from other Peripatetics, Ptolemy or anyone else. I stress that the problems could have been caused by different individuals. One editor may have inserted the catharsis-clause and Andronicus may have kept it while combining some of the papyrus, whether they were in scrolls or not, as mere fragments, into the order we now have in the *Dramatics*. In other words, Andronicus may well have inherited the interpolated catharsis-clause and himself combined, say, Chapters 17, 18, and 20 with the other texts.

Barnes confirms that the later Aristotelian commentators (living at least 200 years after Andronicus) knew of the differences in the copies of a particular work in Aristotle's corpus. It was taken for granted by the commentators that they were rarely, if ever, perusing the one and only authentic scroll by the Master. They knew different manuscripts had different words and they assumed that it was equally possible they were reading a corrected or damaged copy. That is, they gave no absolute priority to the selection that Andronicus considered the canon, and even if they did, this in no way shows that catharsis in *Dramatics* 6 was legitimate, considering all of the aforementioned problems and explanations.

Philodemus and the Neo-Platonists

Any (of the very few) possible references to *Aristotelian* catharsis by Philodemus, who lived at the same time as Andronicus, and by the neo-Platonists, who thrived over four centuries later, are clearly, at best, to the *dialogue* that was the youthful, exoteric work of Aristotle's, when he was still greatly under the sway of Plato. Yet the Athenian himself was a proponent of catharsis in many areas of his thought. I have shown, for example, in *ADMC* the similarity in utility of catharsis for both the Northern Greek and Plato in the sacred rites or when dealing when Corybantism, and without question, the neo-Platonist Proclus speaks of catharsis as being also relevant *to comedy* for Plato's star pupil. *To emphasize, there is no reference to catharsis in our Dramatics until the Arabic commentators.*

Possible Christian Destruction or Modification

Simplicius himself seems to have had no copy of the *Dramatics*, and after him the Roman and Byzantine empires went dark concerning drama until the Arabic scholars and then the discoveries of the Greek manuscripts in the 1400's in Italy. Surely, anyone who owned a copy of the *Dramatics* under Justinian after the bans on both drama and on paganism, if they were brave enough to keep the book knowing what the Christians did to the daughter library at Alexandria, would have kept it well hidden and would have discussed it in whispers, at best.

This topic deserves more exploration. After Simplicius, it is obvious why any scrolls in the Eastern Roman Empire might have been destroyed, kept private *or modified*. Under Justinian's extreme repression, an emphasis on catharsis rather than on pleasure would be more

Appendix 2: The Transmission of the *Dramatics*

compatible with Christian religous doctrine and might allow the work to survive. Otherwise, with the original goal, the treatise almost surely would have been cast into the fire as reprehensible pagan influence. We should not forget that the Christians acted more like the Taliban at times than the gentle Jesus or at least that the Christians happily impersonated Jesus driving the merchants out of the temple with a whip.

The Arabic Influence

Al-Fārābī, the "Second Aristotle" residing in Baghdad, is the very first person in history to write about the definition of tragedy *and he notes that pleasure is the goal.* Catharsis is not even recognized. It is in Persia a few generations later that Avicenna first tries to explain both the definition of tragedy and the clause with catharsis, pity and fear, but he relies on an Arabic translation that came from a Syriac one, hardly a recipe for authentic doctrine. Moreover, he finds *katharsis* so baffling that he simply ignores it. Averroes over a hundred years later translates it in a way that, on the surface, makes philosophical sense of Aristotle's ethical views (as "moderation") but that is impossible as a meaning of *katharsis* in ancient Greek. We saw already how Manuscripts A and B have discrepancies in their definitions of tragedy, with *mathēmatōn* ("learnings") in the former and *pathēmatōn* ("sufferings" or "emotions") in the latter, reminding us of Barnes' words that there was no true canon but differences in the various manuscripts that the commentators like Alexander of Aphrodisias (c. 200 CE) took for granted as the normal state of affairs.

One Final Option

We have now examined the ancient histories along with, for instance, Zeller's take on them, including his mistakes (which should not impugn all of his work because there is still much of value). I can now handle one final objection, which came to me right before publication in private correspondence from a specialist of ancient Greek philosophy. He also recalls Zeller:

> Zeller in *Aristotle and the Earlier Peripatetics* ... collects a lot of impressive evidence. *What was found at Skepsis must have been Aristotle's personal copies, which Andronicus used to correct existing texts.* At least that seems to be the more plausible story. If so, the catharsis passage cannot be so easily dismissed.

First, some of Zeller's evidence was completely misinterpreted by Zeller himself, as we saw, and Zeller missed, e.g., that Chapter 20 was interpolated and had a different title. Second, to jump to the end of the private correspondence's "more plausible story" for the moment, the catharsis passage is not "easily" dismissed. Two rigorous chapters of *ADMC* that include a comprehensive rebuttal of four sets of counter-arguments by one of the acknowledged experts in the world, Stephen Halliwell, demonstrate that the catharsis-phrase is absolutely untenable philosophically. The rigorous demonstration of the illegitimacy of the catharsis-phrase holds no matter which interpretation of *katharsis* one accepts and notwithstanding that pity and fear *in the middle chapters* are legitimate. Third, as revealed in this Appendix, copies of the "in-demand" manuscripts of Aristotle's esoteric works were known or made after the library was restored and returned to the Peripatetics from Scepsis. However, why would at least two copies of each manuscript have existed? If no one cared to comment on the *Dramatics*, then presumably they did not consider it important. In this case, there was no reason to pay for a copyist to replicate it. Alternatively, if they did not consider it important simply because they never viewed it, there may have been only one version of the *Dramatics* until Andronicus or later, and whichever editor modified it set the doctrine for 2000 years.

To re-emphasize a point made regarding Tarán, the more copies that existed, the more likely that commentators would have read the *Dramatics*. Yet the history of even the earliest references to just *a few words that were supposedly in the original treatise* entails just the opposite. Janko, Zeller, Schironi, and Veloso cite Porphyry on syn-

Appendix 2: The Transmission of the *Dramatics*

onym about 260-300 CE, and Janko and Veloso cite the so-called Antiatticist on a very tiny phrase on word-play about 180 CE. The discussion of both topics may have occurred in the book on comedy, because a discussion of synonym does *not* exist in the *Dramatics*.[237] I grant Janko the point about the Antiatticist, if only for the sake of argument, yet I have shown above in the *Comments* of Chapter 20 that there is a very good chance the definition of synonym was already given in *Rhetoric* III 2 and that the references to the other topics discussed in the *peri poiētikēs* are satisfied with the solution I give. That solution, though, shows parts of the *Rhetoric* on metaphor coming from the original *Dramatics*, all of which means, yet again, that the treatises got jumbled at some point in time, with Strabo's account giving the plausible events. One *could* even posit that Andronicus had four pristine copies, all with catharsis, to handle all four branches of manuscripts. This still, however, does not resolve the important problem, and in fact would exacerbate it, why *no one* in Western Europe until Renaissance times remarks on having read the treatise. To emphasize, the more copies that existed, the more likely that somebody would have read and commented on the *Dramatics*.

Furthermore, regarding the Antiatticist, especially since the second roll is lost, there is no guarantee that whoever had the roll on comedy had the roll on serious drama *or vice-versa*, about 460 years after the library was seemingly put into Neleus' descendants' trench in at least some disorder. If drama was unimportant for the Peripatetics after Theophrastus, then any version of the rolls could have vanished as fast as the hundreds of junk books that one sees in Strand Bookstore in New York City or at any bookstore with remaindered items, selling for 25 cents each,—or not selling even for that price, because one needs space to store books and it is not only their acquisition cost that we consider when deciding whether to purchase a volume. Probably this remark is melodramatic (although very fitting on a treatise that deal

---

237   Cf. *ADMC*, p. 526.

with *melos* and drama) and surely the rolls were worth more than the equivalent of 25 cents, but how else do we explain the lack of any commentary on *Dramatics* 1-26 until Al-Fārābī—*1200 years after Aristotle!*—and the loss of the second book? If Andronicus really had a pristine private copy of the manuscripts to correct multiple copies, then presumably he made *multiple copies of the second roll on comedy*, too. Yet, the second roll appears to be completely gone (except, in my view, perhaps the categorization of jests that survives to some extent in the *Tractatus Coisilianus*[238]).

Finally, if there had been more than one copy of the authentic *Dramatics*, including an original that Andronicus used to correct or make additional copies, why did Philodemus and the neo-Platonists Proclus and Iamblichus not know about the treatise in some detail? Philodemus by implication and Proclus explicitly refer to Aristotle's youthful "dialogue" in discussing how catharsis is used by Aristotle against his mentor in both serious drama *and* comedy but they never refer to the *Dramatics*.[239] Of all points, this might be the most influential, proving that the *Dramatics* had only one, or a couple, essentially unknown

---

238   Cf. *ADMC*, pp. 369, 407; and 491-5.

239   Iamblichus does not mention Aristotle's name. Janko reports Philodemus speaking of catharsis in Fragment 46 (for the *On Poets/On "Musical" Dramatists*). However, the passage does not have catharsis *of pity and fear*. Rather it has "the art (of poetry) is something useful with a view to virtue, purifying, as we said, the (irrational) part (of the soul) [Janko's conjecture for "virtue," "irrational" and "of the soul" result from gaps in the manuscript] (Janko, *op. cit.*, 2011, p. 447).

If, however, the goal of "poetry" or "dramatic 'musical' composition" were virtue for the mature Aristotle, why no mention of the subject in any way whatsoever in the tract in which he examines virtue most deeply, the *Nicomachean Ethics,* and notably in III 10, in which he discusses people taking extravagant delight in painting, music and in the theater? There it is a *moderate aesthetic pleasure* that theater- and art-lovers should be concerned with, which is probably the reason that Averroes translated *katharsis* as "moderation." Cf. *ADMC* p. 476 and Chapter 4, in which virtue is not the best end of "music" although it can be an end for music used as education for children.

Appendix 2: The Transmission of the *Dramatics*

versions for a very long time, at least in Western European circles. Given that there might have been only one copy for 700-1200 years, with a new one created only when the older one was crumbling, it would have taken only one editor to interpolate the catharsis-clause to spawn the whole tradition with the four branches.

Considering that the extant manuscripts have gaps, interpolations and inversions, as emphasized by Zeller himself, to whom the modern scholar at hand appeals, it hardly seems plausible to contend that Andronicus *corrected* any bad copy with a pristine original. If anything, he had the badly edited version that came from the original that itself had been corrupted in Scepsis. Using that, Andronicus corrected the copies as much as he could, but either added or left in the catharsis-clause. He certainly left in the inversions, interpolations and some gaps. Again, though, Andronicus is reported not to have edited, merely to have organized the corpus, but I assume that he might have done a little editing in accomplishing his overall task. If he only organized, however, then he simply kept the corrections that the previous editor(s) had made, for good or for bad.

Thus, the hypothesis that Andronicus had a pristine copy of the *Dramatics* with *katharsis* that was used to correct other copies (or to make them), does not come close to withstanding scrutiny.

FINAL SUMMARY AND CONCLUSION

The evidence supporting Posidonius, Strabo and Plutarch on the topic of the library in Scepsis is overwhelming, if necessarily circumstantial. The fact that a few handfuls of the more popular esoteric Aristotelian works were copied and distributed from Theophrastus to Andronicus, and even later, is no counter-evidence to Strabo. More importantly, there is absolutely no ground for thinking that the original, pristine

---

Also, in *ADMC* Chapter 7, I demonstrate that a "(proper) pleasure" is the real goal of tragedy and epic throughout the *Dramatics*.

Dramatics survived into the Renaissance in Rome and Byzantium, and there is a good chance most of the second book on comedy had already been eaten by moths by the time of Apellicon. He was probably left with a few fragments like the categorization of jests that eventually became incorporated into, e.g., the *Tractatus Coisilianus*.

The full history until Avicenna also gives absolutely no evidence—*not one iota*—for the authenticity of catharsis in the *Dramatics as distinct from* the early *On Poets/On "Musical" Composers*. *Proclus is the only one in over 1200 years, until the Arabic scholars, to explicitly connect Aristotle to catharsis in the context of dramatic theory but at best Proclus' reference is to the early dialogue.*

Consequently, given the history of Posidonius, Strabo, and Plutarch; given that al-Fārābī is the very first to speak of the definition of tragedy but with pleasure, quite correctly, as the goal; and given the philosophical considerations *that Tarán shies purposefully away from*,[240] we must conclude that catharsis, pity and fear were incorrectly added into the "mutilated and corrupt" treatise that we possess. In brief, the paleography, even though unanimous in terms of the occurrence of catharsis (but not in terms of the whole catharsis-clause) in all four branches, is unanimous *because of an initial corruption*. The unanimity, therefore, in no way proves the authenticity of catharsis as the goal

---

240 For example, Tarán says "...nor do I ask if he [Aristotle] is consistent in his views or not, etc." (*op. cit.*, p. 221). This is convenient for Tarán because then he does not have to handle the very serious issue of biological division being the process of defining tragedy, with no instance of catharsis, pity and fear appearing in the introductory divisions. Nor does he have to handle Aristotle stating repeatedly that (proper) pleasure and the like are the goal(s) of tragedy. Nor does he have to deal with the complete lack of explanation of catharsis in our treatise, contrary to the promise of *Politics* VIII 7, along with a host of other important matters. Such an approach does the *philosopher* Aristotle a very grave disservice. Unlike Greek dramatists or literary figures, for whom consistency was not as crucial as creativity and style, consistency was extremely important for the founder of logic.

Appendix 2: The Transmission of the *Dramatics*

of all tragedy and cannot outweigh the overwhelming evidence to the contrary.

This Appendix explains very reasonably when, how, and by whom the catharsis-clause was interpolated. *Why* the exact words "catharsis, pity and fear" were written as the goal of tragedy was given at the beginning of this Appendix: catharsis comes out of a later editor's plausible appeal to Aristotle's youthful work and *Politics* VIII 7; similarly with pity and fear, which are legitimate for one (if only one) plot-type in Chapter 13. Even if, however, Apellicon or any hired hands did not interpolate the catharsis-clause before releasing the modified versions to the Peripatetics (or to anyone else), once the library was known to have been edited poorly, as Strabo reports, any number of later Peripatetics, or someone after al-Fārābī in Baghdad, trying to make sense of a gap in the definition of tragedy, might have felt professionally obliged to add the "final cause" to ameliorate the damage and to enlighten future readers. If any editor was working with the only copy that survived, or at least the one that became the basis for other copies, catharsis becomes entrenched, no pun intended, in the *Dramatics*.

Obviously, those other copies were very few in number until the Renaissance, perhaps from lack of interest but also in large part from Christian repression, proof of which is that the work was simply not known in antiquity or Byzantine times. It generated no interest even if read or, because unknown, it did not even get read. In any event, fewer copies meant fewer readers. Maybe one of the few copies or the only copy (with the corruptions) made it to Alexandria and then, before the library was destroyed, to Syria. Whatever the route, and whether or not through Alexandria, either a version by Apellicon or a copy stemming from the one that al-Fārābī read, with modifications, became the source for our four branches of manuscripts. Because the catharsis-clause seemed relatively plausible, all subsequent copyists kept it, even if many did not fully understand it and, for example, continued to use the word *mathēmatōn* ("learnings") rather than *pathēmatōn* ("sufferings") next to *katharsis*.

Halliwell's attempted defense of the treatise being a unified whole confirms that Andronicus or anyone else was not completely foolish and had some reason to think that the texts all belong together, in the current sequence. I trust, however, that the arguments of this *Primer* and of *ADMC* demonstrate that Zeller and others had the more accurate appraisal. The *Dramatics* is hopelessly mutilated and corrupt, even if completely Aristotelian. The parts taken independently, nevertheless, are still valuable. Your mother's diamond necklace may have broken apart and some of its diamonds are in a jewelry box with assorted rubies and pieces of gold. That box, needless to say, still has very valuable contents and should be kept, even if the original necklace is lost.

Epilogue

A little knowledge can be dangerous. A lot of knowledge can be, and in this case was, outright fatal to Petruševski's argument that *katharsis* is inauthentic in *Dramatics* 6. In defending the status quo, *even if it is wrong*, scholars can metaphorically pile as many books on an intellectual revolutionary as the heavy stones that the agents of the Salem witch trials piled on Giles Corey to suffocate him because he denounced the trials (as represented somewhat authentically in Arthur Miller's *The Crucible*).

I say "metaphorically" because no real book was piled onto the modern Macedonian's paper editions. That is, not one attempted rebuttal of his publications was ever printed (to my knowledge). Rather, the private thoughts and conversations of almost all of the specialists of the *Dramatics* of his and the following generation rejected or ignored his view (the two exceptions being António Freire in 1969 and Teddy Brunius in 1973[241]). In effect, the specialists buried Petruševski's view

---

241 António Freire, "A Catarse Tragica em Aristoteles," *Euphrosyne*,

Appendix 2: The Transmission of the *Dramatics*

not in a trench but among the approximately 100,000,000 books in the world that existed by the turn of the millenium (and this may not even take into account articles). The renowned American specialist of the *Dramatics,* Gerald Else, could hardly have been ignorant of Petruševski's views in the 1950's and 1960's, yet Else surprisingly never acknowledges Petruševski's revolutionary stance. As alluded to earlier, to their credit Tarán and Gutas do mention his work and show respect for him. However, to their discredit and, one might say, to their shame, they do not even acknowledge him emphatically denying that Aristotle could have written *katharsis* in the definition of tragedy when they assert that there is *no doubt* that Aristotle wrote the word. If I had not stumbled in the mid-1990's by pure chance upon the remarks about Petruševski by Brunius, perhaps the modern Macedonian would be entirely unknown to Anglo-American philosophers of the 21st century.

Readers may be curious about the more recent developments and whether the view that I champion fares any better than that of Petruševski. A URL for *Errata & Updates* is given in the front of this book to take advantage of digital resources that writers for papyrus or Gutenberg-type presses never had. The link will be periodically updated and will give the most up-to-date summary of the debate that Petruševski began, including reviews of *ADMC* (of which more later) and of this *Primer*, perhaps with replies to those reviews or to misguided criticisms. Correct criticism, and how it impacts my major conclusions, if at all, will also be included, so that this book and the website function almost like a blog or at least function more interactively than books and readers historically interacted, a phenomenon that Plato complained about (a book without the author could not answer any questions the reader had).

---

3 (Lisbon, Portugal: Universidade de Lisboa/Centro de Estudos Clássicos) 1969. Teddy Brunius, "Catharsis," in P. Wiener (ed.), *Dictionary of the History of Ideas*, Vol. 1 (New York, 1973) 264–70 at 270. Cf. *ADMC*, p. 354.

I provide now, then, only a very brief account of the recent developments until right before the publication of this *Primer* in early 2019. The short of it is that my publication from 2003 (*op. cit.*) and Veloso's own publication in 2007 (*op. cit.*) started broadcasting Petruševski's position again, even though both Veloso and I argue that Petruševski did not go far enough in athetizing only *katharsis*. He left pity and fear in the definition of tragedy, without recognizing the grave inconsistencies that result. Based on the two articles (from *Oxford Studies*), some scholars have welcomed Veloso's and my solution to the seemingly unresolvable problem of the meaning of *katharsis* in the definition, accepting the word as illegitimate. A subset of those scholars additionally buy our arguments that pity and fear had also been wrongly interpolated, although others want to keep those two emotions as being critical to all tragedies for the Northern Greek, notwithstanding their agreement with us on *katharsis*.

Other scholars, especially those who have published on Aristotle's treatise and whose reputation and book royalties are at stake, like Heath, Janko, Tarán and Gutas, have been completely silent in public, perhaps hoping that the new, revolutionary position will eventually disappear, as Petruševski's almost did. About a handful of yet other scholars have responded in writing, most with a peripheral remark or two and some with a few, extremely brief paragraphs that can hardly be counted as arguments, much less rigorous arguments. Only one scholar, Halliwell in 2011 (*op. cit.*), as of the publication of this *Primer* has had the curiosity, intellectual courage and professional integrity to try to answer in the requisite detail the arguments from *Oxford Studies*, even if his excellent answer ultimately fails in our opinion (and I emphasize the "if," because readers of this book, *ADMC* Chapter 6, and Veloso's new *Pourquoi*, 2018, with additional reasons by Marwan Rashed in its Preface, will determine whether Veloso, Rashed and I have solidly rebutted Halliwell's answer or not).

Finally, rather than resort to silence or to legitimate argumentation

Appendix 2: The Transmission of the *Dramatics*

based on the ancient texts, a final group of scholars has stunningly resorted to *ad hominem* attacks because Veloso and I would dare question the authenticity of *katharsis* in the definition of tragedy. For example, William Marx, a French scholar, has called Veloso and myself "terrorists" (cf. Veloso and Rashed, 2018, pp. 10 & 376). Pierre Somville, a French specialist of the *Dramatics*, has said that Veloso merely tries to draw attention to himself in Veloso's own article in *Oxford Studies in Ancient Philosophy* in 2007 (cf. Veloso, 2018, pp. 10 & 377). Others have cast similar aspersions, if not as extreme. These are insults, I gather, from desperate individuals foreseeing ignominy, oblivion, or at least loss of respect for their own previous work on the *Dramatics*.

The insults were perhaps predictable, if still deplorable, given the status that Veloso and I had when we published in *Oxford Studies*, as "outsiders" who were not well-known around the world and who had no tenured positions at globally top-ranked universities in ancient philosophy. However, anyone who paid attention to our biographies and bibliographies would have known we came from prestigious Ph.D. programs, had been hired by well-respected universities, and had previously published with world-class houses. It is one thing to be bicycle mechanics, as the Wright brothers were, and to be ignored by the press and the military because even the Ph.D.'s in aeronautical engineering at the time had all been failing themselves in trying to fly (it was not until the French press called the brothers prevaricators and asked for proof that the aviators showed to the world that they could control a plane for more than a few seconds, four years after Kitty Hawk, and in France, not in the USA). It is another thing, and not very prudent, I dare say, to disdainfully ignore the research of scholars who, for whatever reason, were simply not renowned in 2008, after Veloso corrected one of my arguments from *Oxford Studies* but added weight to my whole position with his own article in the world-class publication. At any rate, history will have the final verdict.

Speaking of *Oxford Studies*, Somville especially has been disrespectful of David Sedley, the editor who published both my article and Veloso's. Sedley is one of the finest specialists of ancient Greek philosophy in the last 40 years. By stating curtly and with no supporting counter-argument to Veloso's article itself that Veloso *only published to draw attention to himself*, Somville implies that Sedley published an article (by Veloso) that is mere self-aggrandizement or that Sedley could not distinguish between self-aggrandizement and serious, legitimate scholarship! This is *miaron* (disgusting) and Somville, implicitly and with very poor judgment, insults not only those associated with *Oxford Studies* but the scholars who Veloso explicitly followed, if only in part, all the way back to Petruševski and Smerdel.

Rashed, who, again, writes the *Preface* to Veloso's newest work (*op. cit.*, 2018), is from the Sorbonne and, unlike Veloso and myself, *is* one of the most known *and* respected specialists of ancient Greek philosophy in the world. As alluded to in this *Primer* and as detailed in the Post-Postscript of *ADMC* 6, he has called out the recent *ad hominem* arguments for what they are. More importantly, he has also published in 2016 (*op. cit.*) reasons why Aristotle could not have written *katharsis* in the definition of tragedy. Given Rashed's stature, it is inconceivable (to me) that the previous name-calling and arguments *ad hominem* will continue. Those who have written (or not) on the *Dramatics* and who find the illegitimacy of *katharsis* too hard to believe either will have to stay silent or will have to attempt, like Halliwell, to rebut professionally the arguments of the followers of Petruševski. *This* is how philosophy that best cares about understanding Aristotle proceeds.

I should emphasize, though, that Rashed in 2016 only followed the modern Macedonian in arguing that *katharsis* was wrongly interpolated. Both thinkers keep pity and fear, but this was shortly before my *ADMC* first appeared and Rashed did not know, therefore, my most recent, fuller arguments (in *ADMC* 6), demonstrating that pity (and

Appendix 2: The Transmission of the *Dramatics*

sometimes fear) are excluded *by Aristotle* from a number of plot-types of "tragedy" in *Dramatics* 2-18. The future will determine whether Rashed comes to agree with me on this topic or whether he devises a solution that keeps the two emotions in the definition, a solution that can handle my evidence to the contrary. (Veloso has slightly different arguments for why pity and fear are not legitimate in the definition, and it is unclear to me whether Rashed is now partial to them.)

More details on all of this, including the respective book citations, are given in *ADMC*,[242] but, as a tangential remark and leaving aside *melos* (music-dance) *per se*, I wonder whether academic scholarship is more melodramatic at times than the subject we have been examining in this book!

In 2016, the first edition of my *ADMC* appeared when Veloso submitted his final draft of *Pourquoi* to Vrin Press. Because of publishing delays, his book only appeared in September of 2018, at the same time that I coincidentally published my second edition of *ADMC* in order to correct some editing and formatting issues of the first edition. (As an aside, the reader may be interested in hearing that redoing editions is one of the advantages of the Print On Demand technology that I am leveraging. Because of its flexibility and speed, and because of other reasons briefly explained below on p. 259, footnote 206, I will never allow Cambridge University Press or any other publisher that does not have an ethical recusal policy to control my work again.)

Even though Veloso and I give, e.g., different reasons for pity and fear being illegitimate in Chapter 6, those reasons may be complementary. Resolving, though, all of this and any other current difference in interpretation of Aristotle and Plato is a task for the future.

---

242   *ADMC*, pp. 453-6; cf. also Veloso, *op. cit.*, 2018, pp. 376-7, especially the footnotes.

For the first review of Veloso's new book (Oct. 3, 2018), and more details on the recent (and perhaps still on-going) cultural and intellectual "competition," see:

> https://www.nonfiction.fr/articlecomment-9562-la-poetique-daristote-sans-la-catharsis.htm

The review, by Hicham-Stéphane Afeissa, is in French, but translation programs will give a basic, if occasionally incorrect, understanding for those who do not read French.

For any English reviews of *ADMC*, one of which to my knowledge is in progress, see the following URL (which is case-sensitive at least for the html page):

> http://www.epspress.com/ADMCupdates.html

To conclude, justice is long overdue for those like Petruševski and Smerdel, at least with respect to *katharsis*. Given the arguments here and in *ADMC*, true Aristotelians would wisely protect the 26 chapters and not the one tiny phrase with catharsis, pity and fear that continues to cause the Northern Greek's legitimate theory in the rest of the treatise to be buried like manuscripts in a moist and smelly trench. That generation after generation of scholars could have been mistaken is easily shown. Simply ask how many of them even considered Aristotle to be following the Diotiman meaning of *poiēsis*, when the explanation in the *Symposium* has been within arm's reach since (at least) the Renaissance and when that meaning dissolves immediately a number of the paradoxes that have generated shelf after shelf of convoluted commentaries on the *Dramatics* for over 465 years.

I rest my case.

(Corrective) Glossary

This book is designed to be used in tandem with traditional translations or commentaries, some of which have full glossaries that also cover the fine-grained points that I leave aside in this book. Thus, I only include here the basic terms that previous scholars have misconstrued, emphasized in a different manner, or ignored.

Actor: See *hypokritēs*.

Composer (creator/producer): See *poiētēs*.

Diotiman (narrow) sense of *poiēsis*: See *poiēsis*.

Epic (*epopoiia*, literally, the making of the epic): Usually translated in this context as "epic poetry," which is anachronistic for Plato and Aristotle and which suggests only verse (in hexameter) when it was at least usually song (in hexameter). The *epopoios* (epic-maker) created or sang the verse and in early times accompanied himself with a lyre. Until at least Plato and Aristotle, he also gesticulated and dramatized with facial and vocal expressions (cf. Plato's *Ion* and *Dramatics* 3 & 26). See *rhapsodos* (rhapsode) also.

Gorgian sense of *poiēsis*: see *poiēsis*.

Gorgias (c. 483 - c. 375 BCE): A famous sophist who coined "language and meter" as a new meaning of *poiēsis* about 415 BCE in the *Encomium to Helen* (cf. Notomi, *op. cit.*, pp. 300-4).

Harmonia: The goddess of Harmony; a fitting together (as planks in a ship); music; song (e.g. *Laws* II 665a). Often badly translated as "(musical) harmony" in this context, when no musical harmony in our sense of the word existed in ancient Greek music, in the sense of chords and chordal harmonies. Music was generally just single melodic lines, at least for Plato and Aristotle.

Hypokritēs: plural *hypokritai*. Actors in general, but also actors who were assigned by lot to the dramatists for the competitions. The winners bypassed the random drawing the following year, and thus, when the term is used in conjunction with the competitions, the actors are implied to be very skillful, if not professional (like a footballer competing in the finals of the World Cup).[243]

Lexis: Speech, language, diction, and style. In the *Dramatics*, it typically means speech or language although on an occasion or two it might be diction. In Chapters 19-20 it actually is very broad and subsumes *logos*.

Logos: Speech, language, prose (in contrast to *metron*), ratio, proportion, among many other meanings.

Maker: See *poiētēs*, especially Diotima's "broad" sense of *poiēsis*.

Metron: Meter (such as "hexameter" or "duple meter") or verse (as "poetry" in our sense).

Melopoiia: Making of the *melos*.

Melos: The primary meaning is "limb" (cf. Liddell & Scott Greek lexicon), but in the context of the theater can mean melody, music, or "music-dance," which Liddell & Scott and almost all translators in this context miss (cf. Mathiesen, *op. cit.*, pp. 25-6; also *ADMC*, p. 106).

Mimēsis: Often just transliterated and used as "mimesis" in English,

---

[243] Cf. *ADMC*, pp. 162; 246; and 307.

the source of "mimetic." In ancient Greece, a rich word that in the 5th century BCE originally meant "expression" or "impersonation," of other people, animals, or the gods and then later "representation," "imitation," "copying" or the like (cf. *ADMC* Chapter 3 for the historical details). Like "play" in English, the context determines the precise connotation.

Mime: Sometimes related to the cognates of *mimēsis* but for Aristotle not our notion of an individual acting silently. Rather, a prose (literary) composition conveying some aspect of life, often of the typical citizen rather than of the nobility (cf. *Dramatics* 1).

Mousikē: (i) Arts of the Muses (which can include history and other disciplines that we would not consider "art" *per se*); (ii) music (as the strictly aural phenomenon); or (iii) music and dance (e.g., Plato's *Laws* II, *Alcibiades* 108 and Aristotle's *Politics* VIII 7, although typical translations miss the meaning in the *Laws* and *Politics*).

Nome: different accounts are given, but one is a solo sung to a harp accompaniment. It is unclear whether the soloists were like our popular singers who accompany themselves with a guitar or who had an accompanist. In any event, given that Aristotle says (at the end of *Dramatics* 1) that the nome involved *rhuthmos* (*qua* dance), the soloist must have at least walked or moved in a designed manner (even if improvised), like our rock-and-roll performers simultaneously singing, using an instrument, and engaging in various movements on stage, even if very restricted ones because the performer is "attached" now to a microphone (at least before wireless innovations).

Poet: See *poiētēs*.

Poiēsis: (i) Composition, production, or making (the broad meaning that Diotima gives it, *Symposium* 205). (ii) Poetry (which is the meaning Gorgias gives it starting in 415 BCE). (iii) *Mousikē kai metra*, "music" in the Greek sense and verses (the "narrow" sense that Diotima gives it, *Symposium* 205, in contrast to the broad sense). It seems best in the *Symposium* to mean "music-dance and verse" (for reasons given in *ADMC*, especially pp. 25-6 and 58-61). (iv) The composition of music, dance, verse and plot (this is Aristotle's technical sense in the *Dramatics*, building on the Diotiman narrow sense, with plot as a fourth and final necessary condition).

Poiētikēs: (The art of) *poiēsis*, with "art" (*technē*) presupposed.

Poiētēs: See *poiēsis*; hence, a maker or composer (Diotima's broad sense); or a composer of music, dance, and verse (Diotima's narrow sense); or a composer of verse (Gorgias' sense); or a composer of music, dance, verse and plot (Aristotle's sense).

Rhapsodos (rhapsode): From *rhap-* ("to stitch together") and *odos* ("song," although sometimes badly translated as "poem"). A singer, and later a declaimer, of epic and other kinds of song or verse who, at least in later times, performed other composers' work. In the dialogue *Ion*, the rhapsode Ion chants the Homeric epics. It is not commonly known when precisely the sub-genres of epic that involved only verse without music of any kind branched off. The Greeks often had the same division of labor that we do, involving songwriters and singers, both of whom had their own individual talents.

Rhuthmos: In archaic times, the form or shape of something, whether (given examples from ancient sources) the shape of an image on a ceiling or shield, or of a pair of sandals. By Plato's time, it could also mean the gait of a man or the order in music. At *Laws* II 672 it has the sense of temporal order, but in *Laws* V, of "scales" or "measure" (728e). At *Laws* II 665a and in the *Dramatics* it is used in the context of orchestral art and is "dance," i.e., (the name of) the order of body movement. In Aristotle's *Rhetoric*, it is the numerical limitation of a composition. Generally, from Aristoxenus onwards, it is primarily a temporal ordering (Aristoxenus was to ancient Greek music theory as Euclid was to ancient Greek geometry).

Rhythm: typical translation (and sometimes mistranslation) of *rhuthmos*.

Satyr play: Starting about 490 BCE, from soon after the beginning of the competitions in "serious drama" (*aka* "tragedy") that itself involved three individual plays, the satyr play took the "fourth position." It involved usually a burlesque plot, with a mixture of noble characters and ribald satyrs. The *Alcestis* of Euripides in the competition of 438 BCE was an exception in that no satyrs were included, and this may have been a harbinger of things to come, but unfortunately we have not one extant "tetralogy" from the whole 4th century BCE. The only surviving satyr play is Euripides' *Cyclops*. The satyr play generally provided relief (maybe catharsis?), especially after dramas that tended to end in misfortune for protagonists (but not always, because at least five of Euripides' "tragedies" end happily). At about 340 BCE, the satyr play was dropped from the competition in "tragedy," and the competition became a trilogy.

Tragedy: Often misleading translation of *tragōidia*.

Tragōidia: The origin is still unknown. It seemingly comes from *tragos* and *aoidē/oidē* (ode or song), and apparently either meant for the ancients something like "song of the goat" or "the song of the spelt" (because *tragos* could also mean the wheat, or spelt, that was fermented into the type of beer associated with Dionysian-type performances like the dithyramb from which tragedy came, on some accounts).[244] For Aristotle, though (and for Plato), *tragōidia* only need mean serious drama, because Aristotle states at least three times in the *Dramatics* that the plot can go from misfortune to fortune. In

---

244   Cf. *ADMC*, p. 447.

addition, in Chapter 14, in the ranking of the best "tragedies," the type ending horribly like *Oedipus* is ranked second, below the type like *Cresphontes* ending happily.

Bibliography

Afeissa, Hicham-Stéphane. "La *Poétique* d'Aristote sans la catharsis?" at https://www.nonfiction.fr/articlecomment-9562-la-poetique-daristote-sans-la-catharsis.htm (as of October 3, 2018).

Aristotle

---. *Aristotle's Ars Poetica*, ed. Rudolph Kassel (Oxford: Clarendon Press, 1966).

---. *Aristotle: Poetics*, Greek text with commentary, D.W. Lucas (Oxford: Clarendon Press, 1988); first printing 1968.

---. *Aristotle's Poetics*, trans. James Hutton (New York: W.W. Norton & Co., 1982).

---. *Aristotle: Poetics, with the Tractatus Coisilianus, Reconstruction of Poetics II, and the Fragments of the On Poets*, trans. Richard Janko (Indianapolis: Hackett Publishing Co., 1987).

---. *La Poetique d'Aristote: Texte Primitif et Additions Ultérieures*, trans. and comment. by Daniel de Montmollin (Neuchâtel: Henri Messeiller, 1951).

---. *Aristotle Poetics: Editio Maior of the Greek Text with Historical Introduction and Philological Commentaries*. Leonardo Tarán and Dimitri Gutas (Brill: Leiden and Boston, 2012).

Other translations of *Poetics:*

---. S.H. Butcher (see *op. cit.*)
---. A. Dacier (see *op. cit.*)
---. G. Else (see *op. cit.*)
---. G. Whalley (see *op. cit.*)

Translations of other works by Aristotle:
    ---. *Posterior Analytics,* trans. R.G. Mure (Digireads.com, 2006). Originally published in *The Works of Aristotle,* Vol. 1 (Oxford: Clarendon Press, 1928).

The Complete Works of Aristotle, ed. Jonathan Barnes, 2 vols. (Princeton: Princeton University Press, 1984).
    ---. *Poetics,* trans. Ingram Bywater.
    ---. *Rhetoric,* trans. W. Rhys Roberts.
    ---. *Physics,* trans. R.P. Hardie and R.K. Gaye.

Aristotle in 23 Volumes (Cambridge: Harvard University Press; London: William Heinemann Ltd., 1944).
    ---. Vol. 23 *(Poetics),* trans. W. H. Fyfe. As found on the Perseus Project:
    http://www.perseus.tufts.edu/hopper/text?doc=Perseus%3atext%3a1999.01.005

Athenaeus. *The Deipnosophists, or Banquet of the Learned of Athenaeus,* ed. C. D. Yonge (London: Henry G. Bohn, Covent Garden, 1854).
    ---. Translation by Charles Burton Gulick (Cambridge: Loeb Classical Library, Harvard University Press, 1927).

Aufderheide, Joachim. Review in *Byrn Mawr Classical Review,* 2018.11.53, of William Robert Wians, Ronald M. Polansky (ed.), *Reading Aristotle: Argument and Exposition. Philosophia antiqua, 146* (Leiden; Boston: Brill, 2017). Available on the web as of 11/26/2018 at:
    http://www.bmcreview.org/2018/11/20181153.html

Barnes, Jonathan: See under "Aristotle" for translations.
    ---. *Philosophia Togata II: Plato and Aristotle in Rome,* ed.

by Jonathan Barnes and Miriam Griffin (Oxford: Clarendon Press, 1997).

Battin, Margaret Pabst. "Aristotle's Definition of Tragedy in the *Poetics*," Pts. 1–2, *Journal of Aesthetics and Art Criticism*, 33 (1975) 155–170 and 293–302.

Brunius, Teddy. "Catharsis," in P. Wiener (ed.), *Dictionary of the History of Ideas*, Vol. 1 (New York, 1973) 264–70.

Burke, Daniel. "Bible Museum says five of its Dead Sea Scrolls are fake," at https://www.cnn.com/2018/10/22/us/bible-museum-fake-scrolls/index.html, as given on 10/23/18.

Butcher, S.H. *Aristotle's Theory of Poetry and Fine Art* (London: Macmillan and Co. Ltd., 1923); first printed 1895

Campbell, David A. *Greek Lyric Poetry* (London: Bloomsbury/Bristol Classical Press, 1982).

Carroll, Noël and Sally Banes. "Dance, Imitation and Representation," *Dance, Education and Philosophy*, ed. by Graham McFee, Chelsea School Research Centre Edition, Vol. 7, 13-32 (Oxford: Meyer & Meyer Sport Ltd., 1999).

Corcoran, Clinton. "The Problem of Dramatic Expectation in Aristotle's *Poetics*," in *Greek, Roman and Byzantine Studies* 38 (3), September 1997, 285-294.

Costelloe, B.F.C. and J.H. Muirhead. *Aristotle and the Earlier Peripatetics: Being a Translation from Zeller's "Philosophy of the Greeks,"* in Two Volumes (New York: Russell & Russell, Inc., 1962).

Csapo, Eric. "Choregic Dedications and What They Tell Us About Comic Performance in the Fourth Century BC," *Logeion: A Journal of Ancient Theatre*, 6 (2016) 252-284.

---. "Imagining the shape of choral dance and inventing the cultic in Euripides' later tragedies," *Choreutika: Performing and Theorising Dance in Ancient Greece*, ed. by Laura Gianvittorio, 119-56 (Pisa/Rome: Fabrizio Serra Editore, 2017).

Dacier, André. *La Poetique d'Aristote: contenant les regles les plus exactes pour juger du poëme heroïque* [*Aristotle's Poetics: Containing the most exact rules for judging the heroic poem*] (Paris: Barbin Publ., 1692).

---. *The Preface to Aristotle's Art of Poetry. With Mr. D'Acier's Notes Translated from the French* (London: Dan. Brown, 1705). The Augustan Reprint Society, Publ # 76, 1959, editor Samuel Holt Monk.

Deslauriers, Marguerite. "Aristotle on the Virtues of Slaves and Women," *Oxford Studies in Ancient Philosophy*, Vol. 25. (Winter 2003) 213-31.

Destrée, Pierre. *Plato and the Poets*, ed. by Pierre Destrée and Fritz-Gregor Herrmann (Leiden & Boston: Brill, 2011).

Editors of *Encyclopaedia Britannica*. "Beowulf: Old English Poem." At https://www.britannica.com/topic/Beowulf as of 11/5/18.

El-Abbadi, Mostafa. "Library of Alexandria," *Encyclopædia Britannica*, online at:
https://www.britannica.com/topic/Library-of-Alexandria as of 9/27/18.

Else, Gerald. *The Argument* (Cambridge: Harvard University Press, 1963). First publ. 1957.

Bibliography

Feagin, Susan L. "Reading Plays as Literature," *The Routledge Companion to Philosophy of Literature*, eds. Noël Carroll and John Gibson, 107-116 (New York and London: Routledge, 2016).

Fendt, Gene. *Love Song for the Life of the Mind: An Essay on the Purpose of Comedy* (Washington D.C.: Catholic University of America Press, 2011).

Ferrari, Giovanni. "Aristotle's Literary Aesthetics," *Phronesis* 44 (3) (1999) 181-198.

Fitton, J.W. "Greek Dance," *Classical Quarterly*, New Series, Vol. 23, No. 2 (November 1973) 254-274.

Freire, António. "A Catarse Tragica em Aristoteles," *Euphrosyne*, 3 (Lisbon, Portugal: Universidade de Lisboa/Centro de Estudos Clássicos) 1969.

Gallop, David. "Animals in the *Poetics*" in *Oxford Studies in Ancient Philosophy*, Vol. VIII (1990) 145-171.

Gould, Rebecca. "The *Poetics* from Athens to al-Andalus: Ibn Rushd's Grounds for Comparison," *Modern Philology*, 112.1 (2014) 1-24.

Griffith, Mark. "Cretan Harmonies and Universal Morals: Early Music and Migration of Wisdom in Plato's *Laws*" in *Performance and Culture in Plato's Laws*, ed. Anastasia-Erasmia Peponi, 15-66 (Cambridge and New York: Cambridge University Press, 2013).
---. *Greek Satyr Play: Five Studies* (Berkeley: California Classical Studies, 2015).

Grote, George. *Aristotle*. Ed. by Alexander Bain and G. Croom Robertson, 2nd edition with additions (London: John Murray, Albemare St., 1880).

Gudeman, Alfred. *Aristoteles: Peri Poiētikēs* (Berlin: Walter de Gruyter, 1934).

Habib, M.A.R. *A History of Literary Criticism: From Plato to the Present* (Hoboken/Oxford: Wiley-Blackwell Publishing, 2005).

Halliwell, Stephen. "Aristotelianism and anti-Aristotelianism in Attitudes to Theatre," *Attitudes to Theatre from Plato to Milton*, ed. Elena Theodorakopoulos, Nottingham Classical Literature Studies, Vol. 7, 57-75 (Bari: Levante Editori, 2003).
---. "Ancient Beginnings," in *The Routledge Companion to Philosophy of Literature*, eds. Noël Carroll and John Gibson, 3-12 (New York and London: Routledge, 2016).
---. *Between Ecstasy and Truth: Interpretations of Greek Poetics from Homer to Longinus* (Oxford: Oxford University Press, 2011).
---. *Aristotle's Poetics* (Chapel Hill: The University of North Carolina Press, 1986).

Heath, Malcolm. "Aristotle on the best kind of tragic plot: re-reading *Poetics* 13-14," in R. Polansky and W. Wians (eds.), *Reading Aristotle: Exposition and Argument*, 334-351 (Leiden: Brill, 2017).

Herrmann, Fritz-Gregor. See Destrée.

Hordern, J.H. *Sophron's Mimes. Text, Translation, and Commentary* (Oxford: Oxford University Press, 2004).

Bibliography

Janko, Richard. See under *Aristotle* for translation of the *Poetics*.
---. *Philodemus: The Aesthetic Works. Vol. I/3: Philodemus, On Poems Books 3-4, with the Fragments of Aristotle, On Poets* (Oxford: Oxford University Press, 2011).
---. *Philodemus' On Poems and Aristotle's On Poets, Cronache ercolanesi*, 21 (1991) 5-64.
---. Book Reviews, book review of Tarán and Gutas, in *Classical Philology* 108 (2013) 252-7; also at http://www-personal.umich.edu/~rjanko/review%20Gutas%20&%20Tar%E1n.pdf.)

Kenny, Sir Anthony. *Aristotle POETICS* (Oxford: Oxford University Press, 2013).

Lada-Richards, Ismene. *Silent Eloquence: Lucian and Pantomime Dancing* (London: Duckworth, 2007).

Laertius, Diogenes. *Lives of the Eminent Philosophers*, trans. R.D. Hicks, 2nd ed. (Cambridge: Harvard University Press, 1972); first published 1925.

Lawler, Lillian. *The Dance in Ancient Greece* (Middletown, CT: Wesleyan University Press, 1964).
---. *The Dance of the Ancient Greek Theatre* (Iowa City: University of Iowa Press, 1964).

Liddell, Henry George and Robert Scott. *Greek-English Lexicon*, 1968 impression; first ed. 1889.
---. Revised and augmented throughout by Sir Henry Stuart Jones with the assistance of Roderick McKenzie (Oxford: Clarendon Press, 1940).

Lindsay, Hugh. "Strabo on Apellicon's Library," *Rheinisches Museum für Philologie*, Neue Folge, 140. Bd., H. 3/4 (1997) 290-298.

Lobel, E. *The Greek Manuscripts of Aristotle's* Poetics (Oxford: Oxford University Press, 1933).

Lorenz, Konrad. *On Aggression*, trans. by Marjorie Kerr Wilson (New York: Harcourt, Brace & Company, 1966); originally published by Deutscher Taschenbuch, 1963.

Marchetti, Christopher C. *Aristoxenus "Elements of Rhythm": Text, translation, and commentary with a translation and commentary on POxy 2687* (Ph.D. diss., Rutgers University, NJ, 2009).

Margoliouth, D.S. *The Poetics of Aristotle* (London: Hodder and Stoughton, 1911).

Mathiesen, Thomas J. *Apollo's Lyre: Greek Music and Music Theory in Antiquity and the Middle Ages* (Lincoln, NE/London: University of Nebraska Press, 1999).

Mayhew, Robert. "*Peri iambōn:* A Note on Riccardianus 46 and the Lost Second Book of Aristotle's *Poetics*," *Hermes*, 144 (2016/3) 374-9.

McKirahan, Richard. "The Place of the *Posterior Analytics* in Aristotle's Thought, with Particular Reference to the *Poetics*," *Apeiron* 43/2-3 (2010) 75-104.

Meyer, Susan Sauvé. *Plato Laws I and II*: Translated with a Commentary (Oxford: Clarendon Press, 2015).
---. "Legislation as a Tragedy: On Plato's *Laws* VII, 817B-D," *Plato and the Poets*, ed. by Pierre Destrée and Fritz-Gregor Herrmann, 387-402 (Leiden & Boston: Brill, 2011).

Moore, Robert H. *Effective Writing*, 4th ed. (New York: Holt, Rinehart and Winston, Inc., 1971). First printing 1955.

Mulroy, David. *Early Greek Lyric Poetry*, trans. with an Introduction and Commentary by David Mulroy (Ann Arbor, MI: The University of Michigan Press/Ann Arbor Paperbacks, 1999).

Munteanu, Dana Lacourse. "Aristotle's Reception of Aeschylus: Reserved Without Malice," in *Brill's Companion to the Reception of Aeschylus,* ed. Rebecca Kennedy, 87-108 (Leiden: Brill, 2017).

Nagy, Gregory. *Poetry as Performance,* published online in 2009 by the Center for Hellenic Studies, with the permission of Cambridge University Press:
http://chs.harvard.edu/CHS/article/display/5581 (orig. publ. by Cambridge Univ. Pr., 1996).
---. *Pindar's Homer: The Lyric Possession of an Epic Past* (Baltimore: The John Hopkins University Press, 1990). Accessed online, October 2015, at:
http://chs.harvard.edu/CHS/article/display/5262
---. "Genre, Occasion, and Choral Mimesis Revisited—with special reference to the 'newest Sappho'," *Classical Inquiries: Studies on the Ancient World from Center for Hellenic Studies.* Published online 2015.10.1 at:
http://classical-inquiries.chs.harvard.edu/genre-occasion-and-choral-mimesis-revisited-with-special-reference-to-the-newest-sappho/

Natali, Carlo. *Aristotle: His Life and School*, ed. by D.S. Hutchinson (Princeton: Princeton University Press, 2013).

Nicholls, Matthew. "Greek manuscripts," for the British Library. Available as of 1/3/2019 at https://www.bl.uk/greek-manuscripts/articles/ancient-libraries.

Notomi, Noburu. "Image-Making in *Republic* X and the *Sophist*," in *Plato and the Poets*, ed. by P. Destrée and F. Herrmann, 299-326 (Leiden & Boston: Brill, 2011).

Petruševski, M.D. "La Définition de la Tragédie Chez Aristote et la Catharsis," in *L'Annuaire de la Faculté de Philosophie de l'Université de Skopje*, 1 (Skopje, Macedonia, 1948).
---. "Pathēmatōn Katharsin ou bien Pragmatōn Systasin?," *Ziva antika/Antiquite vivante* (Skopje: Societe d'etudes classiques Ziva Antika, 1954).

Phillips, Tom and Armand D'Angour, eds. *Music, Text, and Culture in Ancient Greece* (Oxford: Oxford University Press, 2018).

Plato

Plato: *Symposium*, trans. with Introduction and Notes, by Alexander Nehamas and Paul Woodruff (Indianapolis & Cambridge: Hackett Publishing Company, 1989); also reproduced in *Plato: Complete Works*, ed. John Cooper, *op. cit.*, 1997.

The Republic, Vol. 1 and 2, trans. Paul Shorey. Loeb Classical Library (Cambridge: Harvard University Press, 1956).

Platonis Opera (Greek text), ed. John Burnet (Oxford: Oxford University Press, 1903).

Plato in Twelve Volumes, Vol. 9, trans. Harold N. Fowler (Cambridge: Harvard University Press; London: William Heinemann Ltd., 1966).
---. *Ion*, trans. W. R. M. Lamb.
---. *Laws*, Vols. 10 & 11, trans. R. G. Bury.
---. *Symposium*, trans. Harold N. Fowler.

Bibliography

Plato: The Complete Works, Editor John Cooper & Assoc. Editor D.S. Hutchinson (Indianapolis/Cambridge: Hackett Publishing Co., 1997).

Rashed, Marwan. "*Katharsis versus mimèsis*: simulation des émotions et définition aristotélicienne de la tragédie," *Littérature*, Vol. 182, No. 2 (2016) 60-77.
---. Also see Veloso, *Pourquoi*.

Ross, W.D. *Aristotle: A complete exposition of his works & thought* (New York: Meridian Books, Inc., 1959).

Scaliger, Julius Caesar. *Poetica*. 1561. In *Select Translations from Scaliger's Poetics*, trans. F.M. Padelford, 136-143 (New Haven: Yale University Press, 1905); as found in *Critical Theory since Plato*, ed. Hazard Adams (New York: Harcourt Brace Jovanovich, Inc., 1971).

Scott, Gregory. "The *Poetics* of Performance: The Necessity of Performance, Spectacle, Music, and Dance in Aristotelian Tragedy," in *Performance and Authenticity in the Arts (Cambridge Series on Philosophy and the Arts)* eds. Salim Kemal and Ivan Gaskell (Cambridge: Cambridge University Press, 1999) 15-48.
---. "Purging the *Poetics*," *Oxford Studies in Ancient Philosophy*, Vol. 25 (Winter 2003) 233-264.
---. *Aristotle's Favorite Tragedy: Oedipus or Cresphontes?*, 2nd ed. (New York: ExistencePS Press, 2018); first published in 2016.
---. *Aristotle on Dramatic Musical Composition: The Real Role of Literature, Catharsis, Music and Dance in the POETICS*, 2nd ed., 2 vols. (New York: ExistencePS Press, 2018); first published in 2016. (Often shortened to *ADMC*.)

Simonides. See Campbell and Mulroy.

Smerdel, Anton. *Aristotelova Katarsa* (Skopje: Južna Srbija, 1937).

Storey, Ian. Review of Carl Shaw, *Euripides: Cyclops. A Satyr Play (Companions to Greek and Roman Tragedy*, 2018). *Bryn Mawr Classical Review* 2018.10.24, available as of 10/15/18 at:
http://www.bmcreview.org/2018/10/20181024.html

Strabo. Editor H. L. Jones, *The Geography of Strabo* (Cambridge, Mass.: Harvard University Press; London: William Heinemann, Ltd., 1924).

Veloso, Cláudio William "Aristotle's *Poetics* without *Katharsis*, Fear, or Pity," *Oxford Studies in Ancient Philosophy,* Vol. 33 (2007) 255-84.
---. *Pourquoi la Poétique d'Aristote? DIAGOGE*, with a Preface by Marwan Rashed (Paris: Vrin, 2018). (Sometimes shortened to *Pourquoi.*)

Whalley, George. *Aristotle's Poetics: Translation and with a Commentary by George Whalley*, ed. by John Baxter and Patrick Atherton (Canada: McGill-Queen's University Press, 1997).

Woodruff, Paul. *Antigone: Translated with Introduction and Notes* (Indianapolis and Cambridge: Hackett Publishing Company, 2001).

Zeller, Eduard. See Costelloe.

Index

Symbols
27 chapters 25
80-line miniature 209
(comic) mime actors 45
"-composer [using plot/representation]" 133
"merely" necessary conditions 157
"mixed" manner 147
"music" and verse 45
"-*poios*" 133
-*poios/-poious* 130
"–*poios/poious/poioi*" 45
"professional" actors 92

A
'Abbās I 281
Abū Bishr Mattā 42
Academy 9
Achilles 220
acroatic 261
acting 227, 228, 230
actions 111, 142
actor 93
actors 58, 77, 93, 162, 164
actor's art 206
actors' excessive delivery 227
adage 90
Adeimantus 147
ADMC (see *Aristotle on Dramatic Musical Composition*)
adorning language 208
Aegisthus 183, 189
aeidō 201
Aeschylus 10, 20, 53, 58, 81, 118, 137, 158, 188
aestheticians 43, 221
aesthetic pleasure 292
A Funny Thing Happened on the Way to the Forum 245
Afeissa 302
Agamemnon 182, 183, 205
Agathon 61, 137, 184
agglomeration 179
aggression 246

agōn 164, 224
agōnos 162, 164
al-Andalus 284
Alcestis 53
Alcibiades 47, 232
Alexander 269
Alexander of Aphrodisias 289
Alexander the Great 52, 57
Alexandria 251, 253, 258, 272, 279
Alexandrians 274, 276
Alexandrine grammarians 266
Alexandrine library 275
amazement 93, 231
American Midwest 230
Ammonius 269
Amphiaraus 199, 202
amphitheaters 43
analabontes 173
ancient commentary 269
Andromeda 79
Andronicus 289, 293, 295
Andronicus of Rhodes 256, 276
animals other than man 60
AnonC 259
anonymity 260
AnonymousC 259, 195
antecedent causality 71
Antheus 184
Antiatticist 280, 290, 291
Antigone 185, 191, 192, 197
antiquities market 259
ants 60
aoidē 307
apathes 197
Apellicon 253, 254, 265, 279, 287
apolabontes 173, 174
Apollo 136
Apollo's Lyre: Greek Music and Music Theory in Antiquity 180
Arabic scholars 274
Arabic translation 3
archaic Greek 69
archetype 41, 100

archetype Omega 284
arête 144
Aristarchus 274, 276
Aristophanes 34, 79
Aristotelian categories 273
Aristotelian Scholarchs 275
Aristotle on Dramatic Musical Composition 1
Aristotle's death 41
Aristotle's Favorite Tragedy 194
Aristoxenus 69
arrangement of incidents 161
art 60, 111
art for art's sake 222
artifact 59
artificial 59
artificial products 60
artistic aspects 56
arts 46
arts of the Muses 7, 8, 47
Astydamas 210
Athenaeus 251, 144, 266, 117
Athenian Stranger 143
athetized 100
Attalic kings 253
Attalid 254
Attalids 257
Attalus 255
Aufderheide 195
aulēsei 142
aulētikēs 102
aulos xi, 102
aural experience 70
automatic correction 21
autonomous 222
autonomy of art 221
Averroes 3, 44, 166
Avicenna 3, 14, 43, 289, 44, 62, 120, 166

B
bad copying 258
bad copyists 253
Baghdad 281

ballet 116
Banes 103
bare language, namely prose 121
Barnes 268-272, 278, 287
Baumgarten 222
be-causes 71
beginning, middle, and end 77
Bekker 13, 26
Benefits of Laughter 246
Benesh 79
Beowulf 283
Bernays 16, 173, 180
best men 224
best plot-types 181
best tragedy-type 34
best type of tragedies 198
better, equal or worse 141
bibliophile 253
biological 57
biological analogy 153
biological definition 214
biological division 17, 156, 159, 169
biological frameworks 57
biological metaphors 11
biological paradigms 71
biology 57, 245, 59
birth of tragedy 71
blind reviewer 259
blonde-haired 19
blueprint 77
Bournonville mime 118
break dancing 50
broad sense of "doing/making" 104
Broadway 31
Browning 209
Brunius 297
brutal implementation 43
Burke 258
Butcher 27, 73, 106
Bywater 27
Byzantine 39
Byzantium 293

Index

C
Caesar 278
Callicles 17, 34
Callippides 227
Camargue 230
Cambridge University Press 259
capacity 90
captured sailors 137
Capulets 192
Carcinus 202, 202, 210
Carroll 103
Cassander 252
Cassandra 205
Castelvetro 156
Catalogue of Diogenes 275
catharsis 3, 14, 214, 54, 36, 166, 292, 222, 225, 232, 233
catharsis-clause 75, 158, 167, 172, 174, 250, 264-5, 289
cause 60
censorship 56
Centaur 121, 132, 133
Chaeremon 77, 79, 80, 120, 121, 132, 133
chance 60
chants 217
chapter 25
Chapter 27 76
character 31, 81, 111, 142, 144, 199, 200, 215, 216
characters 222
children 292
Children of Paradise 61
children's jumping 112
children wildly jumping 67
choral art 114
choral beginnings 58
choral dance 180
chord 66
Choregic Dedications 39
choreia 143
chorus 81
chorus dance performers 117
Christianity 279
Christians 279
Christian values 62

Christian West 6
cinematic tragedy 244
cinquecentro 22
clarification 2, 14, 160
clarify pity and fear 15
classification of metaphors 208, 209
classifications 73
Cleopatra 278
climax 201
clogging 151
Clytaemnestra 16, 183
codex form 40
codices 40
cognate ending of *poiēsis* 8
collection of Aristotelian texts 82
collection of essays 180
Collection of the Art of Theodectes 210
color 111
Comastes xi
combination 111
comedy 31, 35-6, 292, 49, 54, 76, 55, 77, 102, 136, 158, 171
Comments 25
commerce 271
commonplace Greek 14
competent scribe 158-9
competition 92
complex 73, 90
complex tragedy 82, 170, 203
complication 77, 127, 201
complication and dénouement 201
complications 98
composer 13
composer of "musical" drama 13
composition 46
Connery 36
conservatism 18
Constantinople 43
content 147
contest 224
contradiction 202
Corcoran 178
Coriscus 252

Index

Corneille 55
corps de ballet 111, 115, 117, 142, 143
Corybantism 240, 288
cowboys 230
Creon 192
Cresphontes 19, 34, 81, 182, 194
criticism 74
Csapo 39, 180
Cyclops 53

D

Dacier 25, 182
dais 50
Danaus 177
dance 240, 31, 50, 88, 94, 111, 113, 115, 120, 180, 231
dancers 62
dancing 142
D'Angour 79
Darwin 11, 57
Dead Sea Scroll 259
De Anima 57
Debureau 61
decent spectators 227
dedications 39
definiendum 159
definiens 159, 160, 174
definition of comedy 101
definition of tragedy 72, 157
Deipnosophists 118
deliberation 60
delivery 77, 227
Delphi 41
Demetrius 252
Demetrius of Phaleron 252
Demodocus 217
de Montmollin 209, 93
dénouement 77, 99, 127, 201
derived necessary conditions 163
descendants of Neleus 271
designer's art 92
Deslauriers 19
dianoia 204

diction 69, 101, 161, 204, 226
differentiae 214
digital technology 280
dinner party 126
Diogenes Laertius 209
Dionysiac ritual 155
Dionysian Dramatic Victories 209
Dionysus 49, 79
Diotima 7, 18, 45, 46, 63, 96
Diotiman meaning 301, 65
Diotiman sense of *poiēsis* 8, 10, 87, 98
direct discourse 146
direct object 33, 66
discoveries 21, 200
disgust 187
disgusting 19
dithyramb 49, 76-7, 94, 95, 104, 147, 148, 154
dithyrambic 136
dithyrambic poets 77
dithyramb-making 102
dithyrambopoiētikē 102
divergences in character 143
divergences of character 142
divisions 159
dogs 227
doing 7
Dorian dialect 126
double-oboe 102
double structure 189
Dover 46
drama 31, 49, 245
dramatic composer 20
dramatic literature 80
Dramatic Records 209
Dramatics 11
drunkenness 226
dunamin 90
dunamis 56, 91, 162, 229

E
Eastern Georgia 281-2
Eco 36

Index

Editio Maior 40
editors 260
educated guesses 280
educated women 224
educating the youth 137
education 292
effective writing 68
efficient 71
efficient cause 75
eidōn 90
eight of the nine plot-types 197
eikonopoios 8
ekdedomenoi logoi 261
El-Abbadi 279
elegeiopoious 45, 121, 128, 129
elegiac poets 121, 128
elegiacs 121
elegiac (verse) makers 45
eleventh century 43
Elizabethan dramatists 62
Else 296, 27, 93, 122, 122, 207
embellished language 160
emotion 142
emotions 111
Empedocles 121, 128, 131, 135, 150, 221
Emperor Justinian 6
Emperor Theodosius I 279
empirical knowledge 56
empiricist 55
empiricist *non plus ultra* 10
enactment 146
encomia 49
end in nature 60
enemies 197
enemies harming enemies 191
enthrallment 285
entomologist 269
epic 49, 50, 244, 213, 214, 51, 231
epic composer 215
epic maker 8
epic poetry 147
epic poets 121, 128

epic rhapsode 217
epic (verse) makers 45
epinicians 49
episode 179
episodic plots 93
epistēmē 56
epopoios 8
epopoious 45, 121, 128, 129
equivocal 33
Erastus 252
Eratosthenes 279
errors 261
esoteric 14, 199, 199, 261, 266
essential conditions 17, 18, 157, 230
ethical compass 31
ethical instruction 222
ethical rhetoric 6
ethicist mean 223
ethics 55, 222, 223
Eucleides 267
Eumenes II 254, 257
Euripides 34, 53, 53, 79, 182, 188, 191, 137, 192, 201
Euripides' plays 162
Europeans 43
Eurydice 192
exoteric 14, 138, 199, 201
exposition 215
express 13, 108
expression 65, 108

F
fake fragments 258
Fall of Miletus 20
famous definition of tragedy 14
fatal flaw 181
Feagin 79
feet 146
feminists 18
feminist scholars 46
Fendt 17, 55, 56, 60, 166, 196, 239
Ferrari 265
Ferri 127

Index

film 52
final 71
final cause 71
fine language 131
first book 36
first commentary 43
first philosophy 57
first sentence in the treatise 94
fitting together 112
Fitton 49, 69, 79
five major claims 168
flattery 107
flute xi, 102
fool's errand 172
foot 69
form 111, 147
formal 71, 103
formal cause 75
form-content 75, 138
forms of speech 262
foundation 23
foundation of literary theory 23
four branches 283
four causes 71
four discernible lines of manuscripts 40
four kinds of metaphor 208
four possible combinations 191
four sub-categories of tragedy 90
four sub-types of epic 216
four sub-types of tragedy 201, 203
fourth branch 42
fourth wall 57
four types of tragedy 82
Freire 296
French culture 230
Frogs 34, 79
from the ships 272
Fugard 219, 220
full enactment 146
function 227, 228
function of Tragedy 97

G
Galen's summaries 44
Gallop 153
gardians 230
garland 205
gelotopoioi 45
genesis 72
genre 72
Geography 252
Georgia 281
gesture 227, 228
gestures 202
goal 237
goal of tragedy 171
goat-song 35
good characters 21
good plots 87
Gordian Knot 55
Gorgian-English sense of *poiēsis* 9
Gorgian meaning 65
Gorgian sense 9, 13, 45, 119
Gorgias 7, 17, 44, 95, 104, 221
Gould 284
grammar 204, 206
grammatical points 206
Great Library 279
Greek culture 97
Greek-English lexicons 13
Greek Music and Music Theory in Antiquity 180
Greek Satyr Play 189, 237
Griffith 189, 237, 238
Grote 255, 266, 275
Gudeman 55, 167
Gutas 28, 28, 29, 172, 281

H
Habib 119
Haemon 192
Halliwell 59, 72, 262, 223, 295, 298, 300
hamartia 181
harmonia 66, 88, 111, 112, 143, 152, 232
harmonia kai rhuthmos 66, 70

harmony 66
Harmony 112
harmony/melody and rhythm 48
Harpies 189
Heath 195, 259, 265, 298
heirs of Neleus 257
Hellenistic age 269
Herculaneum 275, 280
Herculaneum excavations 275
Hermannus Alemannus 42
Herman the German 42, 284
Hermippus 278, 287
Hesiod 69
hexameter 76
Hipparchus 279
history 72, 148
History of Animals 71, 72, 74, 76
history of comedy 54
history of drama 54
Homer 50, 52, 121, 128, 130
Homeric epics 217
Homeric Problems 52, 81, 213, 209, 221, 213
Homer the first tragedian 154
Hordern 126
horror 197
house 60
human being 18
humanism 245
human nature 245
Hutcheson 222
Hutchinson 268
Hutton 162, 205, 210
hymns 49
Hypermestra 177
hypocrite 164
hypokritai 304
hypokritēs 304
hypokritōn 162, 164

I
iambic 121
iambics 148

Iamblichus 292
iambs 54
Ibn Rushd 284
Ichneutai 53
idiosyncratic phrases 260
Ikalto 281
Iliad 50
imitate 13, 142
imitation 65, 226, 106, 226
imitation in voice 227
impersonate 13, 142, 226
impersonation 65, 147, 226
importance of dance 180
importance of plots 75
incidents 205
individual dramatist 72
inherent tonal rhythms 66
instrumental music 94
intellectual enjoyment 15
intelligence 60
intermingling all the verse-forms 132
interpolation 172, 276
interpolations and inversions 276
invective 54, 148
inversions 276
Ion 50, 217
Iphigenia 19, 81, 182
irrational 35
Italian *cinquecentro* 22

J
Janko 292, 27, 202, 58, 155
Jason 192
jest 226
jests 54
Jowett 47
just by nature 186
Justinian 6, 280, 288, 43, 62
just in particular 186
Justnes 259

K

kai 7
Kant 222
Kassel 28
katharsis 2, 14, 36, 189
Kenny 12, 16
kinds 87, 90
kithara xi, 47, 137, 142
kithara-playing 102, 111
kitharistai 137
kitharistikēs 102
kitharōdoi 137
kitharsei 142
kōmōdopoiois 45
Koran 6, 44

L

Labanotation 79
Lada-Richards 62
Laertius 209
lampoons 158
language 31, 65, 68, 88, 82, 111, 204, 211, 216
language and verse 6
Latin version 42
laughable 58
Laurentius 267
law courts 67
Lawler 136, 180
Laws 13, 47, 66, 67, 102, 224, 232
Laws 665a 114
learnings 41
Lécythe à figures noires xi
Lesbos 254
Les Enfants du Paradis 61
lexis 68, 161, 202, 161, 204, 205, 216, 204, 216
library 252
library of Alexandria 252
Licymnius 77
likely impossibility 219
limb 69, 146
Lindsay 252
literary catharsis 240

literary theorist 78
literary theorists 205
literary tragedy 52
literary view of tragedy 80
literature 31, 106, 124, 125, 145
Lobel 40
logical sequence 82
logō 111
logois psilois 121
logos 65, 88, 151, 161
Lorenz 246
lost second "book" 36, 54
love songs 49
lower-case 40
Lucas 28, 231
Lyceum 14, 32, 97, 103, 199
Lynceus 177
lyric or choral makers 45
lyric poetry 123

M

machine 162
Madagascar 11
made by nature 60
major types 216
maker of images 8
makers 46
making 7, 45, 46
making of the choral composition 91
mallon 190
Maltese 22
man 18
manner 75, 146
Manuscript A 158, 284
Manuscript B 158, 224, 284
manuscript rolls 159
manuscript tradition 39
Marceau 61
Marchetti 69
Margoliouth 102, 136
Marlowe 62
Marx 299

Index

material 71
material cause 75
mathēmatōn 289, 41, 158, 295
Mathiesen 69, 180
Mayhew 158, 213
McKirahan 119
meanness 208
means 75
means of mimesis 13, 32, 66, 140
measure 112
Medea 192, 197
Medieval 62
Medieval religious pageants 62
melei 136
melody 66, 69, 146, 162
melody/music and dance 48
melopoiia 91, 216, 218
melopoiias kai rhuthmōn 163
melopoioi 45
melos 69, 136, 146, 161, 180, 216, 218, 232
melpesthai 69
melpō 69
Melpomene 69
memorization 79
men-de-de pattern 113
merē 101
Merope 194
metaphor 82, 211, 204
metaphorical types 208
metaphysics 57
meter 68
meters 149
meters alone 122
meters/verses are part of *rhuthmos* 122
metra 7, 22, 46, 149
metres 67
metrical 67
metrical forms 122
metrō 136
metrois 121
metron 68, 149, 150, 151
Meyer 20

miaron 19, 187, 192, 197
Middle Ages 42, 62
middle chapters 19
Miller 296
mime 77
mime in the literary sense 77
mimeîsthai 106
mimes 76, 94, 121, 126, 145
mimesis 75, 87, 104, 119, 148, 226
mimēsis 13, 305, 65, 102, 103, 142
mimētikós 106
mimicry 226
minstrels 21
misfortune to fortune 19, 176
missing second book 171
mistake 181
mistakes regarding stage effects 138
mixed comic and serious 242
mixed (enactment) 146
mixed-verse 133
moderation 289, 166
modern definition of rhetoric 68
modern literary tragedy 244
modes of mimesis 75, 138, 148
Moerbeke 100
monastery 281
monastery at Ikalto 281
monstrous 63
Montagues 192
mood 204
morality plays 62
moral purposes 222
moriōn 90, 100
moths 271
Mount Vesuvius 275
Mourelatos 171, 63
mousikē 7, 8, 46, 47, 70, 102, 163, 231, 232
mousikē kai metra 7, 12, 45
mouth 207
MSI 280
multispectral imaging 280
Munteanu 155

Muse 69
Muse of tragedy 69
Muses 7, 8
Museum of the Bible 258
music 70, 78, 88, 136, 137, 201, 217, 232
musical catharsis 239
musical harmony 66
musical interludes 61, 144
musical theater 31
music and dance 7, 10, 47
music-dance 69, 180
music-dance-verse 12, 32, 47
music-dance-verse making 46
music in ancient Greece 180
music (in the Greek sense) 36
muthos 161, 215
muthous 90
mutilated 264
Mynniscus 227

N
Nagy 49, 218
narration 146
narrative 21, 226
Natali 268
natural 59
natural capacity 73
natural gestures 150
natural science in verse 121, 128
natural scientist 121, 128
necessary conditions 17
necessity 60
Nehamas 47
Neleus 252, 260, 267, 283
neo-Platonists 224, 264, 288, 292
Nestorian patriarch of Baghdad 281
Net Fishers 53
New Comedy 91
Nicocrates of Cyprus 267
Nicomachean Ethics 292, 144, 194
nome 136, 305
nomes 76-7, 95, 136

Northern Greece 9
Notomi 7, 50, 218
noun 206
nouns 277
novel 125
novels 124, 145
number 112
numerical limitation 67, 68, 152

O

oboe 102, 142, 202
oboe-playing 102, 111
ōdais 143
ōdē 143
Odyssey 50, 189, 217
Oedipus 34, 194, 197
Of Tragedies 209
oidē 307
Oklahoma! 245
older lads 224
Omega 284
On Composers 169
On Dramatic Musical Composers 169
On Interpretation 151
On "Musical" Composers 202, 261
On Poets 202, 202, 209
On Speaking 58
on stage 52
On the Art of Poetry 43
On the Soul 57
On Tragedy 209
opera 10, 31
opsis 6, 92, 216
Oration 58
orator 67
orchēsei 142, 143
orchēsesin 143
orchēsis 115, 116, 117, 143, 153
orchestōn 111, 115
orchestra 117, 146
orchid *Angraecum sesquipedale* 11
order 114

ordered body movement 50, 66, 112, 143
ordered voice 143
ordinary people 252, 256
Orestes 16, 182, 183, 189
Orestes-Aegisthus 194, 197
organic unity 74
original 41
origins of drama 54
origins of *poiēsis* 153
Orpheus 238
other people 131
outliers 159
Overview 25

P

paeans 49
paganism 279
pageant-wagons 62
painter 109
painters 141
painting 94, 104, 141
paleographic strictures 100
paleography 87, 100, 159
panpipe-playing 111
panpipes 115
pantomime 31, 31, 61, 150
pantos 61
parchment 39
Parisinus Graecus 41
parts 56, 87, 90, 100
parts of tragedy 178
passage on language 120
pastoral drama 188
pathēmatōn 41, 289, 42, 158, 295
Peele 62
Peisistratos 57, 58
Peisistratus 267
performance 80, 162, 228
Pergamum 41
peri de problēmatōn kai luseōn 213
peri iambōn 158
Peripatetic 287

Peripatetic scribe 287
peripeteia 177
peri poiēseōs 210, 210, 212, 262
Peri poiētēn 261
peri poiētikēs 291, 43, 208, 210, 314, 233
peri poiētōn 274
Perseus Project 23
Persia 3, 43
Persian shah 281
Persian war 72
persuasive speaking 67
Petruševski 3, 15, 55, 100, 173, 167, 195, 296-7, 300
Phaedrus 63, 72, 74, 90, 138
Philadelphus 267, 276
Philebus 151
Philip of Macedonia 57
Phillips 79
Phillis the Delian 118
Philocles 81
Philodemus 58, 288, 292
photosynthesis 59
phusica 57
phusiologon 121, 128, 133
Phyrnichus 20
Physics 57, 60
Pindar 218
pity 19
pity and fear 15, 18, 175, 166, 176, 197
plagiaulos xi
Plato 7, 45, 75, 224, 106, 232
Platonic diaeresis 159
Platonic dialogues 145
Platonists 213
play 33, 66, 142, 215
pleasure 34, 171, 232
pleasure is the goal 34
pleasure through mimesis 148
pleasure through pity and fear 181, 233
plot 31, 93, 94, 200, 215
plot as fourth condition 33
plot in a literary sense 126
plot of a silent film 215

Index

plots 58, 75, 77, 90
plot-types 19
Plutarch 41, 251
poems 218
poet 13, 20, 121, 128
poetic art forms 88
poetic arts 75
poetic formalism 223
poetic Greek forms 33
Poetics 43, 209
poetry 6, 7, 77, 120
poiein 121, 128
poiēseōs 46
poiēsis 6, 7, 32, 45-7, 54, 56, 63, 65, 90, 104, 125
poiētai 46
poiētēs 7, 8, 13, 20, 45, 119, 140, 163, 220, 221
poiētikēs 65, 138, 206
poios 8
political public assemblies 67
Politics 15, 54, 70, 72, 224, 232, 233
Politics VIII 7 36
Polycrates of Samos 267
Polyneices 186
Porphyry 273, 290
Porter 205
portrait-painter 8
Posidonius 251, 252, 268, 276
possible combinations of means of mimesis 123
Posterior Analytics 72
potential 56
potential (*dunamis*) of tragedy 92
potential (*dunamis*) of verse and prose 91
power 56, 90
precursor of tragedy 33
principles of criticism 213
principles of merely written drama 78
pristine version 279
Proclus 292
producing 45
prologue 58, 179
proper delivery 227
proper pleasure 76, 172, 174, 214

proportion 65
prose 65, 67, 122, 142, 144, 145, 208
prose examples 125
prose rhythm 67
proverbs 126
psuchagōgei 274, 285
psuchagōgia 274
psyche 56
psychology 245, 57
Ptolemaic navy 279
Ptolemies 271
Ptolemy 267, 272, 279, 287
Ptolemy I 252
Ptolemy Philadelphus 266
public debates 78
public libraries 79
published writings 199
punctuation 40
pure language 120, 122
purely literary phenomenon 149
purely literary tragedies 21
pure narration 227
purgation 2, 14, 160
purgation of the tendency to laughter 171
purification 2, 14, 16, 160
purificatory 189
purificatory rites 16
pursuit of Hector 220

Q

qualitative 98, 178
qualitative part 97
quality 101
quantitative 101
quasi-definition 214

R

Racine 55
radio 52
random pleasure 232
Rashed 168, 298-300
ratio 65

Index

reading 77
real goal of tragedy 34
reasoning 82, 216
recitation 51
recusal policies 260, 301
Red Lion 62
reed instrument 102
religious festivals 137
religious pageants 62
Renaissance 301, 25, 35, 55, 148
re-present 108
represent 13
re-presentation 110
representation 65, 103
representations 111
Republic 52, 75, 142, 147, 154, 226
reversal 177
rhapsode 51, 215, 217, 219
rhapsodes 21, 50, 217, 218
rhapsodes gesticulate 51
Rhetoric 36, 54, 67-8, 77-8, 82, 122-3, 131, 152, 164, 171, 193, 197, 205, 208, 211, 224, 233
rhetoricians 78
Rhetoric III 262
Rhetoric III 2 291
rhuthmō 111, 143
rhuthmos 21, 66, 88, 112, 119, 120, 139, 143, 149, 232, 306
rhuthmos kai harmonia kai melos 160
rhythm 21, 66, 67, 68
rhythmical gestures 111
Riccardianus 41, 158
Richard III 187
Richards 315
rock-and-roll performers 114
role 31
Roman editors 82
Roman marketplace 3, 41
Rome 251, 253, 293
Romeo and Juliet 192
Ross 171, 224
Royal Danish Ballet 118

S

Salem witch trials 296
Sappho 49, 218
Sardis 72
satire 54
satyr drama 155
satyr play 31, 52, 77, 91, 188, 225, 237
satyr plays 53, 115
satyrs 52, 115
Scaliger 35, 55, 62
scene-painting 58
scenery 82
scenery-maker 8
Scepsis 252, 254, 276
Schironi 273
scientific knowledge 56, 72, 73
scribes 159
script 79
scripts 80
sculpture 94
Seabrook 280
secondary meaning 134
second-best tragedy 193
second branch 41
second mode of mimesis 141
Sedley 299
seeds 153
self-published 259
sentence-types 206
separately 111, 121
separately and in combination 140
separately or in combination 87, 88, 113
sequentially 95
serious Broadway plays 10
serious drama 19, 35, 198
Serracino 22
set designer 138
Seven Generals against Thebes 118
seven possible combinations 88
Shakespeare 9, 62
Sharp 259
shocking 19, 186

Index

Sigma 284, 172
sign-language 150
silent film 215
similar titles 262
simile 208
simple 73, 90
simple and complex plots 175
simple narration 226
simple or spectacular tragedy 82
simple plots 93
simple tragedy 203
Simplicius 269, 280, 288
Simpson 44
sing and dance 83
sing and dance in a tragedy 69
singers 218
Sisyphean struggle 167
Sisyphean task 172
six necessary conditions 157
six necessary parts 100
skeuopoios 8, 45
Smerdel 55, 167, 300
Socrates 126, 226
Socratic dialogues 94, 124, 126
Socratic philosophers 252
Solmsen 122
solo 136
Somville 299-300
song 66, 101, 202, 217, 232
song-composer 47
song-dance 69
songs 218
song-stress 69
song-writer 47
sophia 274
sophist Gorgias 44
sophists 7
Sophocles 58, 61, 137, 185, 188, 191, 197, 201
Sophron 121, 125, 126, 145
Sosistratus 51
soul of tragedy 31
spatial order 112

species of literature 32
spectacle 6, 92, 138, 162, 165, 216, 231
spectacle maker 45
spectacular 90
spectacular effects 92
spectator 202
speech 65, 202, 68, 204, 205, 204
speeches of professional writers 78
spelt 307
sphodra 186
spiders 60
stage 202
stage-craft 204
staged tragedy 244
stage effects 138, 199
Stagira 9
standard of correctness 222
Stephanus 13
stepping rightly 47, 114
Storey 53
story-ballet 215
story ballets 31
storytelling 147
Strabo 41, 251, 58, 258, 268, 276
straight plays 31, 220
strict Christian values 43
strolling minstrels 114
structure of incidents 215
style 69, 161
St. Zenon's monastery 281
sub-kinds 91
sub-kinds of comedy 91
subset of tragedy 51, 93
sub-types 35
sub-types of tragedy 201
Sulla 253, 268
Sultan 137
Surette 32
Swan Lake 215
syllables 207
Symposium 7, 18, 45, 46, 47, 63
synecdoche 47, 144

Index

synonym 211
synonyms 208, 209
Syracuse 137
Syriac-Arabic branch 258
Syriac-Arabic translations 289
Syriac translation 3, 42
systematic classification of the arts 75

T

tale-telling 147
tap dance 151
Tarán 28-9, 87, 94, 97, 100, 122, 158, 294
Tarán and Gutas 283, 297, 298
Tauris 182
taxis 114
taxonomy 73, 75, 88
taxonomy of arts 113
teaching geometry 131
technais 46
technical aspects of dance 163
technical term 32
teleologist 265
Telestes 117, 144
television 52
temporal art 179
temporal order 112
temporal ordering 22
tendency to laughter 171
tetralogy 53, 225
Thamyras 137
that for the sake of which 71
theatrical arts 113
The Book of Mormon 245
The Crucible 296
The Encomium to Helen 44
Themistius 58, 154
The Name of the Rose 36
Theodectes 210, 177, 210
Theodosius I 279
Theophilus 279
Theophrastus 252, 260, 265
theoretical plays that could be done 59

theory of definition 10, 18
the sake of an end 60
Thespian 57
Thespis 54, 57, 58
third branch 41
third mode of mimesis 146
thought 204
three aspects of *mimēsis* 103
three-dimensional shape 71
three-fold schema 147
three forms of drama 52
three means of mimesis 96, 98
three means of mimesis concomitantly 95
three modes of mimesis 75, 138
thunder 226
time-travel 219
Timocrates 267
Timothy I 281, 282, 283
Toledo 284
totality of the parts 91
Trackers 53
Tractatus Coisilianus 27, 292
tragedy 31, 35, 102, 136, 244
tragedy of character 82, 91, 170, 203
tragedy of suffering 82, 91, 170, 203
tragedy's limit 156
tragicomedy 242
tragōidia 19, 35, 198, 225, 307
tragos 307
translation 22
translations 20, 28
Treatise on the Art of Poetry 209
trench 257, 269
trilogy 53, 188
trimeters 121, 124
triple meter 149
Trojan Women 197
Troy 182
Tryannion 276
tune 111
twenty-seven chapters 182
two-dimensional colored shape 71

Index

two pipes 102
Tyrannion 253, 267, 276, 287
tyrannos 57, 58
tyrant 57

U
unaccompanied 121
unaccompanied words 121, 124
unconvincing possibility 219
underground 81
underworld 203
unified organic whole 83
unities of time and place 156
unity 74
universal characters 54
universal themes 54
universities in Italy 62
univocal 33, 65
unscrupulous translators 258

V
variant readings 269
vases 137
vellum 39
Veloso 168, 298-302
verb 206
verse 20, 67, 68, 121, 128, 136, 142, 144, 208
verses 121, 124
victory odes 49
villain 222
virtue 292, 144
voice 111
vulgar 35, 225
vulgar gesture 231

W
wand , 205
West Side Story 10, 245
Whalley 119
whole via a part 47
William of Moerbeke 284, 42
witness 284

women 19
Woodruff 47, 185
woodwind xi
word-smithing 120
wordsmiths 119
Wright brothers 299
writer of speeches 77
writers of metrical verses 47
writing 68

X
Xenarchus 121
Xi 284

Z
zealous 254
Zeller 159, 210, 256, 260, 265, 296
zoology 59

ABOUT THE AUTHOR

After working in ballet, Gregory Scott finished his doctoral dissertation, *Unearthing Aristotle's Dramatics: Why There is No Theory of Literature in the Poetics,* under Francis Sparshott at the University of Toronto, while also studying there under one of the esteemed 20th-century scholars of the *Poetics*, Daniel de Montmollin. He then taught for four years as a full-time philosopher at universities in the U.S. and Canada. Afterwards, he engaged in a post-doctoral fellowship under Sarah (Waterlow) Broadie at Princeton University (Philosophy) while simultaneously directing the doctoral program in dance education at New York University (NYU).

Scott has published on Aristotle's theory of drama in Cambridge and Oxford University presses and on the philosophy of dance in scholarly journals such as *Dance Research Journal.* His "Twists and Turns: Modern Misconceptions of Peripatetic Dance Theory" appeared in *Dance Research,* Edinburgh University Press, 2005, and in 2016 he published the first edition of his books *Aristotle's Favorite Tragedy: Oedipus or Cresphontes?* and *Aristotle on Dramatic Musical Composition: The Real Role of Literature, Catharsis, Music and Dance in the POETICS.* The revised second editions of both books appeared in 2018.

Scott has taught *The Meaning of Life* and *The Art and Theory of Dance* from 1995 in Humanities at NYU (SPS) and is in the final stages of a book entitled *Aristotle's "Not to Fear" Proof for the Necessary Eternality of the Universe* (anticipated publication Spring 2019). He can be reached at gls62@columbia.edu.

www.ingramcontent.com/pod-product-compliance
Lightning Source LLC
Chambersburg PA
CBHW070528010526
44118CB00012B/1075